Creating
H llywood
Style
Movies

with Adobe® Premiere® Elements 7

Carl Plumer

Peachpit Press

Creating Hollywood-Style Movies with Adobe® Premiere® Elements 7
Paul Ekert & Carl Plumer

Peachpit Press
1249 Eighth Street
Berkeley, CA 94710
510/524-2178
Fax: 510/524-2221

Find us on the web at: www.peachpit.com
To report errors, please send a note to errata@peachpit.com
Peachpit Press is a division of Pearson Education
Copyright © 2009 by Paul Ekert and Carl Plumer

Senior Editor: Karyn Johnson
Production Editor: Becky Winter
Tech Editor: Steve Grisetti
Copyeditor: Rebecca Rider
Compositor: Danielle Foster
Proofreader: Scout Festa
Indexer: Rebecca Plunkett
Interior Design: Anne Jones
Cover Design: Mimi Heft

ISBN-13: 978-0-321-60621-1

ISBN-10: 0-321-60621-3

9 8 7 6 5 4 3 2 1

Printed and bound in the United States of America

Both Carl and Paul would like to thank everyone whose remarkable efforts have made this book what it is today! Our thanks to you all.

Acknowledgments

We want to thank Karyn Johnson for guiding us through the amazing process of turning a concept into reality. Thanks, too, to Steve Grisetti, for his helpful technical review; to Rebecca Rider, our incredible copy editor; to Becky Winter and Danielle Foster, for their production work; to Scout Festa, for catching errors during proofreading; and to all the great people at Peachpit Press who helped make this book possible. Thanks to the companies and individuals who enthusiastically contributed sample clips for this book—your contributions are essential to the success of these projects. And to the people at Adobe, our thanks for putting Premiere Elements 7 out here for all of us in the first place.

About the Authors

Paul Ekert is a filmmaker who writes and edits his own productions and is the author of *Pinnacle Liquid Edition 6 for Windows: Visual QuickPro Guide* and *Avid Liquid 7 for Windows: Visual QuickPro Guide* (Peachpit). Besides his film and technology pursuits, Paul is developing a fiction portfolio that includes his first novel, *Ordinary Monsters*, published in December 2008. Further work from Paul can be found at www.PaulEkert.com.

Carl Plumer has worked professionally as a writer, web developer, multimedia designer, help systems developer, and documentation manager for high tech companies including Oracle, Computer Associates, and Avid. At Avid, he helped design one of the very first home video editing applications, Avid Cinema. Carl is also the author of *Easy Adobe Premiere Elements 2* (Que) and the previous edition of this book.

Contents

Introduction

Today, thanks to the Internet and video sharing sites such as YouTube, you can find video just about anywhere. You'll find it on your hard drive, on your iPod, and on your iPhone. You can even upload video for the entire world to see on dozens of video sharing and video blogging sites, and you can view homemade video shorts on cable channels such as Current TV and, occasionally, CNN.

So here you sit with your camcorder and your computer, eager to join this exciting world, but you find that despite all this change and energy, the whole digital video experience is lacking something; it's missing that one key ingredient necessary to keep you involved and interested. . . Fun!

The fact is, editing video is hard work. Getting the right shots in the first place is no easy feat. Then you have to capture your footage onto your computer, gather all your music, create titles, and duct tape the whole thing together; this can make for hours of painstaking effort, and you might only end up with a video production that still has you wishing you could have done it better, could have created something a little more special. This is the bane of every video editor's life.

But let's get back to the fun!

This book shows you how to create your own Hollywood special effects and have fun at the same time. The techniques you explore in this book don't require much, if anything, in the way of special equipment, and they don't require a whole lot of time investment either. However, the small movies you learn to create will impress your family and friends (and you) and will, no doubt, spark some new creative thinking of your own. In fact, if you come up with some great suggestions, let us know. They just may end up in the next edition of this book!

Along the way, while you are having fun and being creative, you also learn more about Adobe Premiere Elements 7 than you ever thought possible. In fact, by learning how to execute these special effects, you learn skills that translate well into your other editing projects—those that have no special effects angle to them.

In fact, these projects teach you about Premiere Elements 7 in a way that no other book can.

Where the Fun Is

Let's face it: special effects are where the fun is, where the "wow" factor is. They are what people want to see and what you want to create, otherwise you wouldn't be reading this book. It's by going through the projects in this book that you learn how to put the "wow" into your own films.

The projects in this book are organized to build one upon the next, but you don't need to follow them sequentially; that said, some of the earlier chapters contain information you need to know, so try not to skip them. Once you have the information in these earlier chapters under your belt, feel free to pick a chapter that looks interesting and have at it.

Before you plunge straight in, however, give yourself some time to work through the steps and study the illustrations. If you skip a step or miss a setting for an effect, the thing might fall apart on you; but so what? Back up a step or two, and start again—and don't forget the undo key (Ctrl-Z).

Although it's important to follow the steps exactly, it's equally important, once you get comfortable with your new skills, to experiment. We recommended certain settings throughout to achieve an effect that we believe is appropriate or simply cool. Feel free to mess around with any or all of the controls and settings as you go—even throw a few other effects into the mix. You may discover something that we are not even aware of and, in the process, create an awesome effect of your own!

Ultimately, by following the clear, step-by-step projects in the book, you learn to think about timing, splitting and syncing clips, matching audio to video, and other concepts that until now, you might not have given much thought to. You get hands-on experience using the audio files, effects, and clips on the accompanying DVD, and have loads of fun along the way! Here are just a few things you learn to do:

- Create a freeze frame and animate it.

- Add music and use SmartSound in your projects.

- Create a scrolling *Star Wars*-style title.

- Alter the flow of time in your movie.

- Add a picture-in-picture effect in the style of the hit TV series *24*.

- Create fun effects: "beam up" a friend, make him fly, or turn him into a ghost.

- Use the Crop effect to create the illusion of clones.

- Create and animate a light saber.

- Edit out unwanted words and objects with ease.

- Custom-build a unique "look" for your movie.

- Create a movie trailer using InstantMovie.

And this is just scratching the surface of what Premiere Elements 7 can do! Many effects come standard with Premiere Elements, so what you see in this book is a mere sampling of what Premiere Elements 7 is capable of. Browse through the Effects panel and Transitions view and apply the effects to clips on the Timeline and see what you come up with. Combine effects and play with the controls in the Properties view.

You will be genuinely surprised by what you can accomplish with a little creativity and a video-editing package as powerful as Premiere Elements 7.

The System Specifications for Premiere Elements 7

Video editing requires a lot of computer horsepower; creating special effects requires even more. If you are already editing your videos, you are probably aware that video editing is a high-end task for your computer. To underline this, we've listed the following minimum system recommendations for Premiere Elements 7, as laid out by Adobe.

TIP Projects that require special effects where changes are applied to each frame in a clip, to many clips in a video track, to many tracks in a project, and to both video and audio tracks at the same time obviously require more than the minimum specification.

◆ Intel Pentium (or compatible) 1.3 GHz processor with SSE2 support; 3 GHz required for HDV (High Definition Video)

◆ Microsoft Windows Vista (32-bit only), Windows XP, or Windows MCE (Media Center Edition) (XP and MCE require Service Pack 2)

◆ Windows Vista: 1 GB of RAM; 2 GB required for HDV

◆ Windows XP and MCE: 512 MB of RAM; 1 GB required for HDV

◆ 4.5 GB of available hard-disk space (for the basic install of Premiere Elements 7)

◆ Color monitor with 16-bit color video card

◆ 1024 x 768 monitor resolution (preferably better)

◆ Display and sound drivers compatible with Microsoft DirectX 9 or later

◆ DVD-ROM drive (compatible DVD burner required to burn DVDs)

◆ DV/i.LINK/FireWire/IEEE 1394 interface to connect a Digital 8 or DV camcorder, or a USB2 interface to connect a DV-via-USB-compatible DV camcorder (other video devices supported via the Media Downloader)

NOTE Users of HDV (High Definition Video) material require even more horsepower than users of SD (Standard Definition) material.

The Secret of Working with Special FX

There's a secret to creating your special effects clips. You need to think about creating your movie as the process of assembling a number of smaller clips into a final, finished video movie. Work on your special effects clips as separate projects—the smaller the better. If you have a scene where the special effects are only used for a minute or two, cut that section out of the longer clip and start a new project for that section. For an example of this, see the final section of Chapter 16; you combine the end result of this chapter with a Title sequence you build in Chapter 4 to create a movie with a stunning title introduction from two separate AVIs.

Working in smaller, compartmentalized sections of your overall movie also adds less strain to your computer; this allows you to cut down on render times and be in less danger of ruining an entire Timeline sequence just by making one "small" change. In the end, you will even find it easier to work this way because you can even go back and make changes to individual Timelines and reimport them as you need to into the larger project.

And that's it! Have fun, be creative, and think outside the box. And if you get a chance, write to us at PaulEkert@PaulEkert.com or CarlPlumer@gmail.com. We'd love to hear from you about your experiences and new ideas.

Hollywood Movie Titles:
Adding a WOW Factor

MEDIA:

clouds.avi
Swans.avi

COMPLEXITY:	Simple	Moderate	Complex
SKILL LEVEL:	Easy	Intermediate	Advanced

Introduction

Adding titles to a movie can provide an instant professional touch, giving your projects depth and power. This chapter has you taking titles to another level by first demonstrating how to start a project, add tracks, and rename those tracks. Then you'll learn how to add media to your project and Timeline. Once you've learned the basics, you'll dive in and create a title and then learn how to fill that title with a video clip of flowing clouds. Doing so has a dramatic "wow" effect that your audience will appreciate. It also gives your production the feel of a broadcast television show.

With the techniques from this project under your belt, you may be inspired to plan, or even storyboard, a real show. The subject of the show could be something along the lines of a Welcome To My Life video that takes the viewer around your house and your town. When making family videos, think creatively. This doesn't mean you have to stage everything, just get everyone involved in the project. Even a movie about cleaning out the garage could become a great family video if you do it with enough planning and enthusiasm.

Once you get a nice opening title, you can always reuse it and perhaps create a weekly five- or ten-minute "broadcast" of your own. A number of web sites exist that make it easy to upload videos and video blogs, or vlogs. Your friends and family might even get used to tuning in to your weekly online show!

What You'll Learn

Preparing the Project

Adding Media to Your Project

Adding Media to the Timeline

Creating the Main Title Text

Flying Solo: Adding the Fill Clip to the Timeline

Filling the Title with Clouds

Creating a Drop Shadow for the Title

Adding a Fade Out to All Media Clips

Making Adjustments, Rendering, and Exporting

Preparing the Project

As with all of the projects in this book, you will start by creating a new project, creating any extra tracks you might need, and renaming those tracks into something a little more user friendly. This last step is especially important if you attempt complex Movie effects. You will also deselect the audio tracks for three of those tracks in order to see more of the Timeline without using the scroll bar at the end.

Note that the sample files supplied on the DVD are for use on an NTSC (National Television System Committee) Timeline. If your default Project Settings are not NTSC, change them now by clicking the **Change Settings** button and choosing **NTSC > DV > Standard 48kHz**.

Name the Project, Add a Track, and Rename All the Tracks

1. Start Adobe Premiere Elements 7 and at the splash screen, click the **New Project** button. If Adobe Premiere Elements 7 is already running, choose **File > New Project**.

2. Browse to a large local hard drive, create a folder named **Peachpit**, and create a new project inside that folder called **Chapter 1 – Seethrutitle**.

3. Once the Premiere Elements interface opens, if the My Project panel is in the Sceneline, click the **Timeline** button to switch to the Timeline.

   NOTE *You need to switch to the Timeline because you will be working with multiple clips on multiple video tracks.*

4. Right-click in the track header area and from the contextual menu choose **Add Tracks**.

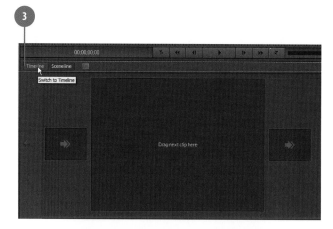

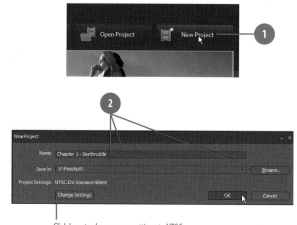

Click here to change your settings to NTSC.

5 The default on the Add Tracks dialog is to add one track. Use the Add Tracks dialog as follows:

◆ If this brings the total number of video tracks to four, leave this setting and click **OK**.

◆ If not, change this number as needed so that you will have at least four video tracks available for this project.

6 Right-click in the track header area and from the contextual menu, deselect **Show Audio Tracks**. This allows you to see all the upper video tracks without having to use the Timeline scroll bar on the right of the Timeline.

7 Right-click the actual name of the track and from the contextual menu choose **Rename**. Change each track to the following:

◆ Video 1: **Background**

◆ Video 2: **Drop Shadow**

◆ Video 3: **Fill Layer**

◆ Video 4 : **Main Title**

IMPORTANT *You should now have a minimum of four video tracks on the Timeline, all named as shown in the screenshot.*

There should now be four video tracks on the Timeline.

Adding Media to Your Project

In this task, you import some media clips (AVI files, in this case) from the DVD that comes with this book. Getting media can also involve capturing movie footage from your HD/DV camera, or some similar device, or importing from your hard drive. For further details on these features, please refer to Adobe Premiere Elements Help. For this project you need to import **clouds.avi** and **Swans.avi** from the DVD. Swans will be your background clip over which your title will be superimposed. This can be any clip at all, but it should contain some movement. This is video after all, not photography.

Get Media from the DVD

1. If it is not already active, select the **Organize** tab, and then click the **Get Media** button to access the Import panel.

2. Choose the **DVD (Camcorder or PC DVD Drive)** button.

3. When the Media Downloader appears, click the **Advanced Dialog** button to switch to advanced mode, and from the source Get Media From list, choose your DVD drive.

   NOTE *Once you have selected the DVD drive, the various media files begin to appear. On some systems this may take a few moments.*

4. To the left of the Media Downloader are the save options. Click the **Browse** button and create a folder on the hard drive where you want the imported media to be stored. For example, the **Peachpit** folder.

5. Click the **UnCheck All** button once to deselect all the files (otherwise you will end up importing *everything*), then scroll down through the available media clips and locate **Swans.avi** and **clouds.avi** and place a check next to the filenames.

6. Click the **Get Media** button. Premiere Elements copies the media from the DVD onto your hard drive and adds it to the Available Media list.

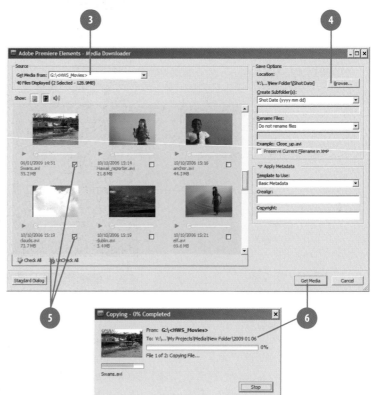

4

Adding Media to the Timeline

In this task, you'll get the "background" clip and drag it on the Timeline. This is a simple procedure and one that you should be familiar with since dragging is the main way of doing pretty much everything in Adobe Premiere Elements. Throughout this book you are asked to drag many times, so you might as well get comfortable with the concept now.

Drag Media to the Timeline

1. Select the **Edit** tab to switch to the Edit workspace and then click the **Project** button to display the Media panel if it is not already available.

2. Choose the **Swans.avi** clip for this project by clicking the thumbnail in the Media panel.

3. From the Media panel, drag the **Swans.avi** clip to the Background track on the Timeline.

    IMPORTANT *Be sure to drag the **Swans.avi** clip so the front (the head) of the clip lines up with the very front (the head) of the Background track. Otherwise you will end up with a blank playing gap at the start of your Timeline.*

4. Click the **Zoom In** button ("+ ") a couple of times until the background clip occupies about two thirds of the Timeline. Click the **Zoom Out** ("-") button if you go too far. Or you can use the slider along the top of the Timeline.

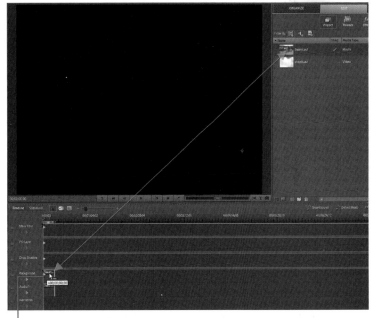

Creating the
Main Title Text

For your title, you will use sturdy, block-style lettering (**Arial Black**), which will enable the viewer to better see the clouds inside the title. You'll also make the title as large as you can while leaving plenty of the background clip showing. However, you have to be careful not to go outside the safe text boundary that surrounds the title area.

Type, Color, and Position Your Title

1 Make sure the Timeline cursor is at the very start of the Timeline by pressing the **Home** key on the keyboard; then click the **Add Default Text** button (the "T" icon) at the bottom of the Monitor panel.

2 In the text box on the Monitor panel that currently reads Add Text, type **WINTERSWIM** in capital letters with no space between the two words.

3 Using the arrow keys on your keyboard, move the cursor so that it's between WINTER and SWIM, then press **Enter** on your keyboard. This places the two words on separate lines, like this:

WINTER
SWIM

> **IMPORTANT** *If you click on or off the Add Text box, Add Text will no longer be highlighted. Be sure to highlight all of the text in the Add Text box again before you start typing.*

"Add Text" appears here. Simply start typing to overwrite it.

Did You Know?

The See-Through Title effect works best with short titles. Long words, and titles containing too many words, don't work as well as short ones. Think of your basic blockbuster title. You don't often see full, literary-style titles in blockbusters. You see, instead, titles like *The Ring, Scream,* and *Titanic*. Today, *The Adventures of Huckleberry Finn* would simply be *FINN! All Quiet on the Western Front*, simply *QUIET!* and *Psycho* would be. . . Ah, bad example. . .

Make Adjustments to the Text

① Click the **Center Text** button on the Properties view to center the text.

② Right-click the WINTER SWIM text and select **Font**.

③ From the list of fonts, choose **Arial > Black**.

Did You Know?

You can customize titles with your favorite fonts. Any font that you install in Windows XP will also show up in Premiere Elements. If you install a new font while Premiere Elements is running, you may need to restart it before it shows up in the font list. This feature enables you to use any font, including free fonts, in your video productions. The right font can set the tone of a movie and can make for a truly personal statement that identifies your films as yours.

Set the Font Color

① Click the **Color Properties** button.

② In the Color Properties dialog, the color of the text should be pure white. If it is not, change it by entering the following settings:

- ◆ R: **255**
- ◆ G: **255**
- ◆ B: **255**

③ Click **OK**.

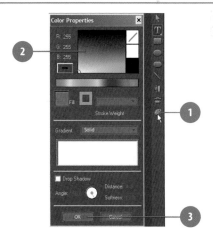

Reposition the Title Text

1 Center the title horizontally by clicking the **Horizontal Center** button.

2 Center the title vertically by clicking the **Vertical Center** button.

3 Click the **Selection Tool**.

4 Drag the title up so that it aligns with the top of the inner Safe Title Margin.

Move and Resize the Title Clip

1 Click the Timeline to exit the Titler, and the Winter Swim title, Title 01, will be created in the first available track; in this case, the Drop Shadow track.

2 Reposition the **Title 01** clip you just created by dragging it from the Drop Shadow track and dropping it onto the Main Title track.

   IMPORTANT *Be sure to line up the head (the start) of the Title 01 clip with the beginning (the head) of the Main Title track.*

3 Grab the tail (the end) of the **Title 01** clip and stretch it across the Main Title track until it is the same length as the **Swans.avi** clip on the Background track.

4 Press **CTRL-S** to save your project or you can choose **File > Save**.

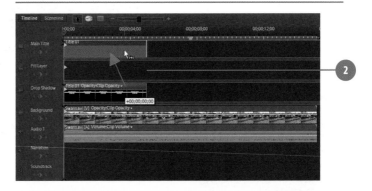

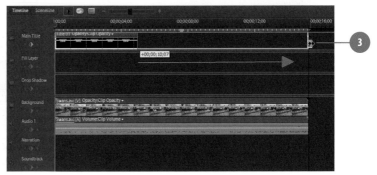

Flying Solo: Adding the Fill Clip to the Timeline

Throughout this book you are given chances to use skills you learn by "Flying Solo." The Flying Solo sections are here to reinforce the learning experience, but you will also find hints and memory joggers in these sections so that you don't feel completely abandoned. In this section, you drag the **clouds.avi** to the Timeline and resize the clip: two skills you already learned in this chapter. For this project, a royalty-free video clip has been provided, courtesy of Artbeats (**www.artbeats.com**), called **clouds.avi**.

Hints on Adding the Fill Clip to the Timeline

1. Drag the **clouds.avi** clip to the Fill Layer track (*Hint: clouds.avi thumbnail; Media panel; drag & drop; destination-Fill track*).

   NOTE *Make sure the **clouds.avi** clip starts at the head of the Timeline.*

2. If the Videomerge message appears, click **NO** because you do not require that effect for this project.

3. You may need to **Zoom Out** the Timeline to see the end of **clouds.avi** (*Hint: Zoom slider under Monitor panel*).

4. The length of **clouds.avi** should be reduced until it is the same length as the other media clips (*Hint: grab tail; drag toward head [the start] of the Timeline*).

5. When you are finished, the **clouds.avi** media clip should be directly below the title and be of the same length (duration).

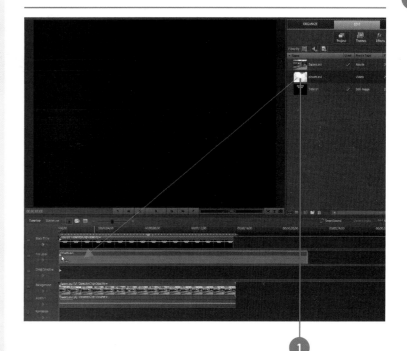

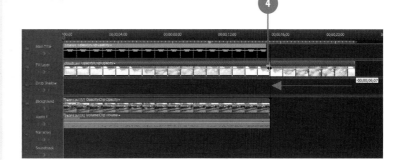

Filling the Title with Clouds

Now that you have two media clips (the background **Swans.avi** clip and the title fill clip, **clouds.avi**) and your title on the Timeline, here's where the real fun begins. You'll apply a Premiere Elements video effect called the Track Matte effect to the fill clip on the Timeline. You'll then point that effect at the **Title 01** clip and the title text will then magically be filled with **clouds**. You'll like it and your audience will be awestruck.

Use the Track Matte Key to Fill the Title

1. Make sure the **clouds.avi** clip is selected by clicking the clip in the Timeline. It will have a purple bar running along the top when it is selected.

2. If it is not already open, click the **Edit** tab to select the Edit workspace and then click the **Effects** button to view the Effects panel.

3. In the Effects search field, type **track**. The Track Matte effect appears in the Keying folder in the Video Effects section of the Effects panel.

4. Drag the **Track Matte Key** effect onto the **clouds.avi** clip on the Fill Layer track.

5. With the **clouds.avi** clip still selected, click the **Properties** button to access the Properties view. If it is not already open, click the triangle next to the **Track Matte Key** effect to reveal the effect's controls.

6. From the Matte menu, select **Main Title**. Leave the other Track Matte Key options (Composite Using and Reverse) as they are.

   TIP *Note that in the Monitor panel, the effect is applied instantly. The clouds now show through the title text. You may have to move your CTI (Current Time Indicator) along the Timeline to see the effect if it happens to be placed off of the clips on the video tracks.*

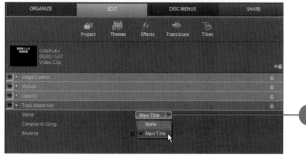

Creating a Drop Shadow for the Title

Although the effect looks good, it has no dimensionality to it; that is, it looks a little flat. There isn't much differentiation between the background and the title. In fact, if you were to use, for example, a clip of the ocean inside your title and your title overlaid a scene of the beach, it could be difficult to tell the title from the background. You can fix this easily using the ever popular drop shadow. To apply a drop shadow you first need to create a duplicate of the **Title 01** clip. Then Fly Solo to add it to the Timeline and resize its length.

Create a Duplicate of the Title 01 Clip

1 If it is not already open, click the **Edit** tab to select the Edit workspace and then click the **Project** button to display the Media panel.

2 Right-click the **Title 01** clip in the Project view to bring up the contextual menu and choose **Duplicate**.

3 Right-click the duplicate clip, **Title 01 Copy**, in the Project view, and from the contextual menu choose **Rename**.

4 Rename the copy **Drop Shadow**.

Did You Know?

Using this workflow, you need to create a separate clip for shadows. You may be saying to yourself, "Hey, why didn't I just add a drop shadow to the title I already have?" Consider this: Had you used the Titler's drop shadow capabilities for the **Title 01** clip (the one with the sky now floating in it), the **clouds.avi** clip would show through the drop shadow as well. This is because the Track Matte Key effect works by allowing the second clip to appear through the matte's white space. And since there's a little white in the drop shadow, a bit of the clip shows through. By using a second clip (a copy of the first **Title 01** clip), you get a nice, clean drop shadow and retain your crisp see-through title. For the shadow to work, it must be on the right track, and this is behind (below) both the Title 01 track on the Main Title track and the **clouds.avi** clip on the Fill Layer track.

Flying Solo: Place the Shadow Clip on the Timeline

1 Add the **Drop Shadow** title to the Drop Shadow track.

2 If the Videomerge message appears, click **NO** because you do not require that effect for this project.

3 Trim the **Drop Shadow** title so that it is the same length as the other clips on the Timeline.

Create the Drop Shadow

1 Double-click the **Drop Shadow** title on the Timeline (on the Drop Shadow track *not* in the Media panel) to open the Titler.

2 Click the **Color Properties** button to access the Color Properties dialog.

3 On the Color Properties dialog, add a drop shadow to the text by selecting the **Drop Shadow** check box.

4 Set the following drop shadow parameters:

- ◆ Angle: **140**
- ◆ Distance: **20**
- ◆ Softness: **40**

5 Click **OK**.

6 Click anywhere on the **Timeline** to exit the **Titler**.

> **TIP** *For these settings, you can type the numbers in directly, or you can use your mouse to slide across and adjust them that way. For the Angle setting, you can use the knob control if you choose. Also, feel free to adjust these settings as you see fit. You can see the changes you make in the Titler in real time. Move the Color Properties dialog out of the way to see the Titler, if necessary.*

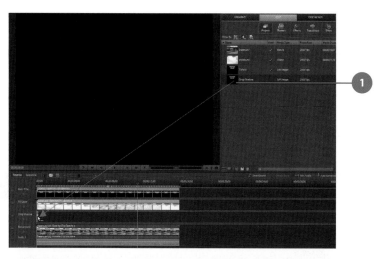

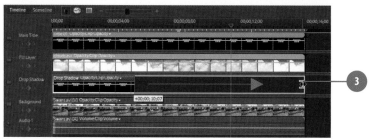

Adding a Fade Out
to All Media Clips

You want to have a gentle "fade to black" for your video and title clips at the end of the movie. Premiere Elements provides you with a very simple way to do this. On each clip's Properties view there is a Fade Out button tucked away inside the Opacity and Volume controls. You'll now click each of the clips in turn and then use the opacity Fade Out and volume Fade Out button to complete this project.

Fade Out All of the Clips on the Video Tracks

1. Click the **Title 01** clip once on the Main Title track to select it.

2. Click the **Properties** button to display the Properties view.

3. In the Properties view for the **Title 01** clip, click the little triangle next to Opacity to display the effect controls and click once on the **Fade Out** button.

4. Repeat Steps 1–3 for the other three tracks until your Timeline looks like the screenshot on this page.

5. Lastly, with the **Swans.avi** file selected, click the little triangle next to Volume to display the controls. Click once on the **Fade Out** button to fade the volume to zero at the same time as the clips fade to black.

6. Press **CTRL-S** to save your project or you can select **File > Save** from the menu.

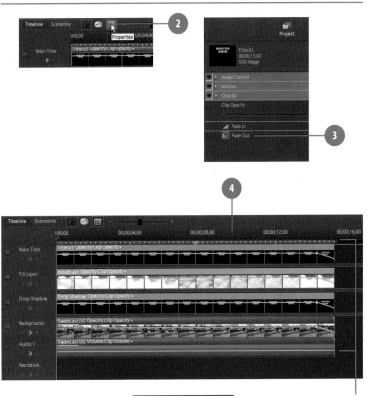

All of the video clips with fade outs applied

Making Adjustments, Rendering, and Exporting

Before you finish this project, make any final tweaks as needed, and you are ready to save, render, and make your movie. Make sure the final saved project file and your exported AVI are placed in the correct folders because you will need both the project and the exported movie later in this book.

Well done. You have completed *Chapter 1* and on the way you learned plenty of core skills and a few special effects tricks, including how to use the Matte Track effect, an effect that you will soon learn has 1001 useful applications in the world of video special effects.

Finish the Project

① Once you have played back your clip and made the necessary adjustments, press the **Enter** key to render your project.

② When the render is complete, and you have made all your final adjustments, press **Ctrl-S** to make a final save of your project.

> **TIP** *Make sure you remember where you saved this project (the **Peachpit** folder you created at the start of this chapter is a good bet) because you will revisit this project in Chapter 3, where you will add some mood music to your movie.*

③ Finally, export your work as an AVI file (a standard Microsoft movie file) by selecting the Timeline, if it is not already selected, and then choosing **File > Export > Movie**.

④ When prompted, browse to the **Peachpit** folder and create a **New Folder** called **HSMovies_Final Renders** and save the exported file as **Chapter 1_Seethrutitle.avi**.

> **NOTE** *This final render will be used again in Chapter 21, as will many of your other renders from this book.*

⑤ Exit or minimize Premiere Elements and browse to the **Peachpit** folder and then open the **HSMovies_Final Renders** folder. Double-click the **Chapter 1_Seethrutitle. avi** file to play it in your default media player.

> **TIP** *You can optionally bring this final render into a larger project, show it on your computer, upload it to an Internet video sharing site, or burn it to a DVD. For more details on these functions, please refer to the Adobe Premiere Elements Help.*

As the project renders, Premiere Elements provides you with status information, including the estimated time to complete and a progress bar.

The finished project running in Windows Media Player, showing the full see-through title effect with drop shadow, superimposed over the background video.

Hollywood Movie Titles:
Using Color and Motion

MEDIA:

retro-footage.avi

2

COMPLEXITY:	Simple	Moderate	Complex
SKILL LEVEL:	Easy	Intermediate	Advanced

Introduction

Aside from conveying essential information, titles can set tone and style and add fun to a movie—not to mention letting the video editor show off a bit. This chapter explores using fonts, motion, and color to create a retro '60s intro-title look. This technique can be a lot of fun to put together and can quickly turn an ordinary movie into a cool "happening" with a real '60s-style flair.

There's a lot to learn here; you'll use keyframes, motion effects, and the Crop effect, as well as techniques such as timing and synchronization. These are essential skills for any video editor seeking to create enjoyable and interesting movies.

Once you have completed this project, you'll find that the skills and knowledge you acquire creating this simple (but cool, baby!) effect will be something that you can apply to a variety of projects in a number of different ways.

The only barrier is your imagination.

What You'll Learn

Installing New Fonts

Flying Solo: Preparing the Project

Creating, Cropping, and Coloring a Freeze Frame

Flying Solo: Creating the Second and Third Freeze Frames

Creating Credits for Each Freeze Frame

Animating the First Actor's Freeze Frame and Credits

Understanding Motion and Keyframes

Flying Solo: Animating the Second and Third Actor's Freeze Frame and Credits

Creating an Opening Title

Flying Solo: Creating the Closing Titles

Making Adjustments, Rendering, and Exporting

Installing New Fonts

To enhance the retro look of this project, you will add two '60s-style typefaces to the Windows font collection. These two fonts, Alba and Chick, were created by Ben Balvanz, a pioneer in the field of electronic type design, and have a distinctive 1960s feel to them. They will help give this project the retro look you need; you'll use the Alba font for the actor's credits and the Chick font for the opening and closing titles. To keep from repeating this in a later chapter, you will also install the Jedi font, which you'll use in Chapter 4 to create a Star Wars opening title.

Install Three New Fonts to Windows

1 From the Windows Start button, select **Control Panel**.

2 On the Control Panel, select **Appearance and Themes**.

> **NOTE** *These steps and illustrations refer to the default setup of Windows XP. If you have Windows XP in Classic View, select **Fonts** from the Control Panel at this time.*

3 From the See Also box on the left side of the screen, select **Fonts**.

4 When the Fonts folder opens, select **File > Install New Font**.

5 In the Add Fonts dialog, use the **Drives** menu to locate your DVD drive.

> **TIP** *Be sure the DVD supplied with this book is in your DVD drive.*

6 Navigate to the Fonts folder on the DVD.

7 The Alba (True Type), the Chick (True Type), and the Star Jedi Hollow (True Type) fonts show up in the list of fonts. Click the **Select All** button to highlight all three fonts and then click **OK**.

> **NOTE** *After the fonts have been installed, close the **Fonts** folder and close the **Appearance and Themes** window.*

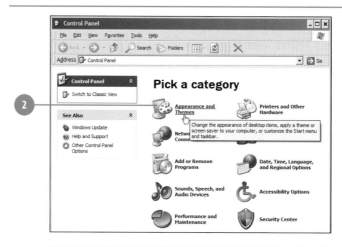

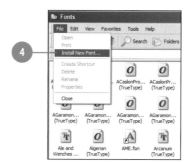

Flying Solo: Preparing the Project

The first steps in creating this effect are the same basic steps you will use for virtually all of the projects in this book: begin a project, name the tracks, and get your media clips. For this project, the video clip is **retro-footage.avi**. In Chapter 1, you learned the necessary techniques to perform all of these tasks, so Fly Solo now and see how much you can remember. Hints and tips are listed within the following steps to help you out, but if you get really lost, peek back at Chapter 1 for more detailed instructions.

Start a Project, Customize the Timeline, and Import Some Media

1 Start **Premiere Elements** and create a **New Project** called **Chapter 2 -Retrotitle** (*Hint: use the New Project at the Splash screen or File > New > Project if Premiere Elements is already open; save in the Peachpit folder created in Chapter 1*).

> **NOTE** *The sample files supplied on the DVD are for use on an NTSC Timeline. If your default Project Settings are not NTSC, change them now by clicking the **Change Settings** button and selecting **NTSC > DV > Standard 48kHz**.*

2 If the Timeline is set to the Sceneline, switch to the **Timeline** (*Hint: Timeline button*).

> **NOTE** *You need to switch to the Timeline because for this project you are working with multiple clips on multiple video tracks.*

3 Deselect audio tracks 2 and 3 (*Hint: right-click Track Header; deselect Show Audio Tracks*).

4 Rename tracks 1 and 2 to the following (*Hint: Right-click the track name; select Rename*):

- ◆ Video 1: **Main Video**

- ◆ Video 2: **Titles**

5 Import the **retro-footage.avi** media clip from the DVD (*Hint: Get Media; DVD (Camcorder or PC DVD Drive) button; Advanced button; select DVD drive; UnCheck All; check retro-footage.avi*).

> **TIP** *Full instructions for importing media into Premiere Elements 7 can be found in the Chapter 1 section, "Adding Media to Your Project".*

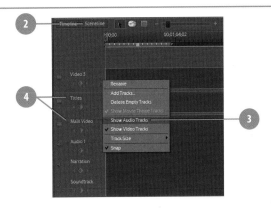

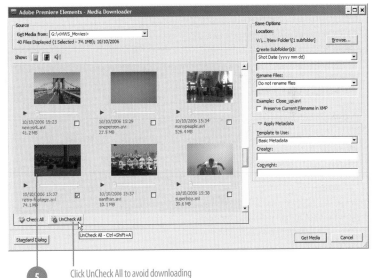

Click UnCheck All to avoid downloading *all* the clips on the DVD!

6 Once the clip appears in the panel, switch to the **Edit** workspace (*Hint: Edit tab; Project button*).

7 Drag the **retro-footage.avi** clip to the Main Movie track on the Timeline.

> **TIP** *Make sure the start of the media clip is at the head of the track.*

8 Use the **Zoom In** or **Out** controls so the **retro-footage.avi** clip occupies about two-thirds of the Timeline. Move on to the next section when your Timeline looks similar to the one opposite.

Did You Know?

You can play most clips in the Preview panel. While you are using the Edit Workspace, you can play clips from the Media panel and the Timeline in Premiere Elements by simply double-clicking them. After you double-click, the Preview panel opens. This panel contains some of the same controls found on the Monitor panel. Specifically, you'll find the following buttons: Play/Pause, Step Back, Step Forward, Set In Point, Set Out Point. You'll also find a miniature timeline and a timecode display.

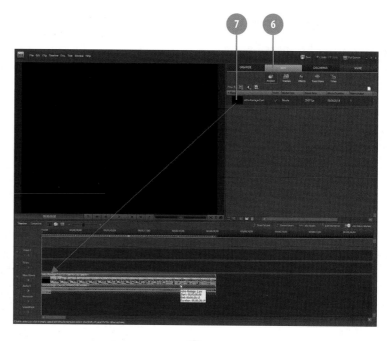

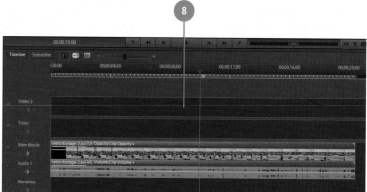

Creating, Cropping, and Coloring a Freeze Frame

Now that your Timeline is set up correctly, you will begin this project in earnest by creating a still, or freeze frame, from the video. You will then resize it to add focus, and recolor it to add coolness. Each of your retro stills will have its own bright color, so as the stills appear on screen, each makes its own unique statement. You'll be using shades of orange, magenta, and green for these stills.

Use the Freeze Frame Feature to Create a Still Image

1. Move the **CTI (current time indicator)** 10 seconds into your clip, to **00;00;10;00**. This is the frame that you'll use as your first still.

   TIP *You can move directly to the 10-second mark by typing* **10;00** *into the CTI.*

2. Click the **Freeze Frame** button under the Monitor panel to access the Freeze Frame dialog.

3. In the Freeze Frame dialog, click the **Insert In Movie** button (the 5-second default is fine for this project).

Crop the Image Using the Crop Effect

1 If it is not already selected, click the **Edit** tab to select the Edit workspace and then click the **Effects** button to view the Effects panel.

2 In the Effects search field, type **Crop**.

3 Drag the **Crop** effect onto the freeze frame (**retrotitle_FF.bmp**).

4 Access this effect by clicking the **Properties** button to view the Properties view **with the clip selected on the Timeline** and then click the triangle next to the **Crop** effect to reveal its controls if it is not already open.

5 Make the following adjustments to the Crop effect.

- ◆ Left: **45.5**
- ◆ Top: **0.0**
- ◆ Right: **36.7**
- ◆ Bottom: **0.0**

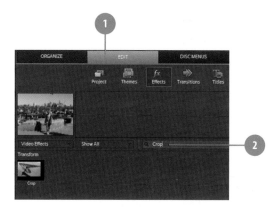

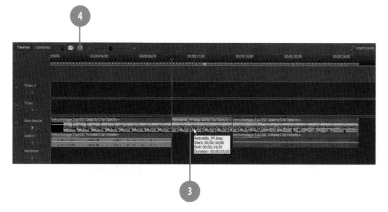

Color the Image Using the Color Balance (RGB) Effect

1 If it is not already selected, click the **Edit** tab to select the Edit workspace and then click the **Effects** button to view the Effects panel.

2 In the Effects search field, type **rgb**.

3 Drag the **Color Balance (RGB)** effect onto the freeze frame (**retrotitle_FF.bmp**).

4 Click the **Properties** button to access the Properties view and then click the triangle next to the **Color Balance (RGB)** effect to reveal its controls if it is not already open.

NOTE *You may need to close one of the other effect's controls by clicking the triangle or scroll down to see the Color Balance (RGB) controls.*

5 Make the following changes to the Color Balance (RGB) effect:

- ◆ Red: **200**
- ◆ Green: **30**
- ◆ Blue: **40**

TIP *Optionally, you can use the sliders in the Color Balance settings area.*

6 Click the **Done** check mark when you have finished.

7 Press **Ctrl-S** to save your project, or you can select **File > Save** from the menu.

Did You Know?

You can paint by numbers. RGB refers to **R**ed, **G**reen, and **B**lue, a standard color format for online use. By mixing these colors much as you would paint, you can create virtually any color you can imagine. You mix your colors with the Color Balance (RGB) effect by changing the number for each color, from 0 to 200.

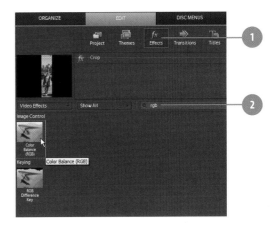

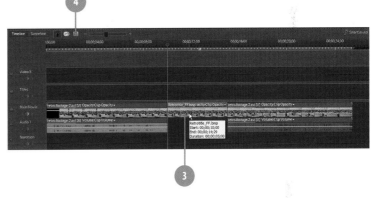

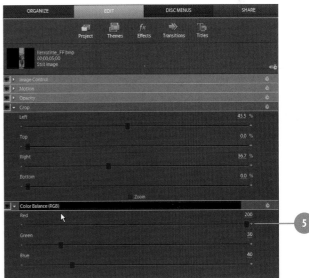

2

Flying Solo: Creating the Second and Third Freeze Frames

Now that you have your first snapshot cropped and colorized, Fly Solo down the Timeline and repeat this technique to create two more freeze frame images; then crop and color them using the techniques you have just learned. The procedure for taking the snapshot, creating the shape with the Crop effect, and colorizing the clip is exactly the same as for the first snapshot. The difference will be in the crop and color settings. To help you out, hints and settings appear in the following steps. If you lose your way, refer back to the procedure for creating, cropping, and colorizing the first freeze frame.

Hints for Creating, Cropping, and Coloring the Second and Third Freeze Frames

1 Move the **CTI** to the 18-second mark and use the **Freeze Frame** button to create the second freeze frame (*Hint: Insert to Movie*).

2 Add the **Crop** effect and use these settings: Left **39.1**; Top **0.0**; Right **48.2**; Bottom **0.0**.

3 Add the **Color Balance (RGB)** effect and use these settings: Red **200**; Green **30**; Blue **130**.

4 Move the **CTI** to the 26-second mark and use the **Freeze Frame** button to create the third freeze frame (*Hint: Insert to Movie*).

5 Add the **Crop** effect and use these settings: Left **43.0**; Top **0.0**; Right **38.7**; Bottom **0.0**.

6 Add the **Color Balance (RGB)** effect and use these settings: Red **50**; Green **200**; Blue **50**.

7 Move to the next section when your Timeline looks something like the screenshot shown.

Did You Know?

Choose any color for your next project.
It doesn't matter which colors you choose for your stills in your next project. You can "colorize" each still in a different shade of blue, for example. Or, you can make each one a primary color: red, yellow, and blue. For a 4th of July video, you could colorize each clip red, white, and blue. For a Holiday clip, perhaps you should choose reds and greens.

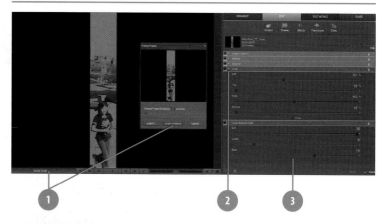

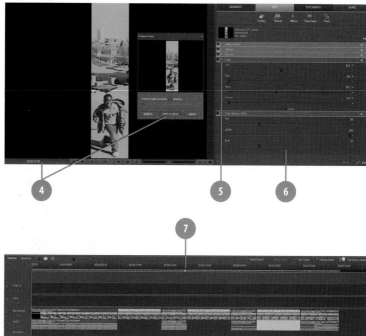

Creating Credits for Each Freeze Frame

Now that you have created all of your still images, you need the identifying credits to match. You'll create three "actor credits" using the Premiere Elements Titler; once you have all of the pieces in place, you will be ready to animate them using the Motion effect in the Properties view.

Create Credits for the First Actor

1 Move the **CTI** to **00;00;10;00**, which is the beginning of the first freeze frame (**retro-title_FF.bmp**) on the Main Movie Timeline.

2 Click the **Add Default Text** button under the Monitor panel.

3 In the panel, change the font to **Alba**, the font size to **48**, and click the **Right Align Text** button to change the alignment to right-aligned.

4 When you launch Titler, the default "Add Text" text should already be selected; if it is not, drag your mouse across the text in the **Titler** and type **Miles W as "Sketch"** to replace it.

5 Move your cursor after **as** and before **"Sketch"** and press **Enter** on your keyboard so that your text looks like the text in the illustration to the right.

6 Click the **Selection Tool** (the arrow at the top of the Titler buttons).

7 Grab the text box and drag it so that it is on the left side of the colored still.

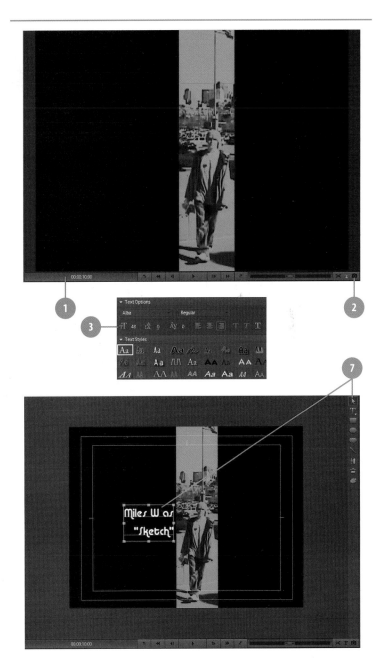

Create Credits for the Second Actor

1. Move the **CTI** to **00;00;18;00**, which is the beginning of the second freeze frame (**retrotitle_FF_1.bmp**) on the Main Movie Timeline.

2. Click the **Add Default Text** button under the Monitor panel.

3. In the Properties view, change the font to **Alba**, the font size to **48**, and the alignment to **left-aligned**.

4. Replace the "**Add Text**" text in the Titler with **Viola Barkley as "Sing"**.

5. Move your cursor after **Barkley** and before **as** and press **Enter** so that your text looks like the text in the illustration.

6. Click the **Selection Tool** (the arrow) and move the text box so that it is on the lower-right side of the screen, next to the actor.

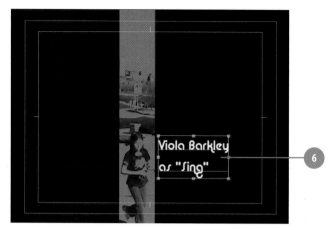

The Titler should look like this after you've created the second actor's credits.

Create Credits for the Third Actor

1. Move the **CTI** to **00;00;26;00**, which is the beginning of the third freeze frame (**retrotitle_FF_2.bmp**) on the Main Movie Timeline.

2. Click the **Add Default Text** button under the Monitor panel.

3. In the Properties view, change the font to **Alba**, **48**, **right-aligned**.

4. Replace the "**Add Text**" text in the Titler with **Joey Donuts as "Ben Ten"**.

5. Move your cursor after **Donuts** and before **as** and press **Enter**.

6. Click the **Selection Tool** and move the text box so that it is on the lower-right side of the screen, near the actor (as shown in the screenshot on the right).

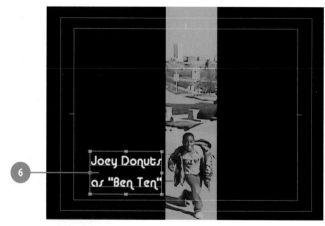

The Titler should look like this after you've created the final actor's credits.

Animating the First Actor's Freeze Frame and Credits

Now you are ready to start animating all of the freeze frames and credits you've created. The idea is to move them in and out of the audience's frame of vision, adding to the overall funky feeling generated by the outlandish colors. To do so, you'll use one of Premiere Elements' most powerful effects features, the Motion effect. The Motion effect is one of Premiere Elements' fixed effects, meaning that the effect is available for all clips and doesn't need to be applied to a clip first from the Effects panel.

Use the Motion Effect

1. Move the **CTI** to **00;00;10;00**, which is the beginning of the first freeze frame (**retro-title_FF.bmp**) on the Main Movie Timeline.

2. Click the first freeze frame (**retrotitle_FF.bmp**) and click the **Properties** button to open the Properties view.

3. In the Properties view, click the **Show Keyframes** button.

4. Click the triangle next to **Motion**, and then click the **Toggle Animation** button for **Motion**.

5. Enter **14;29** into the CTI display to send the **CTI** cursor **00;00;14;29**.

6. Inside the Motion controls, change the Position to **360 725**.

   TIMESAVER *Premiere Elements automatically places a keyframe here at the change in Position. For more information on these features, see the following sidebar entitled "Understanding Motion and Keyframes."*

7. In the Properties view or on the Timeline, move the **CTI** back down the Timeline to **12;15**.

8. Change the Position here to **360 240** (the default position for Motion).

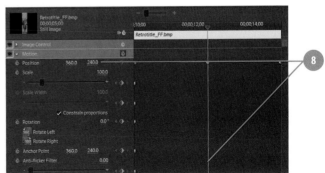

Understanding Motion and Keyframes

A key part of creating the Retro Titles effect is the use of motion. Motion is one of the effects in Premiere Elements that you can control with keyframes. Video clips are made up of frames. *Keyframes* are the key points in a clip where something significant, or key, happens, such as when a video clip changes size, speed, direction, or opacity, for example, or when an audio clip changes volume.

The Motion Effect

For the purposes of this effect, you want to create motion—in other words, you want to *animate*—both the actors' stills and the credits. To do this, use Premiere Elements' Motion effect, which is a default effect for every visual media on the Timeline, including video clips, stills, and titles.

To animate a clip, you first set a start point, an end point, and one or as many middle points as are needed. Each point is defined using a keyframe and each keyframe marks the frame where a change takes place.

You don't need to set keyframes for every frame in a clip, however. Premiere Elements takes care of the "in between" changes for you. This is known as *tweening*, a term that comes from the animation (cartooning) world (as does the term keyframe).

For example, if you have a keyframe that has the clip starting in the lower-left corner of the screen and a keyframe that has the clip ending in the upper-right corner, Premiere Elements will tween (in other words, provide you with) all of the changes to the clip for the intervening frames across the screen.

Using the Motion effect, you can control the position of any clip over time, as well as its scale (size) and scale width (proportionally or not; that is, with or without distorting it), and you can even rotate it (as well as set its rotation anchor point). By default it is in the center of the screen.

Motion and speed are set by the keyframe's position in the Properties view Timeline for the clip. The default motion types are Linear and Auto Bézier, which are the temporal (time) and spatial (space) types, respectively. These can be changed by right-clicking a keyframe and selecting a different temporal or spatial type. The contextual menu that appears when you right-click also contains options for copying, cutting, and pasting keyframes.

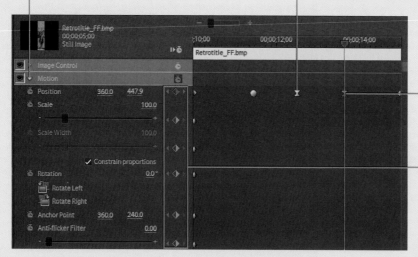

Selected keyframes in the **Properties** view Timeline are blue. Unselected keyframes are gray. Many of the temporal keyframes have their own shape. For example, Linear is a triangle while Auto Bézier is a circle.

You can navigate from keyframe to keyframe using the "go to next" keyframes buttons; one button moves the **CTI** one keyframe to the right (forward), the other one keyframe to the left (backward). Note that these are interactive buttons that light up when the **CTI** is on a keyframe, showing which action you can take. The center (round) button is for adding or removing keyframes. Keyframes are also added automatically any time you make a change to a setting.

Controlling the Timing of a Clip

In the preceding example, the speed at which the clip travels diagonally across the screen is uniform for the given duration of the clip. If you want to speed up or slow down how the clip moves at any point, you can add additional keyframes. How far apart or close together these keyframes are controls how fast or slow the clip plays.

For example, if near the end of the clip you were to add another keyframe at the middle of the screen, then the clip will take a relatively long time to move from the left corner to the center of the screen, after which it would rocket from the center to the upper right.

If, on the other hand, you set this third keyframe very near the end of the clip and very near the upper-right corner, the clip would rocket immediately to the upper right, and then take a relatively long time to go from that point to the end frame in the upper corner.

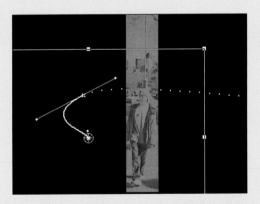

You can control the motion and timing of a clip using a combination of dragging the clip in the **Monitor** panel to define the motion, and setting keyframes and entering numeric values in the **Properties** view to define the timing.

You can also view and manipulate keyframes right on the Timeline. Keyframes are gold when selected and gray when not. You navigate from keyframe to keyframe and add and delete keyframes in the Timeline the same way that you do in the **Properties** view. Using keyframes on the Timeline is best suited for Opacity changes and Volume changes (for audio clips).

Animate the Credits for the First Actor

1 Enter **14;05** into the CTI display to send the **CTI** cursor **00;00;14;05**, where the top edge of the first freeze frame (**retrotitle_FF.bmp**) just passes the bottom of the **Title 01** clip, as shown in the screenshot.

2 On the Timeline, click the **Title 01** clip (the credits for the first actor), and, if the Properties view is not already open, click the **Properties** button to open the Properties view for this title.

3 In the Properties view, click the triangle next to **Motion**.

IMPORTANT *Be sure you click the* **Title 01** *clip just once. This ensures that you are working with the clip as a media clip. If you double-click, you'll open the Titler and you will be working with the clip as a title.*

4 Click the **Toggle Animation** button to create a default Position keyframe at the value of **360 240**.

NOTE *If the keyframes work area is not displayed (as it is in the illustration), click the* **Show Keyframes** *button.*

5 In the Properties view or on the Timeline, move the **CTI** to the end of the **Title 01** clip, **00;00;14;29**.

6 Change the Position here to **940 240**. Premiere Elements automatically places a keyframe here to mark the change in Position.

7 Press **Ctrl-S** to save your project or you can select **File > Save** from the menu.

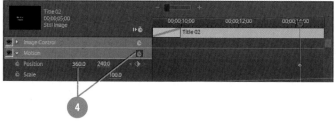

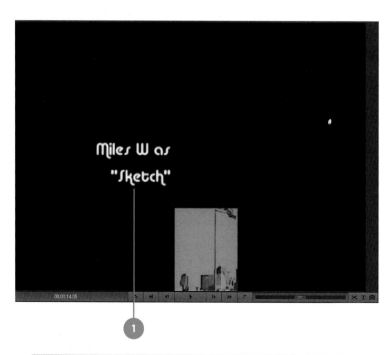

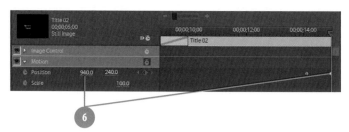

Flying Solo: Animating the Second and Third Actor's Freeze Frame and Credits

In this next section, you take everything you have learned so far and Fly Solo to animate the second actor's freeze frame as well as her credits. Once this is complete, you repeat the experience to animate the third actor's freeze frame and his credits. Don't panic. You'll be using the same keyframing technique you used for the first freeze frame, so if you get lost, refer back to the last section, but don't forget to apply the following settings.

Animate Settings for Second and Third Freeze Frame

1. Move the **CTI** to **20;15** and select the second freeze frame (**retrotitle_FF_1.bmp**).

2. Open the Properties view and then dial open the Motion settings (*Hint: use the Properties button*).

3. Toggle animation **ON** at the default position (*Hint: 360 240*).

4. Move the **CTI** to **20;29** and change the Position settings to **360 -245** (*negative*).

5. Move the CTI to **28;15** and select the third freeze frame (**retrotitle_FF_2.bmp**).

6. Open the Properties view and then dial open the Motion settings.

7. Toggle animation **ON** at the default position (*Hint: - 360 240*).

8. Move the CTI to **30;29** and change the Position settings to **360 725**.

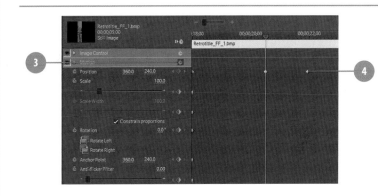

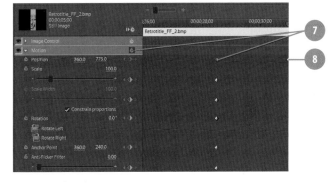

Animate the Second and Third Actor's Credits

1 Move the CTI back to **21;12** and select the credits for the second actor (*Hint: Title 02 clip on the Title track*).

> **IMPORTANT** *Be sure to click just once to ensure that you are working with the clip as a media clip and not as a text clip in the Titler.*

2 Open the Properties view and then dial open the Motion settings.

3 Toggle animation ON at the default position (*Hint: -360 240*).

4 Move the CTI to **22;29** and change the Position settings to **-225** (*negative*) **240**.

5 Move the **CTI** to **30;15** and select the credits for the third actor (*Hint: Title 03 clip on the Title track*).

6 Open the **Properties** view and then dial open the Motion settings.

7 Toggle animation ON at the default position (*Hint: 360 240*).

8 Move the CTI to **30;29** and change the Position settings to **990 240**.

9 Save your work so far (*Hint: Ctrl-S*).

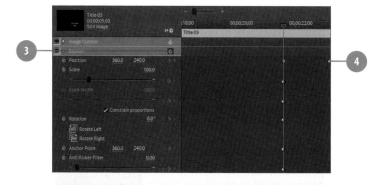

Creating an Opening Title

To finish up the project and create the full "movie credits" effect, you'll create a couple of quick additional titles using the Premiere Elements Titler. The first is an opening title for your movie, which you will call "The Crazy Caper." You will create the title using a particularly '60s-looking font called Chick, created by Ben Balvanz, and you'll add a gradient fill to the font for added grooviness.

Add a '60s-Style Opening Title

1. Press **Home** on your keyboard to return the CTI to the beginning of the Timeline.

2. Click the **Add Default Text** button below the Monitor panel.

3. Change the font to **Chick**; the font size to **72,** and click the **Center Text** button to change the alignment to center-aligned.

4. Type **the crazy caper** to replace the Add Text (you may need to drag your mouse across the **Add Text** first to select it).

   TIP Be sure to press **Enter** on your keyboard after *crazy* and before *caper*.

5. Click the **Vertical Center** button and then the **Horizontal Center** button.

6. Click the **Color Properties** button.

7. In the Color Properties dialog, select **Linear Gradient** from the Gradient menu.

8. Select the first color button by clicking it once and then altering the color values at the top left to R: **50**, G: **250**, B: **200**.

9. Repeat with the second color button, but set these to R: **200**, G: **250**, B: **50**.

10. Click **OK** when finished.

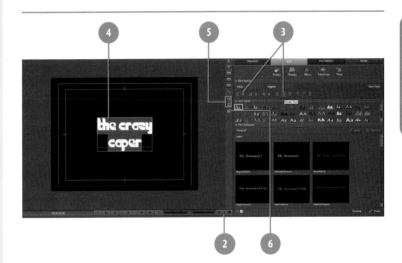

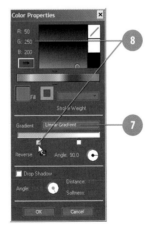

Add a Transition to the Opening Title

1 On the Timeline, select the end (tail) of the Title 04 opening title clip and drag it until it meets the Title 01 clip on the Title track, as shown in the illustration.

2 If it is not already selected, click the **Edit** tab to select the Edit panel and then click the **Transitions** button to view the Transitions view.

3 In the Transitions search field, type **random blocks**.

4 Drag the **Random Blocks** transition and drop it onto the front (head) of the **Title 04** clip on the Title track on the Timeline.

5 Select the **Random Blocks** transition again, and drag it this time onto the tail (end) of the **Title 04** title clip.

6 Press **Ctrl-S** to save your project or you can select **File > Save** from the menu.

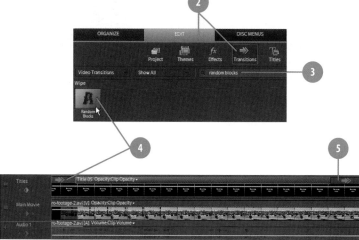

Flying Solo:
Creating the Closing Titles

This is the final clip for this project and you are going to Fly Solo to create a title and a freeze frame. This "caper" is set in Rome, Italy, circa 1966, so you need to create a title to communicate this. You also need to create a freeze frame for the last image of this video by taking one last snapshot and adding it to the end of the clip. You will also use the freeze frame image as the backdrop for your end title. All the settings follow, and all the techniques should by now be familiar to you. Don't worry if you get lost; simply refer back to the previous exercise. Good luck!

Adding a '60s-Style Scene-Setting Title

1. Send the CTI to the end of the Timeline and create a title here (*Hint: End key; Add Default Text button*).

2. Change font to **Chick** and size to **72** and center the text (*Hint: Center Text button*).

3. Type **rome, italy**. Then press **Enter** on your keyboard and type **1966**.

4. Align the text both vertically and horizontally (*Hint: Vertical/Horizontal Center button*).

5. Alter the colors to R: **250** G: **100** B: **230** (*Hint: Color Properties button*).

6. Create a drop shadow using the following settings (*Hint: Color Properties; Drop Shadow check box*): Angle: **130**; Distance: **10**; Softness: **10**.

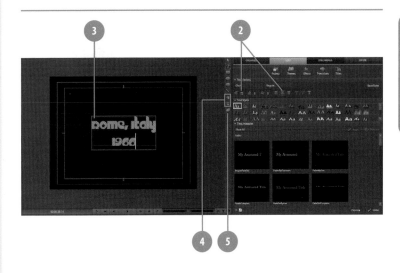

Add a Final Freeze Frame and a Transition for the Closing Title

1. Move the **CTI** to **35;13** and create a freeze frame here (*Hint: Freeze Frame button; select Insert in Movie*).

2. Move the **Title 05** clip from the **Main Video** track to the **Title** track, directly above the final freeze frame (**retrotitle_FF_3.bmp**), as shown in the screenshot.

3. Add the Swirl Transition to the front (head) of the Closing Title (**Title 05**) (*Hint: Transitions button; Type swirl - drag Swirl Transition*).

4. Add a fade to the **Title 05** clip (*Hint: Properties button; Opacity*).

5. Save your project (Hint: Ctrl-S).

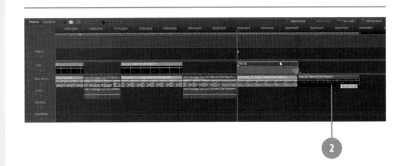

Making Adjustments, Rendering, and Exporting

Well, you've done it! All of the pieces are in place and fully animated and you have your '60s-style opening and closing credits. Test your production by pressing the **Spacebar** to see how it all fits together. If it's not quite right, tweak the timing (move the keyframes around a bit, or add a couple of new ones here or there as needed, shorten the soundtrack, and so on) until it's just right. Then, press **Enter** on your keyboard to render (apply all effects and transitions to the clips) your project.

Finish the Project

1 Once you have played back your project and made the necessary adjustments, press **Enter** on your keyboard to render your project.

2 Once you have made all of these adjustments, press **Ctrl-S** to make a final save of your project.

TIP *Make sure you remember where you saved this project (the Peachpit folder is a good bet) because you will revisit it in Chapter 4, where you add some mood music to your movie, and Chapter 7 where you add a "Movie Look" to the video clips, enhancing the '60s feel of your movie.*

3 Finally, export your work as an AVI file (a standard Microsoft movie file) by selecting the **Timeline**, if it is not already selected, and then choosing **File >Export > Movie**.

4 When prompted, browse to the **Peachpit** folder and then the folder called **HSMovies_Final Renders** and save the exported file as **Chapter 2_retromovie.avi**.

NOTE *This final render will be used again in Chapter 21, as will many of your other final renders from this book.*

5 Exit or minimize Premiere Elements and browse to the **Peachpit** folder and then open the **HSMovies_Final Renders** folder. Double-click the **Chapter 2_Retromovie.avi** file to play it in your default media player.

IMPORTANT *Rendering can take a while, depending upon the speed of your computer and the number of frames that need rendering.*

The completed '60s clip, in all its retro glory, playing in Windows Media player

Hollywood Movie Sound:
Narration, SmartSound, and Sound FX

MEDIA:
SmartSound - Underwater - Ascent.wav
cartoon_stagger.wav
Chapter 1 - Seethrutitle.prel
Chapter 2 - Retromovie.prel

3

COMPLEXITY:	Simple	Moderate	Complex
SKILL LEVEL:	Easy	Intermediate	Advanced

Introduction

What can sound do for a movie? Why even bother with music or special effects? Movies are a visual medium, right? But imagine a Jedi light saber duel without the hum of the saber, the clash of the lasers. Imagine *Jurassic Park* without the roar of T-Rex, or the haunting strike of violins in *Psycho*, warping the visual images to give them an almost literal audio knife-edge!

Audio isn't half the story when it comes to video editing, it's the completion of all that you see, justified in your mind by all that you hear.

To summarize, music and sound effects are very, very important.

In this chapter you'll look at what Premiere Elements can do with sound by adding a musical WAV file to the project you created in Chapter 1, and you'll create your own mood melodies with SmartSound for the project you created in Chapter 2—you'll even add some basic sound effects and create a narration track of your own. You'll also look at balancing the volume of these audio tracks so they don't overwhelm the movie.

Creating a good solid audio track is the squaring of the circle, so if you are tempted to skip any chapters in this book, make sure this isn't one of them.

What You'll Learn

Preparing the Project

Adding Mood Music to a Movie

Mixing the Music Track

Adding SmartSound Music to a Movie

Understanding SmartSound Quicktracks

Flying Solo: Mixing the Retromovie Music

Adding Sound Effects to Your Movie

Creating a Narration Track

Making Adjustments, Rendering, and Exporting

Preparing the Project

In Chapters 1 and 2 you created projects that looked cool but lacked a certain something. Music! In this chapter you add music to those projects and in doing so, learn valuable audio skills that you will use throughout this book and countless times in your own movies. First though, you need to be familiar with reloading projects and creating a working copy.

Work with Saved Projects

1 Start Premiere Elements and select **Open Project** from the splash screen, then select **Chapter 1 – Seethrutitle** (the Premiere Elements project file you created in Chapter 1), or select **File > Open Project** if Premiere Elements is already running on your computer.

> **TIP** You may need to click **Open** and browse to the Peachpit folder if the project you created in Chapter 1 is not displayed.

2 Create a working copy of this project by selecting **File > Save As** and entering the new project name **Chapter 1_Title with Music**. This is to ensure that your original project remains untouched and is available again should you need it.

3 If you are in the Sceneline, switch to the Timeline by clicking the **Timeline** button.

4 Right-click in the Track Header area and from the contextual menu, deselect **Show Audio Tracks**. This allows you to see more of the Timeline by removing unneeded audio tracks.

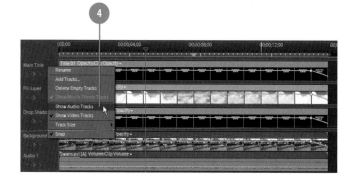

5 When your Timeline looks similar to the one in the screenshot shown, import the **SmartSound - Underwater - Ascent.wav** media clip from the DVD.

TIP *You can find full instructions for importing media into Premiere Elements 7 in the Chapter 1 section "Adding Media to Your Project." Don't forget you need to uncheck all before you make your selection!*

NOTE *The default settings of the Media Down-loader are set not to show audio. To see audio media clips, you need to click the* **Show Audio** *button or press* **Ctrl-U** *on the keyboard. Watch out, Media Downloader rechecks all the files when you do this, so you will need to uncheck all again!*

6 Once you have completed the preceding steps, press **Crtl-S** on your keyboard and move on to the next section.

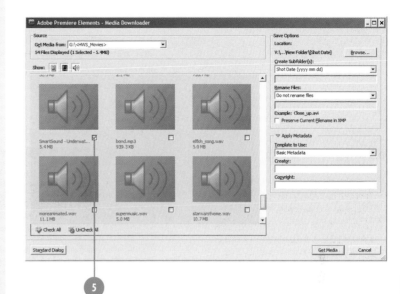

Adding Mood Music to a Movie

The final, and necessary, touch to a good opening credits sequence is to have some music playing "under" the visuals. In the last section, you imported a mellow little tune called **SmartSound - Underwater - Ascent.wav**. This is a small sample from the SmartSound Quicktracks collection (***www.smartsound.com***). You will now add this to the Soundtrack track and then create a fade out for the movie you created in Chapter 1.

Add a Little Music

1. If it is not already selected, click the **Edit** tab to select the Edit workspace.

2. From the Media panel, drag the **SmartSound - Underwater - Ascent.wav** media clip onto the Soundtrack track on the Timeline.

   TIP *Make sure the head of the clip is at the start of the Timeline.*

3. Grab the tail end of the **SmartSound - Underwater - Ascent.wav** media clip and resize it so that it matches the length of the video clips described earlier.

4. Click the **Properties** button to view the Properties view for the **SmartSound - Underwater - Ascent.wav** media clip.

5. Open the Volume setting by clicking the small triangle and then clicking the **Fade In** and then the **Fade Out** buttons.

   INFORMATION *The volume for this media clip will now fade in and out at the beginning and end of the clip.*

6. Press **Ctrl-S** on the keyboard to save your work so far.

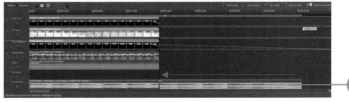

Mixing the Music Track

In the last section you added a musical track to the Chapter 1 movie. This has enhanced it greatly, but it also revealed a few problems. The default volume level for the music track is a little high, and the audio from the **Swans.avi** clip is distracting and not really needed at all. In this next section, you mix the audio levels to get rid of these problems.

Adjust Audio Levels for AVI and WAV Media Clips

1. If it is not already open, open the **Chapter 1 - Title with Music** project by selecting **File > Open** and browsing to where you saved the project.

2. Press **Home** on the keyboard to send the CTI to the start of the Timeline.

3. Click the **Mix Audio** button above the Timeline to open the Audio Mixer.

4. Click the small double arrow icon in the top right of the Audio Mixer box and select **Show/Hide Tracks**.

5. In Show/Hide Tracks, deselect **Audio 2, 3,** and **4**. These contain no audio and are not needed.

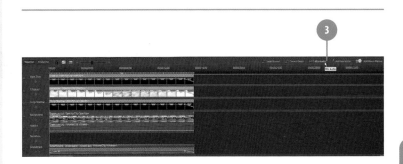

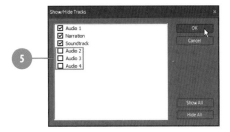

6 Adjust the audio level of the **Swans.avi** media clip to zero dB by moving the Level Slider to the bottom. Close the Audio Mixer when you are finished by clicking the small "x" in the upper right corner of the box panel to close the Audio Mixer.

NOTE *When you let go of the slider, the orange volume indicator on the clip in the Timeline automatically shows the change.*

7 To adjust the **SmartSound - Underwater - Ascent.wav** media clip, you alter the volume directly on the Timeline. Select the clip by clicking it once, then place the cursor midway between the two fade keyframes and over the orange volume indicator line. When you have the mouse in the correct place, the cursor should show a volume indictor next to the arrow (see screenshot).

8 With this new cursor showing, hold down the left mouse button and drag the line downward, keeping an eye on the displayed dB level. Decide yourself what dB level is best, but a setting of -8.3 dB is about right.

NOTE *Even with a fade, the music as it currently stands cuts out a little too harshly. You can cure this by adjusting the end of the music track to run a little beyond the end of the video (10 or 15 frames), then adjust the last fade keyframe to land at this new end point.*

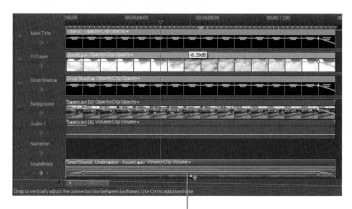

Did You Know?

You can add as many keyframes as you like to an audio level. If an important piece of dialogue would be swamped by music, but otherwise you are happy with the audio level of the music, you can create a keyframe on either side of the dialog and then reduce the audio level between those keyframes. It is worth remembering that gradual decreases and increases in music sound more natural.

Adding SmartSound Music to a Movie

In the last section you brought in a music file created in SmartSound. In this section you learn how to generate your own music with SmartSound and choose a variation on the standard list of music before you save it to your Media panel and add it to the project you created in Chapter 2. For more details about SmartSound and its incredible capabilities, see the sidebar "Understanding SmartSound Quicktracks" later in this chapter.

Add a Little Lounge Music to the Movie

① Following the instructions in the "Preparing the Project" section earlier in this chapter, open your **Chapter 2_Retromovie** project (stored in the **Peachpit** folder), then save a copy to work with called **Chapter 2_With Music**.

TIP *Don't forget to deselect **Show Audio Tracks** so that you can view more of the Timeline without having to scroll.*

② Press **Home** on your keyboard to return the CTI to the beginning of the Timeline tracks and if it is not already selected, click the **Edit** tab to select the Edit workspace.

③ Click the **SmartSound** button just above the Timeline or select the **SmartSound** option from the New Item button above the Media panel.

IMPORTANT *The SmartSound option only appears if you have installed SmartSound Quicktracks on your computer. This is normally installed by default when Premiere Elements is first installed; if it is not, please refer to the Adobe Help file.*

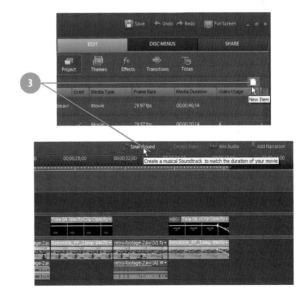

4 The SmartSound Quicktracks for Premiere Elements box appears. Click the **Click here to select music!** hyperlink next to the Name field and the SmartSound Maestro box appears. It is here that you can select your choice of music.

NOTE *You may see a different set of Smart-Sound tracks than appear in the screenshot opposite. What appears all depends on whether you had a previous copy of SmartSound on your computer. See the SmartSound help files for more information.*

5 On the SmartSound Maestro window, select **Owned by me** from the Find Music column.

6 Select **R&B/Funk** from the Style column.

7 Select **Motor City Jam** from the track list and then click **Select**.

TIP *To preview a SmartSound track, double-click the name.*

8 On the SmartSound Quicktracks for Premiere Elements box in the length field, change the default 30 seconds to be slightly longer (10 frames or so) than the length of your movie.

TIP *Your Chapter 2 movie should be around 40;14 (40 seconds and 14 frames), so enter 40 seconds and 24 frames.*

9 Select **Get Down** from the Variation list.

TIP *Click the **Play** button if you want to preview the tune you created.*

10 Click **OK** and you are prompted to save the file. Save the music file to a location on your hard drive and click **OK**. The Quicktracks music file is added to the Media panel and also to the Timeline.

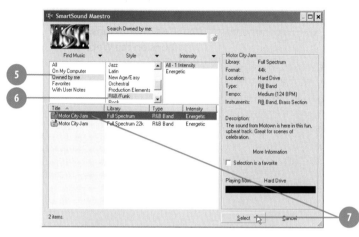

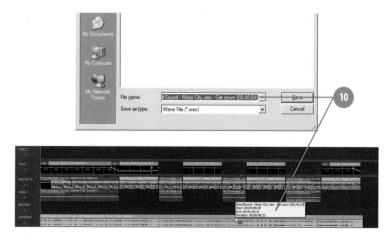

Understanding SmartSound Quicktracks

Quicktracks is an excellent movie-making tool from the people at SmartSound. It allows you to use both the songs that come bundled with the product right off the Quicktracks CD, as well as the hundreds of songs that you can buy on music CDs or download directly from the company's web site.

The music provided with Quicktracks and on the additional music CDs is very similar to the music you'll hear on commercials, corporate presentations, and multimedia and Flash presentations on the Web. What's unique about Quicktracks is that you can choose not just a given tune, but variations on that tune, and you can also choose a custom duration.

For example, if you choose the music selection called "It's Cool" from the list of tracks available with Quicktracks (which SmartSound describes as "Way cool, easy feel jazz with trumpet, sax, piano, bass, and drums"), you'll be able to select from a number of variations on the theme, including:

- Cool
- Sly
- Miles
- Bluesy

Using Quicktracks

To choose a song from Quicktracks, click the **Click here to select music!** link next to the Name field. When you click the prompt, the SmartSound Maestro window appears (shown in figure)—here you can choose the song you want.

But you can also:

- Search for music (on your hard drive as well as on SmartSound's web site).
- Sort and filter the music by category, style, and intensity.
- Listen to selections of the music to help you choose the music that best fits the project you're working on.

Some of the music that comes with Quicktracks is ready to use, and some you need to purchase. You can purchase music on the spot over the Internet, which lets you get right back to your project with just a minor interruption. To see tracks that are available to purchase, select **All** in the Find Music field, then select any track you do not already own and click the **Purchase** button. A preview of your chosen track should play whenever you select it, although an Internet connection is required for this.

3

Flying Solo: Mixing the Retromovie Music

Earlier in this chapter, in the "Mixing the Music Track" section, you learned two different methods to control the audio levels of your media clips. Fly Solo now and adjust the audio of the SmartSound track using the Audio Mixer and the audio level of the **Retro-footage_2.avi** files. You sliced these files apart in Chapter 2 by including freeze frames, so you need to adjust each one individually. Hints and tips are listed below, but if you get lost, just refer back to the "Mixing the Music Track" section.

Make It Smoother

1. Before you proceed, make sure you have saved your work so far by pressing **Ctrl-S** on the keyboard or by using **File > Save**, and then move the CTI to the start of the Timeline.

2. Open the **Audio Mixer** and hide the audio tracks you will not be working with (*Hint: Mix Audio Button; Hide/Show Audio tracks; deselect Audio 1 and 2*).

3. With the CTI at the start of the Timeline, reduce the volume for the first slice of **Retro-footage_2.avi** (*Hint: Audio 1 slider; move to bottom*).

4. Reduce the volume level for the other two slices of **Retro-footage_2.avi** (*Hint: move CTI over the clip; adjust Audio 1 slider to "0"; repeat*).

5. With the Audio Mixer still open, reduce the **Soundtrack** volume to a comfortable level (*Hint: adjust Soundtrack slider*).

   NOTE *SmartSound doesn't usually need a fade in or out if you have entered the correct duration of your Timeline when you're generating the tune.*

Did You Know?

If you want to rip a track from an Audio CD that you own, you need to do that using a different piece of software, then import that media clip using the PC Files and Folders option in the Get Media panel.

Adding Sound Effects to Your Movie

Sound effects are used to mark specific on-screen events, such as a phone ringing. In this next exercise you use unnumbered Timeline markers to mark on the Timeline where the sound effects should go. You then add a sound effect to the Timeline, adjust it for duration, then copy and paste it to two other unnumbered markers on the Timeline.

Import a Sound File to the Media Panel

1 If it is not already open, open the **Chapter 2_ With Music** project by selecting **File > Open** and browsing to where you saved the project.

2 Press **Home** on the keyboard to send the CTI to the start of the Timeline.

3 If the Audio track for the Main Title track is hidden from the previous exercise, right-click directly in the **Main Title** header area and select **Show Audio Tracks**.

4 When your Timeline looks similar to the one in the screenshot opposite, import the **cartoon_stagger.wav** media clip from the DVD.

> **TIP** *You can find full instructions for importing media into Premiere Elements 7 in the Chapter 1 section "Adding Media to Your Project." Don't forget you need to uncheck all before you make your selection!*

> **NOTE** *The default settings of the Media Downloader are set not to show audio. To see the* **cartoon_stagger.wav** *media clip, you need to click the* **Show Audio** *button or press* **Ctrl-U** *on the keyboard. Watch out, Media Downloader rechecks all the files when you do this and you will need to uncheck them all again!*

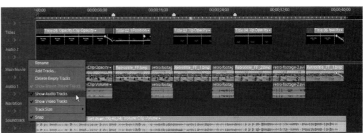

The Chapter 2_Title with Music Timeline with the Audio 2 track showing

Create Unnumbered Markers on the Timeline

1. If it is not already selected, click the **Edit** tab to select the Edit workspace.

2. Move the CTI to the start of the first title (*00;00;10;00*), right-click the CTI and choose **Timeline > Set Timeline Marker > Unnumbered** from the contextual menu to place an unnumbered marker at that location.

3. Repeat step 2 and place a marker at the start of the second and third titles.

   TIP *Use the **Page Down** key to jump up the Timeline.*

Insert and Adjust a Sound File

1. From the media panel, drag the **cartoon_stagger.wav** media file from the Media panel to the Audio 2 track and align it with the first unnumbered marker

2. Zoom in on the Timeline so that you can clearly see the wave form of the audio file, and move the CTI to just after the first sound finishes (indicated by a flat area of the wave form).

3. Click the **Split Clip** button or press **Ctrl-K** to cut the clip at the CTI point.

4. Select the right-hand selection and press **Delete** on the keyboard to remove it from the Timeline.

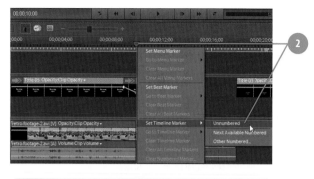

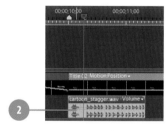

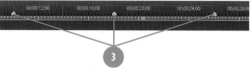

Copy and Paste Sound FX

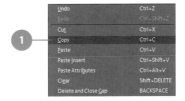

1. With the adjusted sound file selected on the Timeline (indicated by a purple bar running along the top), choose **Edit > Copy** from the menu.

2. Move the CTI to the next unnumbered marker using **Ctrl-Right Arrow**.

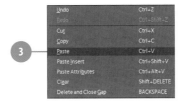

3. Choose **Edit > Paste** from the menu to create a copy of your edited clip at that point.

4. Move the CTI to the final unnumbered marker using **Ctrl-Right Arrow**, and use **Edit > Paste** (or **Ctrl-V**) to insert another copy at this point.

   NOTE *The installation of SmartSound that comes with Premiere Elements does not contain any sound effects, but you can purchase a huge selection online.*

Did You Know?

You can set a marker to the beat of the music. Place your audio media file on the Timeline, then press the **spacebar** to play back. Now every time you hear the beat of the music, press **asterisk key on the number pad of** your keyboard to place an unnumbered marker on the Timeline. Beat markers appear as small musical notes, as opposed to the normal marker icon.

3

Creating a Narration Track

Adding a narration track is one of the most effective ways to enhance a movie, and whether it's a noir voice-over or a documentary's explanation, the method of using this powerful feature remains the same. In this section you add a narration to the Narration track using your own microphone. If you don't have a microphone, skip this section and return when you do.

Work with Saved Projects

1. If it is not already open, open **Chapter 1 - Title with Music** by selecting **File > Open Recent Project** and choosing the **Chapter 1 - Title with Music** project.

2. When the project has finished loading, press **Home** on the keyboard to send the CTI to the start of the Timeline.

Add a Narration

1 Click the **Add Narration** button to open the Record Voice Narration box.

NOTE *To use the narration feature in Premiere Elements, you must have a microphone plugged into your computer. Ensure this is fully working before you continue with this exercise. See your computer handbook and the Adobe help file for details.*

2 Click the **Mic Source** button in the Record Voice Narration window and select which source your microphone is using.

TIP *If you want to hear your voice at the same time you are speaking (not recommended), you need to uncheck **Mute** in the Record Voice Narration window and also use headphones to avoid feedback.*

3 To begin the narration, click the red **Record Narration** button and begin speaking after the 3-second countdown. When you finish, click the stop button and an audio clip containing your narration is added to the Media panel.

4 Adjust the Narration audio level using the **Audio Mixer**.

5 Press **Ctrl-S** to save your work so far.

TIP *If you don't hit stop, the narration automatically comes to an end 30 seconds after the last clip on the Timeline.*

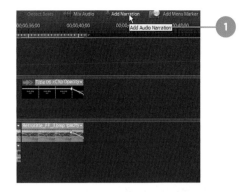

3

Making Adjustments, Rendering, and Exporting

▶

Play your movie by pressing the **Spacebar** and make sure everything looks and *sounds* good. You may want to adjust the audio levels a bit or tweak this or that. Have fun; it's your baby. Once everything is just as you want it, you're ready to share the results, either as a video file or on tape or DVD.

Finish the Project

1 Once you have played back your project and made the necessary adjustments, press **Enter** on your keyboard to render your project.

2 Once you have made all of these adjustments, press **Ctrl-S** to make a final save of your project.

> **TIP** *Make sure you remember where you saved the **Chapter 2_With Music** project (the **Peachpit** folder is a good bet) as you revisit it in Chapter 7 where you add a "Movie Look" to the video clips, enhancing the '60s feel of your movie.*

3 Finally, export your work as an AVI file (a standard Microsoft movie file) by selecting the **Timeline**, if it is not already selected, and then choosing **File > Export > Movie**.

4 When prompted, browse to the **Peachpit** folder and then the folder called **HSMovies_ Final Renders** and save the exported file as **Chapter 2_with music.avi**.

> **NOTE** *You will use this final render again in Chapter 21, as you will use many of your other final renders from this book.*

5 Exit or minimize Premiere Elements, browse to the **Peachpit** folder, and then open the **HSMovies_Final Renders** folder. Double-click the **Chapter 2_with music.avi** file to play it in your default media player.

Hollywood Movie Titles:
The Star Wars Title Effect

MEDIA:

starfield.jpg
244325_OpeningCreditsWilliams.wav

4

COMPLEXITY:	Simple	Moderate	Complex
SKILL LEVEL:	Easy	Intermediate	Advanced

Introduction

Fascination with George Lucas's *Star Wars* movies continues decades after their release and will never really leave us. In this chapter, you learn how to create your own vanishing logo and epic "scrolling story" just like the ones you've come to know and love from the *Star Wars* movies.

You don't need any special equipment or additional software to create this effect, but on the DVD supplied with this book you will find a star field background (complete with a supernova!) provided courtesy of the National Aeronautics and Space Administration (NASA).

You'll also find the jedifont.ttf font on the DVD; you should have already installed this in Chapter 2. Finally, the DVD includes a WAV sample file, 244325_OpeningCreditsWilliams.wav, from the www.StockMusicSite. com web site, which offers many more musical tunes at very reasonable prices. Remember, this is only a sample to give your work that air of authenticity; it is illegal to distribute this with any money-making project.

Although we've supplied you with a convincing starfield, think outside the galaxy on this. You can superimpose your *Star Wars*ian title across any background, including stills and video clips from the videos that you took; they don't need to be from outer space necessarily. In addition, feel free to change the music to anything you like. As long as the music has punch, it will work just fine and will make the title sequence truly your own.

What You'll Learn

Flying Solo: Preparing the Project

Creating Your "Long Ago" Text

Building Your Opening Logo

Animating Your Logo

Flying Solo: Preparing Your Scrolling Text

Making the Scrolling Text Scroll

Changing the Speed

Transforming the Shape of the Scrolling Text

Animating the Scrolling Text

Flying Solo: Adding the Star Wars Theme Music

Flying Solo: Adding Some Project Polish

Making Adjustments, Rendering, and Exporting

Flying Solo: Preparing the Project

By now you should be fairly confident when it comes to setting up a project using Premiere Elements, so Fly Solo to complete the basic tasks you need to begin this project. If you need more help, refer to the "Preparing the Project" sections in Chapters 1 and 2.

Basic Timeline Preparation Skills

1 Create a new project called **Chapter 4_Clone_ Attack_Title** (*Hint: File > New > Project*).

2 Set the Timeline to Timeline View (*Hint: Timeline button to the left of the interface*).

3 Deselect the audio tracks for **Video 2** and **3** (*Hint: Deselect Show Audio Tracks*).

4 Rename (*Hint: Right-click the header*) and change each track to the following:

◆ Video 1: **Background**

◆ Video 2: **Start Title**

◆ Video 3: **Logo**

5 Import the **starfield.jpg** and **244325_ OpeningCreditsWilliams.wav** media clips from the DVD (*Hint: Media Downloader; Show Audio; UnCheck All*).

> **INFORMATION** *The starfield image is brought to you courtesy of NASA. If this one doesn't suit your tastes, visit the NASA web site (**www. nasa.gov/home**) and search for more.*

6 Add the **starfield.jpg** to the Background track. Make sure the head of the image is the start of the Timeline (*Hint: Switch to Edit workspace; drag*).

7 Zoom the **Timeline** in a few clicks (*Hint: click the plus sign next to the zoom slider*).

8 When your Timeline and Media panel look similar to the screenshots opposite, press **Ctrl-S** to save your work so far, then proceed to the next section.

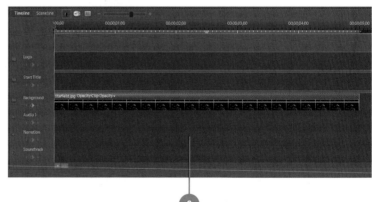

Creating Your "Long Ago" Text

All of the *Star Wars* movies begin with the now universally recognizable, "A long time ago, in a galaxy far, far away…" The beauty of this opening text is how it sets an almost fairytale-like tone in just seven simple words (with "far" repeated), reminiscent of the equally well-known "happily ever after." You can also easily modify the phrase to suit the movie you're putting together, as you will do here with, "A short time ago, in a house not too far away…"

Create the Opening Text

① Click the **Add Default Text** button below the Monitor panel.

② Right-click the default **Add Text** box and select **Cut** from the contextual menu.

③ Click the **Text** key in the Titler if it isn't already selected.

④ Starting in the upper-left corner of the screen, drag a box across the entire screen, down to the lower-right corner, as shown in the illustration. Be sure to stay within the safe margins for titles.

Did You Know?

You can play it safe with margins. Your computer screen can show text and graphics right to the edge of your screen. Therefore, displaying movies online in a media player won't be a problem. But playing it on a television screen is another story. A television screen shows less than a PC monitor and images and titles can appear clipped at the edges. Whenever you create text and titles, be sure to use safe text margins. To display the safe text margins, right-click inside the Monitor panel, select **View > Safe Title Margins**. Optionally, you can display the Safe Action Margins as well.

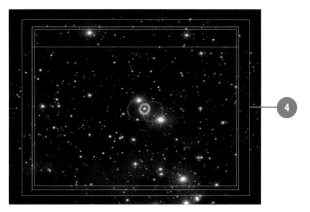

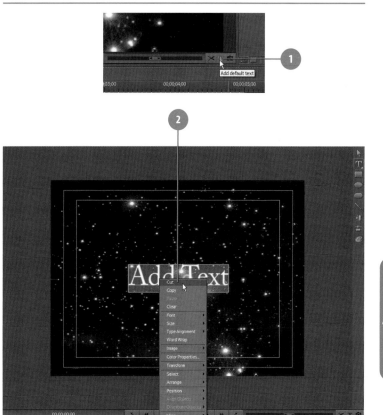

4

Type and Style the Text

1. Type the following text: **A short time ago, in a house not too far away...** (including the ellipses).

2. Press **Ctrl-A** on your keyboard to select all the text you just typed.

3. Right-click inside the text area and from the contextual menu, choose **Font > Arial Narrow > Bold**.

4. Change the font size from the default 64 to 33 by right-clicking again inside the text area and choosing **Size > Other**; then type **33** into the number field and press **OK**.

   TIP *The text all needs to fit on one line. If you are creating different text than the text we're using here and it doesn't quite fit on one line, just reduce the font size a bit more.*

5. Set the justification to centered by clicking the **Center Text** button.

Did You Know?

All of your fonts are here, and out there, too.... All of the fonts that you have installed on your Windows system, including TrueType and OpenType fonts, are available for you to select from and use in your projects here in the Premiere Elements Titler. In addition, thousands of free fonts are available on the Web; these can add a unique look to your titles. One excellent source is Blambot (**www.blambot.com**), a site for comic book artists and fans. Plenty of other font sites are out there, too. Just search for "fonts" or "free fonts" using your favorite Internet search engine.

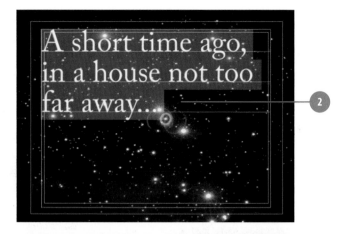

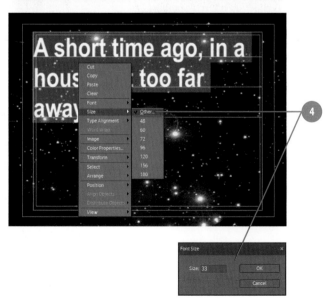

6 Resize the text box by clicking the **Selection Tool** and grabbing the bottom handle of the box; then drag it up to make the box evenly surround the text, as shown in the illustration.

7 Reposition the text so that it sits in the center of the screen by clicking the two centering buttons:

◆ Click the **Vertical Center** button.

◆ Click the **Horizontal Center** button.

8 Premiere Elements should automatically place the new title on the Timeline. If not, drag the title you just created from the **Media** panel to the **Start Title** track on the Timeline so that the head (front) of the clip is at the very beginning of the track.

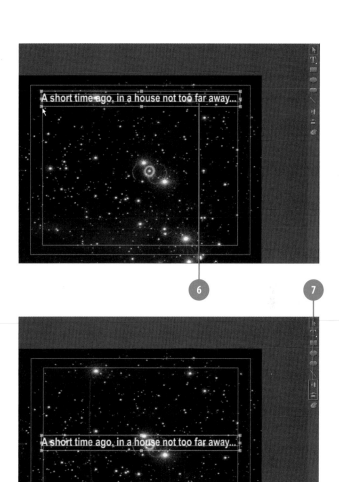

Did You Know?

The Style Properties panel enables you to control all font properties. On the Style Properties panel of the Titler, you'll not only find a full list of all fonts, you'll also find the justification buttons (left, right, and center) as well as the style buttons (bold, italic, and underline). It's here, too, that you set the font size, kerning (the space between letters), and the leading (the space between lines of type in a paragraph).

Create Your Own Style

Save Your Favorite Font Settings as a New Style

As you adjust font properties, you may find you hit on a result that you really like. You don't have to re-create these settings over and over again each time you create a title. Instead, you can save it as your own personal style. Just click the **Save Style** button. Your new style is included with all of the built-in styles at the top of the Titler Properties panel. Premiere Elements saves it at the end of that list, so scroll down if you don't see it. It is even saved with a representation of what the style looks like. If you like your new style so much that you want to use it all the time, right-click it and select **Set Style As Default** from the contextual menu. Until you change it, Premiere Elements uses this style every time you click the **Add Text** button. Better still, the style is available across projects.

Building Your Opening Logo

Every *Star Wars* movie has its instantly recognizable opening logo, and every good parody (or homage) should have it, too. Creating the logo is straightforward. You'll use the Titler to enter this text: **clone attack**. Just be sure you use the font from this chapter. The font is so recognizable that people will understand the reference right away. In addition, the logo behaves a certain way (static and bigger than full screen for the first few seconds, then drifting out to vanish in deep outer space). As long as you follow these few simple rules, everyone will understand the reference.

Set Up Your Logo in the Titler

1 Move the **Current Time Indicator (CTI)** to the end of the Timeline by pressing **End** on the keyboard.

> **NOTE** *If you have not already installed the Jedi font (**Star Jedi Hollow**) please save your project, exit Premiere Elements, and then follow the instructions for font installation you find in Chapter 2. Continue with this exercise when this is done.*

2 Click the **Add Default Text** button under the Monitor panel and the Titler opens with the Add Text automatically selected. Type over it with this text:

clone

attack

> **TIP** *Type the name in lowercase. Be sure to press **Enter** on your keyboard after the first word so that each word is on its own line.*

3 Highlight the text you just typed by dragging your mouse across it or by pressing **Ctrl-A** on your keyboard.

4 Right-click the text and from the contextual menu, select the **Star Jedi Hollow** font.

> **TIP** *Depending on the number of fonts installed on your computer, you may have to select **More** at the top of each list of fonts to navigate to the **Star Jedi Hollow** font.*

Adjust and Stylize the Logo

1 The font looks cool, but you need to adjust the font size and reduce the leading to make it dramatically fill the screen and give it that distinctive *Star Wars* look. To do so, in the Titler Properties panel, enter these settings:

◆ Font Size: **305**

◆ Leading: **-198** (negative)

INFORMATION *Reducing the leading by a negative amount forces the two words to sit on top of each other. You can find the Leading field next to the font size or you can access it via the right-click contextual menu.*

2 Adjust the text justification by clicking the **Center Text** button.

3 Center the two words on the screen this way:

◆ Click the **Vertical Center** button.

◆ Click the **Horizontal Center** button.

4 Click the **Color Properties** button.

5 Select a yellow color by entering these settings:

◆ R: **255**

◆ G: **255**

◆ B: **0**

6 Click **OK**, then click anywhere on the Timeline to exit the Titler.

Relocate the Clone Attack Logo

1. Select the Clone Attack clip and move the title up the Timeline so the head of the new title aligns with the tail of the other two clips.

   TIMESAVER *When moving and aligning clips, use the CTI as a guide. For example, in this case you could first move the CTI to the tail end of the "Short time ago" title clip so that it's at position 00;00;05;00.*

2. Extend the duration of the **starfield.jpg** by dragging the tail of the clip up the Timeline so that it aligns with the tail of the Clone Attack title clip.

3. Zoom the Timeline so that you can see all of the clips on the Timeline.

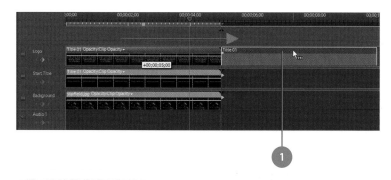

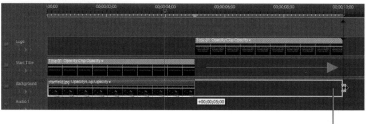

Animating Your Logo

Now that you've created your own version of the *Star Wars* logo, you need to animate it to give it that cinematic touch. In the *Star Wars* movies, the logo waits on the screen for just a second as the music begins to swell. Once the audience is fully engaged, the logo drifts out of the way into outer space to let the scrolling text tell the story. In this section, you'll learn how to animate the logo using keyframes in the motion control settings. For this task, you apply keyframes and then make small adjustments to them to get the effect you need.

Make Your Logo Zoom Off into Space

1 Select the **Clone Attack** logo in the Logo track on the Timeline.

2 Press **Page Up** or **Page Down** as needed to move the CTI to the head (start) of the clip.

3 Click the **Properties** button to see the Properties view for the **Clone Attack** title clip.

4 Click the **Show Keyframes** button to reveal the workspace for adding keyframes, as shown in the screenshot.

NOTE *After you click it, the **Show Keyframes** button becomes the **Hide Keyframes** button.*

5 In **Properties** view, click the triangle next to **Motion** to reveal the effect's controls.

6 Set the **Scale** to **125.0**.

7 Click the **Toggle Animation** button (shown in the screenshot opposite) to turn on the animation functionality of Premiere Elements.

TIP *Premiere Elements automatically places a keyframe at this point.*

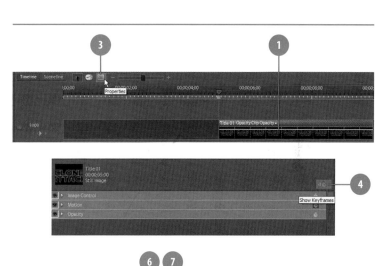

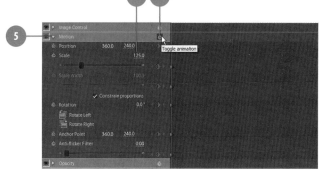

4

8. Move the CTI to the end of the clip by pressing **Page Down** on your keyboard.

9. Set the **Scale** to **0.0**.

   TIP *Premiere Elements automatically places another keyframe at this point.*

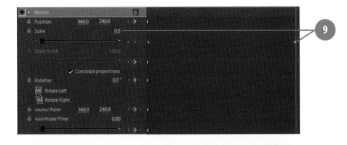

10. You now have a logo that starts at 125 percent and fades away to nothing. However, you really want the Clone Attack logo to pause on screen at 125 percent to fully engage the audience for a few seconds, so move the CTI back to 00;00;08;00.

11. Set the **Scale** to **125.0**.

   TIP *Again, Premiere Elements automatically places a keyframe at this point.*

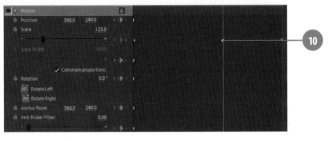

Did You Know?

There is a difference between Render and Realtime. You can optionally render your project at any time, for example, after applying an effect such as a Motion effect. When you apply an effect, Premiere Elements shows you a realtime representation of the effect. This representation allows you to get an idea of how the effect will look, which lets you try different effects and tweak their settings. It's not until you render, however, by pressing **Enter** that you see how the effect truly looks. To show you that a clip has effects applied but not rendered, Premiere Elements places a thin red line above any clip waiting for rendering.

Flying Solo: Preparing Your Scrolling Text

Now that you have your opening text and your logo prepared, your next step is to create some scrolling text. We provided text for this chapter that (somewhat loosely) sticks to the established format, but to save time, you can cut and paste it into the Premiere Elements Titler. Although the copy and paste aspect is new, other elements in this section use skills you should feel comfortable with, so Fly Solo now and set up the Titler so it's ready to receive the pasted text, then copy and paste the text in from the **starwarstext.txt** file you will find on the DVD, before you finally color the text. As always, hints are included to guide you if you struggle.

Create Your Text

1 Move the CTI to the end of the Clone Attack clip (*Hint: Page Up or Page Down*).

2 Open the Titler (*Hint: the Add Default Text button below the Monitor panel*).

3 In the **Titler Properties** panel, set the following font properties:

- ◆ **Arial Narrow**
- ◆ **Bold**
- ◆ Font size: **22**

4 Delete the **Add Text** text (*Hint: Right-click inside the actual text and select Cut*).

5 Create a large text box covering the inner safe area (*Hint: Type Tool; drag from top-left corner to bottom-right corner*).

6 Without leaving the title area, move the newly created title up above the Logo track to create a new track (*Hint: click the actual title; drag to new location; Premiere Elements creates a new track for you*).

NOTE *If you have Premiere Elements configured with more than three video tracks, simply drag the clip to the existing Video 4 track.*

7 Rename the Video 4 track to **Scrolling Title** (*Hint: right-click the Track Header; select Rename*).

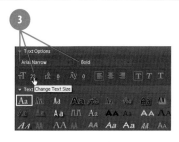

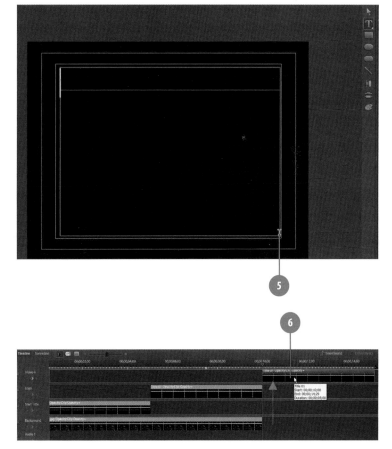

Import the Scrolling Text

1 Jump out to Windows Explorer and navigate to the DVD supplied with this book.

2 Navigate to the **Chapter 4** folder.

3 Double-click the file, **starwarstext.txt**.

> **NOTE** *If you don't have the file association for text files to be opened by Windows Notepad, right-click the file instead, and from the contextual menu, select **Open With** and then select **Notepad**.*

4 Copy the text from Notepad (*Hint: Select All; Edit > Copy or Ctrl-C*).

5 Return to Premiere Elements.

6 Paste the copied text into the text box, then drag the bottom of the box downwards to reveal all of the imported text (*Hint: right-click in the empty text box; select Paste; use Select Tool; drag bottom handle of text box downwards to the bottom of the interface*).

> **NOTE** *The text from the **starwarstext.txt** file you copied should appear. On some systems this may take a few moments; if it doesn't appear after a minute or so, repeat the preceding steps.*

7 Center the text (*Hint: Center Text button*).

Did You Know?

Three choices of paragraph alignment are available in the Titler. Premiere Elements has three paragraph alignment styles: left, right, and center. Die-hard *Star Wars* fans know that the scrolling text is fully justified both to the left and to the right. However, Premiere Elements doesn't have a fully justified setting. Instead, you'll use center, which, once the text is animated to drift into outer space, is a convincing compromise. Just don't tell anyone at a convention!

The text in Notepad, ready to be copied.

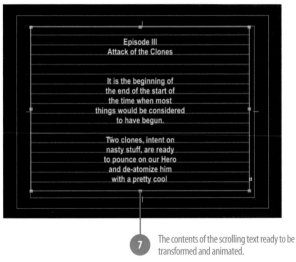

The contents of the scrolling text ready to be transformed and animated.

Color the Text

1 Without leaving the Titler, open the Color Properties box (*Hint: Color Properties button*).

2 Create a yellow color for this text similar to the Logo title (*Hint: R: 255, G: 255, B: 0*).

3 Exit the Color Properties box and then exit the Titler (*Hint: click OK; click anywhere on the Timeline*).

Did You Know?

For more efficient writing and editing, use a word processor such as Microsoft Word. Why not benefit from not only your knowledge of your favorite word processor, but also its built-in spell-checker and other tools any time you need to create longer text? Here's how: First, write your scrolling text in your word processor until you get it just right. Then, use the word processor's thesaurus and spell-checker to finish the passage. Finally, select the text (use the mouse or the shortcut **Ctrl-A**) and copy it to the clipboard (**Ctrl-C**). Back in Premiere Elements, press **Ctrl-V** to paste the text into a text box and you're ready to go.

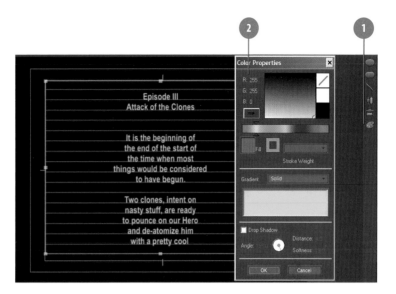

4

Making the Scrolling Text Scroll

If you press the **spacebar** at this point, you'd be disappointed to see that the scrolling text, after all this work, doesn't actually scroll. This is because you need to tell Premiere Elements that you want this text to roll, specifically, from "off camera" to "off camera." This is a simple tweak, but the Roll/Crawl Options button you use to make it happen is tiny and often missed. Refer to the screenshot if you cannot find it.

Make the Text Roll

1 Double-click the scrolling text in the Scrolling Title track on the Timeline to open the text in the Titler.

2 Click the **Roll/Crawl Options** button (it's a tiny icon, so look out for it) to open the Roll/Crawl Options dialog.

3 In the Roll/Crawl Options dialog, under Title Type, select **Roll**.

4 In the Timing (Frames) area, click both of these boxes:

   ◆ **Start Off Screen**

   ◆ **End Off Screen**

   TIP When you click **Start Off Screen**, Preroll is disabled, and when you click **End Off Screen**, Postroll is disabled.

5 Click **OK**.

6 On some systems, you may need to render the Timeline (press **Enter**) to see the scrolling effect.

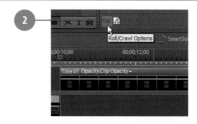

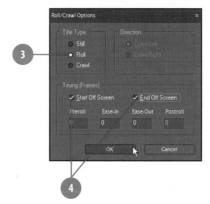

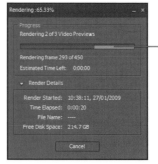

Rendering and exporting your video can take awhile. You can always cancel and go back and finish later. Premiere Elements will pick up where it left off.

Changing the Speed

The text is looking really good for the time that you can see it, which isn't for long enough to appreciate the coolness of your work. You need to slow the whole thing down, and for this you use Time Stretch to increase the number of frames appearing over a much longer duration of time. Effectively, you are creating a slow motion of the title scroll.

Slow It All Down

1 Right-click the **Scrolling** title clip and select **Time Stretch** from the contextual menu.

TIP *If a short menu displays, this is the **Properties** contextual menu. Simply right-click a second time, and the correct contextual menu appears, from which you can select **Time Stretch**.*

TIMESAVER *Optionally, you can click the clip and then press **Ctrl-R** on your keyboard to access the **Time Stretch** dialog.*

2 In the **Time Stretch** dialog, click the **link (chain) icon** until it "breaks" to disconnect the speed from the duration.

3 Click in the **Speed** field and type **6.25**.

4 Click in the **Duration** field and type **00;00;40;00**.

5 Click **OK**. You may want to zoom out on the Timeline to display the entire title.

NOTE *Some systems may need a few moments to update the Timeline after you have made changes.*

TIP *You have now increased the amount of time that this clip displays from the default of 5 seconds to a full 40 seconds, and you've decreased the speed from 100 percent (standard speed) to a more easy-to-read 6.25 percent.*

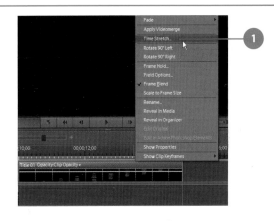

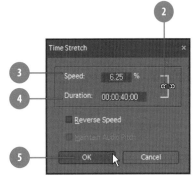

Transforming the Shape of the Scrolling Text

Now that you have created the text, it is scrolling through space and time, and it looks the way you want, you now need to create the appropriate shape of the text block. The *Star Wars* "look" is for the text to start off close to the bottom of the screen and to gradually fade into space, becoming progressively smaller (and harder to read). You make this happen using the Basic 3D video effect to transform the text into the right shape and to make it appear on the right plane.

Change the Perspective

1. If you haven't already done so, click anywhere in a blank area of the Timeline to exit the Titler and then switch to the Edit workspace if that is not already displayed.

2. Click the **Effects** button to view the Effects panel.

3. In the Effects panel text field, type **basic** to bring up the Basic 3D video effect.

4. Select the **Basic 3D** effect from the Perspective Video Effects and drop it onto the **Scrolling Text** title clip on the **Scrolling Title** track.

5. Open the Properties view for the title by clicking the **Properties** button (next to the Zoom Controls), and then click the triangle next to the Basic 3D control to view the effect's controls.

   TIP *You won't see your changes in the Monitor panel unless the CTI is positioned somewhere above the scrolling title clip. So, if the CTI is elsewhere on the Timeline, move it over the clip now.*

6. Adjust the **Tilt** and **Distance** settings (all settings are negative):

   ◆ Swivel: **-1**

   ◆ Tilt: **-65**

   ◆ Distance to Image: **-30**

   NOTE *Leave the other controls—Specular Highlight, and Preview—at their default settings.*

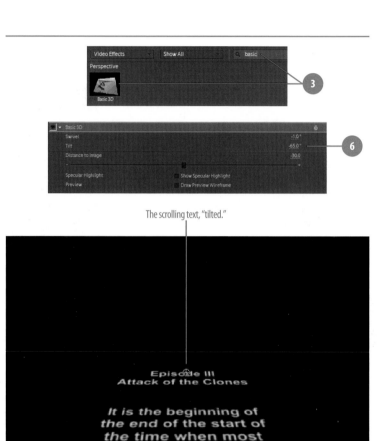

The scrolling text, "tilted."

Animating the Scrolling Text

Now that your scrolling text looks like it should, let's get it to behave correctly. To animate the appearance of the text scrolling off into space and getting smaller as it reaches the vanishing point, you use the same technique that you used with the "Clone Attack" logo, and again, you'll make adjustments using keyframes.

Add the Effect and Adjust the Keyframes

1 Select the scrolling text on the Scrolling Title track on the Timeline.

2 Press **Page Up** or **Page Down** as needed to move to the head (start) of the clip.

3 Click the **Properties** button to open the Properties view for the scrolling text, and then click the **Show Keyframes** button to reveal the workspace for keyframes, if it's not already showing.

> **TIP** You may see the **Hide Keyframes** button, instead, if the **Show Keyframes** button was clicked previously.

4 In Properties view, click the triangle next to **Motion** to reveal the effect's controls.

5 Set the **Scale** to **200.0**.

6 Click the **Toggle Animation** button to turn on the animation functionality of Premiere Elements.

> **TIP** Premiere Elements automatically places a keyframe at this point.

7 Move the CTI to the end of the clip by pressing **Page Down**.

8 Set the **Scale** to **0.0**.

> **TIP** Premiere Elements automatically places another keyframe at this point.

> **NOTE** Once again, on some systems, you may need to render the Timeline (press **Enter**) to see the scrolling effect.

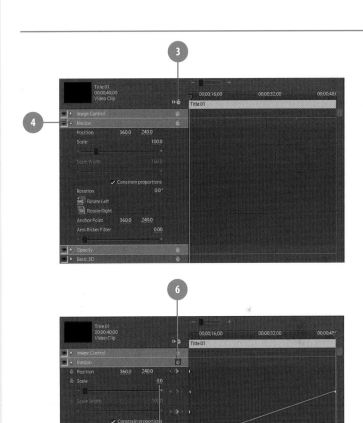

4

Flying Solo: Adding the Star Wars Theme Music

After all that hard work, here is an easy task, one that you can Fly Solo without fear of getting lost. We've supplied a WAV file on the DVD that is suitably dramatic for the title you are creating. You should have already imported the WAV file during the "Preparing the Project" section, so now you just need to "drop" everything and don't let this task be a "drag." And if you need more hints, see the following.

Add the Music to the Timeline

1 Zoom the **Timeline** in or out to show the whole Timeline (*Hint: the plus or minus sign next to the zoom slider*).

2 Add the **244325_OpeningCreditsWilliams.wav** music file to the **Soundtrack** track (*Hint: Edit tab; Project button; use the Force or drag if that works better!*).

TIP *Make sure the head of the music track lines up with the start of the Timeline.*

3 When your Timeline looks similar to the screenshot opposite, press **Ctrl-S** to save your work so far, then proceed to the next section.

TIP *Note the 244325_OpeningCreditsWilliams. wav file is one of many excellent musical tracks available from www.AudioSparx.com. Prices range from a few dollars and their site contains music for pretty much any film project.*

Flying Solo: Adding Some Project Polish

The project is almost complete. You now only need to make small minor adjustments, adding the polish that will make this, and other projects you create, shine with pride. In this section you are given the opportunity to make these tweaks and adjustments while Flying Solo, in order to reinforce the techniques and skills you have learned so far. We've provided you with hints and tips, and if you get lost, refer back to the relevant section in this book to see where you are going wrong. Good luck.

Make Final Tweaks to Your Movie

1 Zoom the **Timeline** in or out to show the whole Timeline (*Hint: the plus or minus signs next to the zoom slider*).

2 Notice that the **starfield.jpg** clip is too short for the length of your movie (*Hint: grab the tail end of the Starfield clip and drag it so it is the same length as the Music clip*).

3 Add a **Fade In** to the start of the **starfield.jpg** and **Title 01** on the Start Title track (*Hint: select clip; Properties button; Opacity; Fade In button*).

4 Add the Gaussian Blur effect to the **starfield.jpg** to punch out those titles (*Hint: Effects panel; type "Blur"; drag the Gaussian Blur effect to starfield.jpg; select clip; Properties button; Gaussian Blur controls; Blurriness to suit—try a value of 3*).

5 Add a **Fade Out** to the end of the **starfield.jpg** (*Hint: select clip; Properties button; Opacity; Fade Out button*).

6 Add a Zoom Blur to the **starfield.jpg** and keyframe it to start at 00;00;41;18 (*Hint: Effect; type "Blur"; drag the Zoom Blur to starfield.jpg; select clip; Properties button; Zoom Blur; move CTI to 00;00;41;18; set zoom to "0"; toggle animation on; use Page Down to move the CTI to the end of starfield.jpg; set zoom to suit; try a value of 100*).

7 Split the Music clip at the 00;00;47;07 point and delete the tail end (*Hint: CTI to 47;07; use Split Clip button or Ctrl-K*).

8 Add a **Fade Out** for the music clip (*Hint: right-click on the clip; select Fade > Fade Out Audio*).

9 When you are happy with your project, press **Ctrl-S** to save your work so far, and then proceed to the final section.

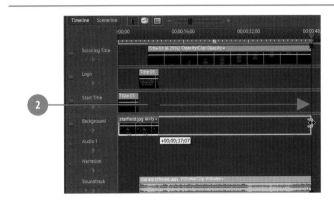

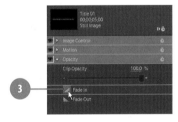

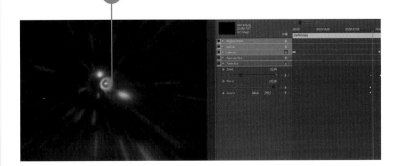

4

Making Adjustments, Rendering, and Exporting ▶

Finish the Project

1 Once you have played back your project and made the necessary adjustments, press **Enter** on your keyboard to render your project.

> **IMPORTANT** *After you select to export your movie, Premiere Elements first renders the entire project (even if you just rendered it yourself). You may have between 1,000 and 2,000 frames and, depending on your computer, it may take anywhere from 15 minutes to over an hour to render. This particular project, because of the scrolling text, can take especially long to render.*

2 Once you have made all of these adjustments, press **Ctrl-S** to make a final save of your project.

3 Finally, export your work as an **AVI** file (a standard Microsoft movie file) by selecting the Timeline, if it is not already selected, and then choosing **File > Export > Movie**.

4 When prompted, browse to the **Peachpit** folder and then the folder called **HSMovies_ Final Renders** and save the exported file as **Chapter 4_Clone_Attack_Title.avi**.

> **NOTE** *You use this final render again in Chapter 16, where you add it to the front of the "Clone Attack" movie you create there.*

5 Exit or minimize Premiere Elements, browse to the **Peachpit** folder, and then open the **HSMovies_Final Renders** folder. Double-click the **Chapter 4_Clone_Wars_Title.avi** file to play it in your default media player.

Play your movie by pressing the **spacebar** and make sure everything looks good. You may want to adjust the audio a bit or tweak this or that. For example, you might want to have the opening "A short time ago..." text appear on screen for a longer time. Remember, however, that changes you make to any given element in this project may cause another element to be out of sync. Once everything is just as you want it, you're ready to share the results, either as a video file, online, or as a DVD.

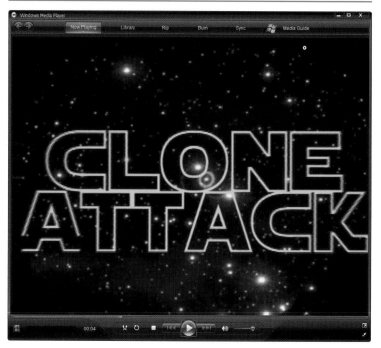

Once the video has been exported, sit back and enjoy the show!

Did You Know?

The Settings button on the Export dialog gives you access to all of the movie's settings. When you click the **Settings** button, the **Movie Settings** dialog displays. Here you can define audio and video quality, movie size, and whether or not you want to export just the audio or just the video part of your project. There's also a check box, on by default, to add the AVI file Premiere Elements creates back into your list of assets in the **Media** panel.

Hollywood Movie Titles: Creating the PiP (Picture-in-Picture) Effect

MEDIA:

24clock.wav
dublin.avi
MinorReleaseL2.mp3
newyork.avi
sanfran.avi
urban.avi

5

COMPLEXITY:	Simple	Moderate	Complex
SKILL LEVEL:	Easy	Intermediate	Advanced

Introduction

If you've followed the television show *24* (or played the game console version), then you're familiar with its dramatic opening: four distinct videos appear on the screen, one after another, each in its own quadrant, each telling its own part of the bigger story. Finally, one of the four video boxes gradually fills the screen and it is that thread of the story that you follow first. These effects are achieved by using what is called a PiP, or Picture-in-Picture.

The PiP is a time-honored movie and television convention that was popular in the 1960s and '70s—*The Thomas Crown Affair* with Steve McQueen used them extensively, and of course the *Brady Bunch* used them famously. In this chapter you'll re-create *24*'s "The following takes place between the hours of..." opening text to give The *24* Effect verisimilitude.

Remember, the techniques you'll use in this chapter are an extension of the title and effects skills you have learned so far. However, now you will also learn to use some preset effects to create a cool *24* PiP opening sequence, and like the techniques you have learned throughout this book thus far, The *24* Effect can be applied to vacation videos, sports videos, and many other projects ("The following birthday party takes place between...").

As you create your next project, think creatively about how you might be able to use a PiP (Picture-in-Picture) effect in your own movies to help tell the story.

What You'll Learn

Flying Solo: Preparing the Project

Flying Solo: Creating the Opening Text

Animating the Opening Text

Creating the Digital Countdown Clock

Animating the Clock Using Title Clips in Sequence

Synchronizing the Clock Clips with the Beep

Flying Solo: Adding the Four Video Clips to the Timeline

Applying a PiP Effect to Each of the Video Clips

Reversing the PiP Effect

Flying Solo: Adding a Soundtrack and a Voice-over

Making Adjustments, Rendering, and Exporting

Flying Solo: Preparing the Project

Although this project looks complicated, using Premiere Elements preset PiPs makes it relatively straightforward. The project incorporates four video clips, one music clip, and one sound effect file (used multiple times). By adding these clips to the Timeline in just the right way, you can re-create your own well-crafted version of the well-known *24* show using just the tools available in Premiere Elements and a little imagination. In this next section, you Fly Solo and make the basic preparations you need to start this project.

Establish Basic Timeline Preparation Skills

1 Create a new project called **Chapter 5 - 24_ PiP_Effect** (*Hint: File > New > Project*).

2 The Timeline should be set to Timeline View (*Hint: Timeline button to the left of the interface*).

> **NOTE** *You need to switch to the Timeline because you will be working with multiple clips on multiple video tracks.*

3 Add two video tracks to the Timeline (*Hint: Add Tracks; Video=2 Audio=0*).

4 Deselect the audio tracks for Video 2 and 3 (*Hint: right-click track header; deselect Show Audio Tracks*).

5 Rename the tracks to the following (*Hint: right-click the header; rename*):

◆ Video 1: **Clock**

◆ Video 2: **PiP 1**

◆ Video 3: **PiP 2**

◆ Video 4: **PiP 3**

◆ Video 5: **PiP 4**

> **TIP** *You will probably need to use the scroll bar to the far right of the Timeline in order to view tracks 4 and 5.*

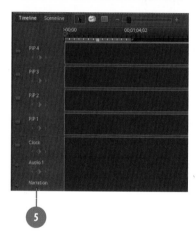

6 Import the following six media clips from the DVD (*Hint: Media Downloader; Advanced mode; Show Audio; Uncheck All; select required media clips*).

- ◆ **24clock.wav**

- ◆ **MinorReleaseL2.mp3**

- ◆ **dublin.avi**

- ◆ **newyork.avi**

- ◆ **sanfran.avi**

- ◆ **urban.avi**

TIP *You can find full instructions for importing media into Premiere Elements 7 in the Chapter 1 section "Adding Media to Your Project." Don't forget you need to uncheck all before you make your selection!*

NOTE *The default settings of the Media Downloader are set not to show Audio media clips. To see any Audio media clips, you need to click the **Show Audio** button or press **Ctrl-U** on the keyboard while the Media Downloader is open. Watch out, Media Downloader rechecks all the files when you do this, so you need to uncheck all again!*

7 Switch to the Edit workspace (*Hint: the Edit tab!*).

8 Press **Ctrl-S** to save your work so far; then proceed to the next section.

Did You Know?

Video clips for this project were prepared from existing clips. The **dublin.avi** clip is a version of Artbeats' **TL302.mov** clip, and the **urban.avi** clip is a version of Artbeats' **TC107.mov** clip. The **newyork.avi** and **sanfran.avi** clips are from the Footage Firm's **brooklynbridge1.avi** and **sanfranpaintedhouses.avi**, respectively.

5

Flying Solo: Creating the Opening Text

At the beginning of every episode of *24*, Jack Bauer, the series' protagonist, sets the stage in a very simple way: he tells you the time of day. The premise of the series is that a story will be told in 24 consecutive 1-hour episodes, each in relative real time. So, for each episode, Jack intones something along the lines of, "The following takes place between the hours of 8:00 AM and 9:00 AM." Fly Solo now and create a simple title from this text. By now you should be very comfortable using the Premiere Elements Titler, but if you get a little lost, there are some hints below to help you out. If you get very lost, refer back to Chapters 1–4 for specific help.

Create Your Opening Text

1 Open the Titler (*Hint: Add Default Text button under the Monitor panel*).

2 Select **Arial Narrow > Bold** as the font, **22** as the font size, and center the text (*Hint: right-click the text; choose Font; right-click the text; choose Size > Other; Center Text button*).

3 Enter the text (all caps): **THE FOLLOWING TAKES PLACE BETWEEN 8:00 AM AND 9:00 AM.**

> **IMPORTANT** *When you type, your new text should replace the default Add Text in the text box on the screen. If it doesn't, select **Add Text** with your mouse and then start typing.*

4 Center the text (*Hint: Vertical and Horizontal Center buttons*).

5 Change the color of the text to a deep gold (*Hint: Color Properties button; R:240 G:186 B:24*).

6 Exit the Titler when you are finished by clicking anywhere on a blank area of the Timeline.

7 Press **Ctrl-S** to save your work so far.

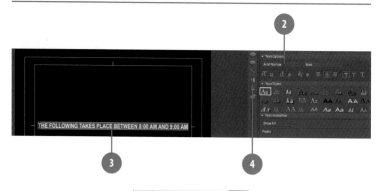

Animating the Opening Text

Now that you have your opening text created, it's time to animate it so it looks as if it's being typed, gradually appearing from left to right across the screen. In other video editors, this effect might take a lot of time to set up, but with Premiere Elements, you just need to apply one of the excellent presets available to you.

Spice Up the Text with a Cool Looking Preset

1 If you have exited the Titler, double-click **Title 01** in the Timeline (*not* in the Media panel) to reopen the Titler.

2 Under Text Animation, change the menu selection from **Show All** to **Fades**.

3 Select the preset **FadeInByCharacters** and a blue square appears around your selection. Click the apply button to add this preset to your title.

NOTE *You can also get a preview of how this preset will display by clicking the small **Play** symbol that appears in the center of the selected preset.*

4 Exit the Titler when you are finished by clicking anywhere on a blank area of the Timeline, then press **Ctrl-S** on your keyboard to save your work so far.

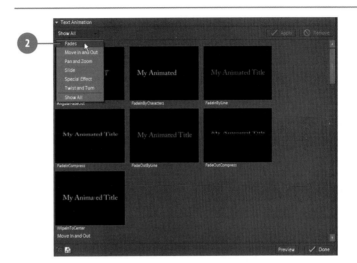

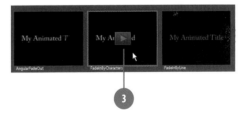

5

Creating the Digital Countdown Clock

To create the illusion of a digital clock ticking on the screen, you create a series of "digital clock" titles, each displaying a time that is one second later than the title that preceded it. You add a beep to this effect in a later task to enhance the effect. Again you are Flying Solo with only the hints to help you. Good luck.

Create the Prototype Clock Title

1 Send the **CTI** to the end of the Timeline, then open the **Titler** (*Hint: End key; Add Default Text button under the Monitor panel*).

2 Select **Arial > Black** as the font, **50** as the font size, and then center the text (*Hint: right-click the text; select Font; right-click the text; select Size > Other; click the Center Text button*).

3 Replace the Add Text with **07:59:55**.

IMPORTANT *When you type, your new text should replace the default **Add Text** in the text box on the screen. If it doesn't, select **Add Text** and start typing.*

4 Change the color of the text to a deep gold (*Hint: Color Properties button; R:240 G:186 B:24*).

5 Center the text (*Hint: Vertical and Horizontal Center buttons*).

6 Exit the Titler when you are finished by clicking anywhere on a blank area of the Timeline. Then press **Ctrl-S** to save your work so far.

NOTE *If the Title 02 clip you just created is not on the Clock track, correct this by dragging and dropping.*

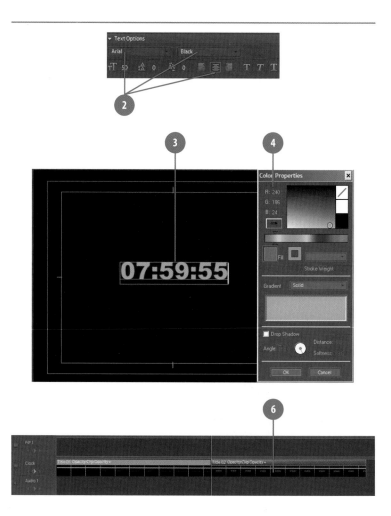

Adjust the Duration for Title 02 on the Timeline and on the Media Panel

1 Make sure you have exited the Titler and that the Edit workspace and Media panel are displayed (*Hint: click anywhere in the Timeline to exit Titler; Edit tab; Project button*).

2 Open the Time Stretch box (*Hint: Right-click Title 02 clip; select Time Stretch from the contextual menu*).

3 Set the **Duration** to 00;00;00;20 (20 frames!).

4 Close the **Time Stretch** dialog.

5 In the Media panel, right-click the **Title 02** clip and again select **Time Stretch** from the contextual menu.

6 Set the **Duration** to 00;00;00;20 here as well (20 frames!).

7 Close the **Time Stretch** dialog.

Did You Know?

You can download digital fonts from the Web. Free fonts are available from many sources on the Internet and many variations on that "digital" look would work well for the clock you're building here. The digital numerals aren't essential, so you're building your clock for this project using a standard Windows font. However, if you want that digital look, use your favorite Internet search engine and search for free fonts. One of our favorite sources for free fonts is **www.pizzadude.dk**. Of their many free fonts (pizzadude also has fonts for sale), **DigitaldreamFat.ttf** is perfect for this project. If you'd rather purchase your font directly from a more well-known font company, Monotype's web site, **www.fonts.com**, has a huge browsable and searchable font collection.

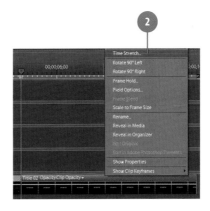

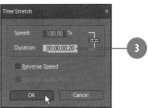

Animating the Clock Using Title Clips in Sequence

Animating the clock involves nothing more than creating five duplicates of your original clock title clip, dragging the duplicates onto the Timeline in sequence, and resetting the time for each of the duplicate clips so that the clips, when played, appear to be one clock ticking off the seconds leading up to 8:00 AM: 07:59:55, 07:59:56, 07:59:57, 07:59:58, 07:59:59, 08:00:00...

Create Five Copies of the Title 02 Clip and Add Them to the Timeline

1. Right-click the **Title 02** clip in the Media panel and select **Duplicate** from the contextual menu.

2. Right-click the **Title 02 Copy** clip you just created and select **Rename** from the contextual menu.

3. Rename the clip **56**.

4. Drag the **56** clip to the Timeline, directly next to the Title 02 clip.

5. Double-click the **56** clip to open the Titler.

6. Change the clock readout for this clip so that it reads **07:59:56**.

7. Fly Solo now and create four additional titles in the same way (by repeating Steps 1–6) until you have title clips on the Timeline named 57, 58, 59, and 8:00. Edit the clips on the Timeline using the Titler so that the clips read as follows:

   ◆ 57 Clip: **07:59:57**

   ◆ 58 Clip: **07:59:58**

   ◆ 59 Clip: **07:59:59**

   ◆ 8:00 Clip: **08:00:00**

   TIP *As you work, move the CTI over the latest "clock" clip on the Timeline so that you can view your progress in the Monitor panel.*

07:59:56

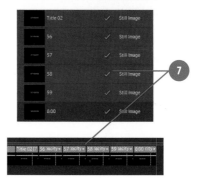

Synchronizing the Clock Clips with the Beep

To give the clock more credibility (and to more exactly match the clock on the TV show), you're going to add a sinister "beep, beep, beep" as the time changes on your clock. You'll be using a sound effect file called **24clock.wav**, placing a copy of it at the beginning of each of the "clock" title clips.

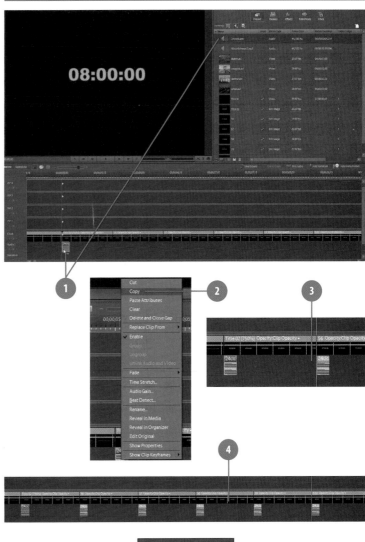

Add a Beep Each Time the Clock Changes

1 From the Media panel, drag the **24clock.wav** clip onto the Audio 1 track on the Timeline so that it lines up with the start of the Title 02 clip on the Clock track.

TIMESAVER Use *Page Up* or *Page Down* to move the CTI so that it lines up with the head of the title clip, and drag the **24clock.wav** file and line it up to the CTI.

2 Right-click the **24clock.wav** clip on the Timeline (*not* in the Media panel) and choose **Copy** from the contextual menu.

3 Press **Page Down** twice to move the CTI to the start of the 56 title and press **Ctrl-V** on the keyboard to paste the **24clock.wav** to the Timeline.

4 Repeat this procedure until all of the "clock" clips have an associated **24clock.wav** clip on the Audio 1 track, as shown in the screenshot.

5 Right-click the last **Beep**, the one under title 8:00, select **Time Stretch**, and change the **Duration** to 00:00:00:06. This gives it a longer, more dramatic beep on the final click of the clock.

5

Flying Solo: Adding the Four Video Clips to the Timeline

In this next task, you add the four video clips to the Timeline that eventually populate the four PiPs in each corner of the screen. The lower-left and lower-right PiPs work perfectly as is, but in a later task, you'll need to make a very small adjustment to the upper-left and upper-right PiPs so that they are positioned correctly in relation to the digital clock you created. For dramatic effect, you won't add video until the third beep at the 06:10 mark (6 seconds and 10 frames). Of course, adding video to the Timeline should be a relatively easy task for you now, so Fly Solo, follow the clues, and build this section of the project using your own knowledge and the various hints dotted about the text.

Add Video to the Timeline

1 From the Media panel, drag the following clips to the following tracks at the following CTI positions (*Hint: move the CTI to the Timeline position; use Page Down; drag the clip to the CTI*):

- **newyork.avi clip > PiP 1 track > 00;00;06;10.**

- **sanfran.avi clip > PiP 2 track > 00;00;07;00**

- **urban.avi clip > PiP 3 track > 00;00;07;20.**

- **dublin.avi clip > PiP 4 track > 00;00;08;10**

NOTE *If you get a Videomerge message when you drop any of these clips to the Timeline, select **No** because you will not be needing that feature in this project.*

2 When you are done, the video clips are arranged in a stair-step fashion (as shown in the screenshot) so that each clip starts a few beats after the preceding clip, synchronized with the "beep." You may need to use the Timeline scroll bar at the far right of the Timeline to see all the tracks.

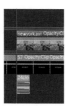

newyork.avi clip > PiP 1 track > 00;00;06;10.

sanfran.avi clip > PiP 2 track > 00;00;07;00

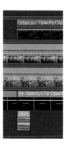

urban.avi clip > PiP 3 track > 00;00;07;20.

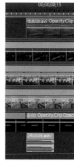

dublin.avi clip > PiP 4 track > 00;00;08;10

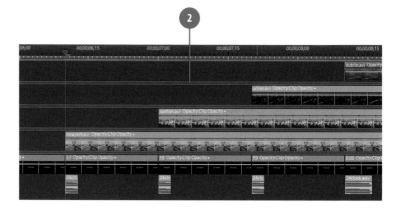

Applying a PiP Effect to Each of the Video Clips

Now that the Timeline is populated with the four video clips you need, it is time to apply a different PiP to each clip to create the *24* look you want. Because the clips are staggered, adding the PiP effect creates the visual experience of multiple smaller video screens popping open on the screen revealing action and the storyline details beat by beat. In this section, you also tweak the upper-left and upper-right PiPs so that they don't clash with the Clock title in the middle of the screen.

Apply a Unique PiP to Each Clip

1 If it is not already open, select the **Edit** tab to open the Edit workspace and then click the **Effects** button to switch to the Effects panel.

2 On the Effects panel, change the selection from **Video Effects** to **Presets**.

3 Type **PiP 40% LL** (LL stands for lower-left) into the text field.

> **NOTE** *There is a gap between the word PiP and the number 40 and between the % symbol and LL, but there is no gap between the 40 and the % symbol. Don't forget the % symbol; otherwise your search will show no results.*

4 Drag the **PiP 40% LL** PiP onto the **newyork. avi** clip in the PiP 1 track on the Timeline.

5 Add the following PiPs to the three remaining video clips:

 ◆ **sanfran.avi: PiP 40% UR** (upper-right)

 ◆ **urban.avi: PiP 40% UL** (upper-left)

 ◆ **dublin.avi: PiP 40% LR** (lower-right)

> **TIMESAVER** *You only need to change the last two letters of the PiP in the text box, for example from **LL** to **UR**, to find the next PiP.*

> **IMPORTANT** *Be careful when you are selecting a PiP. PiPs have very similar names and it's easy to pick the wrong one. You may need to scroll down first to find the correct PiP.*

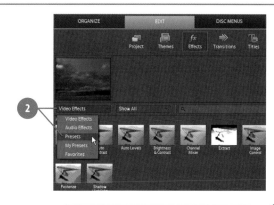

5

Adjust the Upper-Left and Right PiPs

1 Click the **sanfran.avi** clip in the upper-right corner of the Monitor panel.

2 Open the Properties view by clicking the **Properties** button, then click the triangle next to Motion to reveal the effect's controls.

3 Adjust the *vertical* Position of the PiP (the second number in the pair) to **102**.

4 Repeat Steps 1–3 for the **urban.avi** clip in the upper-left corner of the **Monitor** panel.

NOTE *You can also click the Motion bar to highlight the click, then drag the image in the Monitor Panel upward to a new position. Hold down Shift to restrict motion to vertical.*

Reversing the PiP Effect

To finish the visual aspect of this project, return the **newyork.avi** clip to full size, indicating to the audience that this is the storyline that is followed first. To do this, split the **newyork.avi** clip in two and apply a different PiP to the second half so that it grows to fill the entire screen, just as in *24*.

Expand a PiP Back to Full Size

① Scrub the **CTI** to 00;00;09;00.

② Click the **newyork.avi** clip in the PiP 1 track to select it.

③ With *only* the **newyork.avi** clip selected, click **Split Clip** in the Monitor panel.

④ On the Effects panel, type **PiP 40% LL Scale Up**.

⑤ Drag the **PiP 40% LL Scale Up to Full** PiP onto the *new* **newyork.avi** clip you just created (the one that starts at 00;00;09;00).

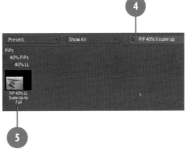

5

Flying Solo: Adding a Soundtrack and a Voice-over

What's an action-adventure style opening (or even a parody of it) without an exciting soundtrack? On this book's DVD, there is just the thing, a tense track from the TwistedTracks folks called **MinorReleaseL2.mp3**. Fly Solo to finish this exercise, and if you feel really brave, tackle the optional stage of adding the "The following takes place…" narration track under the opening title.

Add the Dramatic Music

1 If it is not already displayed, open the Media panel (*Hint: Edit tab; Project button*).

2 Add the **MinorReleaseL2.mp3** clip to the Soundtrack track on the Timeline.

> **IMPORTANT** *Be sure that the start (head) of either the **MinorReleaseL2.mp3** clip or the **SmartSound** clip is at the very beginning of the Soundtrack track.*

3 Hold down the **Ctrl** key on the keyboard, then add the **MinorReleaseL2.mp3** clip to the Soundtrack track for a second time, placing it behind the first mp3 clip on the Timeline.

> **NOTE** *Pressing the Ctrl key is needed the second time you add the MinorReleaseL2.mp3 because otherwise Premiere Elements might attempt to ripple edit all the other clips into a new position. Not what you want! Holding down the Ctrl key while dragging and dropping avoids this problem.*

4 Add a fade out to the mp3 (*Hint: Properties button; Volume Control; Fade out*).

> **NOTE** *Alternatively you can Open SmartSound, create an Intro tune that is around 10 seconds long, and place it at the head of the track.*

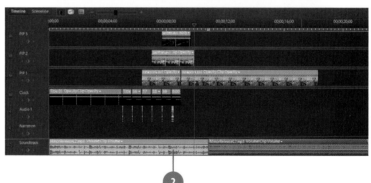

Add the V/O (Voice-over)

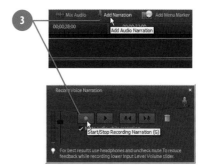

1 If it is not already displayed, open the **Edit** workspace (*Hint: Edit tab*).

2 Move the CTI to the start of the Timeline (*Hint: If you need help here, we have a problem, Houston*).

3 Add the narration, **"The following takes place between the hours of 8:00 AM and 9:00 AM"** at this point (*Hint: Add Narration button; Record; Stop*).

4 Press **Ctrl-S** to save your work so far.

> **TIP** *Once you have added the Music track and any V/O, don't forget to use the Audio Mixer to bring all the volume levels down to an acceptable decibel. You may also want to watch out for musical intros that swamp the clock beeping!*

Making Adjustments, Rendering, and Exporting

Play your movie by pressing the **spacebar** and make sure everything looks right. If it doesn't, make some adjustments until you like what you see. If everything looks good, you are ready to save your work one last time and export your movie to the format of your choice. When you export, Premiere Elements first renders the project (applying effects and transitions to the clips on the Timeline) and then creates the file.

Finish the Project

1. Once you have played back your project and made the necessary adjustments, press **Enter** on your keyboard to render your project.

2. Once you have made all of these adjustments, press **Ctrl-S** to make a final save of your project.

3. Finally, export your work as an AVI file (a standard Microsoft movie file) by selecting the **Timeline**, if it is not already selected, and then choosing **File > Export > Movie**.

4. When prompted, browse to the **Peachpit** folder and then **HSMovies_Final Renders** and save the exported file as **Chapter 5_ The24effect.avi**.

   NOTE *You will use this final render again in Chapter 21.*

5. Exit or minimize Premiere Elements and browse to the **Peachpit** folder; then open the **HSMovies_Final Renders** folder. Double-click the **Chapter 5_The24effect.avi** file to play it in your default media player.

   TIP *You can optionally bring this clip into a larger project, show it on your computer, upload it to an Internet video sharing site, or burn it to a DVD.*

   NOTE *Rendering can take awhile, depending upon the speed of your computer and the number of frames that need to be rendered.*

Once the movie has been exported, sit back and enjoy your own version of the show *24*.

Hollywood Movie Looks:
Using Preset Effects

MEDIA:

Chapter 1_Title with Music.prel

6

COMPLEXITY:	Simple	Moderate	Complex
SKILL LEVEL:	Easy	Intermediate	Advanced

Introduction

Premiere Elements 7 comes with a great selection of effects that you can use to enhance or even artificially degrade the visual experience, creating the illusion of an Old Film effect or a more stylized artistic effect. Using a combination of effects, it's also possible to build a unique "Movie Look" that can add the cool factor to your movies.

You can use these effects to create a certain visual resonance, allowing the audience to identify immediately with the scene they are watching. An example of this appears in the TV series *Joan of Arcadia*. Most scenes in this show have a golden, almost sunny aspect, representing a more optimistic setting, but a few scenes, such as those in hospitals and, in particular, those involving the police, are cast in blue, visually queuing the audience into accepting these situations as being more serious.

In this chapter, you look at using and combining effects to build up a portfolio of Movie Looks to enhance the visual aspect of your projects.

What You'll Learn

Flying Solo: Preparing the Project

Applying the Air Brush Effect

Movie Looks in the Video Effects Folder

Movie Looks in the Presets Folder

Applying the Old Film Effect

Adding Some "Flash" to the Clip

Flying Solo: Adding Some Period Music

Flying Solo: Applying Some Camera Shake

Making Adjustments, Rendering, and Exporting

Flying Solo:
Preparing the Project

In Chapter 1 you created a cool-looking project and then in Chapter 3 you added music to it. In this section, you reload the project from Chapter 3 and add a Movie Look, enhancing it even more. By doing so, you prove the old rule that in movie making, "nothing is ever finished, only abandoned." Now Fly Solo and use the skills you've learned so far to load the old project and tweak the Timeline slightly to prepare for the work ahead.

Load a Saved Project

1 Start Premiere Elements and open the **Chapter 1_Title with Music** project you modified in Chapter 3 (*Hint: open Project [from the splash screen] or File > Open Project [if Premiere Elements is open]*).

TIP *You may need to click Open and browse to the **Peachpit** folder if the Chapter 1 project is not displayed.*

2 Create a working copy of this project (*Hint: File > Save As; Chapter 1_Movie Looks*).

NOTE *This is to ensure that your original project remains untouched and is available again should you need it.*

3 If you are in the **Sceneline**, switch to the **Timeline** (*Hint: Timeline button*).

4 Deselect audio tracks 2 and 3 to see more of the Timeline (*Hint: right-click Track Header; deselect Show Audio Tracks*).

5 When your Timeline looks similar to the one in the screenshot opposite, press **Ctrl-S** to save your work so far.

Applying the Air Brush Effect

In this first step you learn just how quickly you can make radical transformations to regular video by adding the Air Brush effect. You also stylize it slightly to enhance this cool-looking effect, which comes standard with Premiere Elements 7.

Add the Air Brush Effect

1. If it is not already on display, click the **Edit** tab to open the Edit workspace, then switch to the Effects panel by clicking the **Effects** button.

2. Type **air** in the text box.

3. Select the **Air Brush** effect and drag it onto the **Swans.avi** clip on the Background track of the Timeline.

4. Play this back to see the stunning new look you have given this video—you've added an artistic feel that looks good in combination with the see-through title you created in Chapter 1.

    NOTE *You could have added this effect to the title as well, but you probably wouldn't see much difference.*

5. If you want to tone down this effect, or ramp it up to the extreme, click the **Properties** button to open the Properties view for **Swans.avi**, then open the Air Brush settings by clicking the triangle next to Air Brush and adjust the slider to suit.

    TIP *Try a setting around 25 for the best effect.*

6. Press **Ctrl-S** to save your work so far.

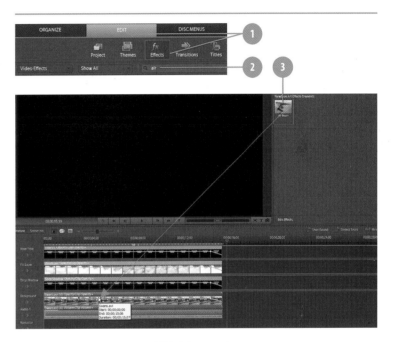

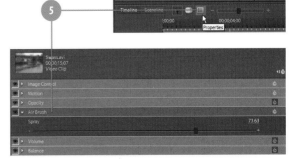

Movie Looks in the Video Effects Folder

The following are a few of the effects available from the Video Effects folder, used here to demonstrate how easy it is to create some cool-looking Movie Looks with just a couple of mouse clicks.

The Extract effect

The Posterize effect

The Invert effect

The Pastel Sketch effect

Movie Looks in the Presets Folder

If you open the Presets folder (by clicking the menu in the Effects panel—see the screenshot), you'll find even more presets to play with. Again, this is just a small sample and we encourage you to experiment to get the most from this exciting area of Premiere Elements. Don't forget, you can combine any number of presets to create new and unique looks.

The Tint Blue preset effect

Selecting the Presets folder

The Narrow Bevel Edges preset effect

The Tint Red + Increase Saturation preset effect

6

Applying the Old Film Effect

Although the previous example showed an artistic leaning, a more widely used Film Look example comes standard with Premiere Elements 7: The Old Film effect. This "look" attempts to degrade your video material and make it look as though it is something that was created in the early days of black-and-white, hand-cranked cameras. In this section, you create this effect, complete with sepia lines and scratches, and you do it with a single bound using the Old Film effect. You also have a chance to tune this effect to your personal taste.

Add the Old Film Effect

1 Use **File > Save As** and save your project as **Chapter 1_ Old_Film_Effect**.

2 Select the **Swans.avi** media clip on the Background track and if the Properties view is not already open, click the **Properties** button to view it.

3 Click the actual **Air Brush** text to highlight it, and then press **Delete** on your keyboard to remove it from the media clip.

4 Switch to the Effects panel if it's not already visible by clicking the **Effects** button.

5 Type **old** in the text box.

6 Select the **Old Film** effect and drag it onto the **Swans.avi** clip on the Background track of the Timeline.

7 Now drag the **Old Film** effect onto the **Clouds.avi** media clip on the Fill Layer track.

NOTE *Adding this effect to the Title will have no direct effect in this project.*

8. Select the **Swans.avi** clip and then click the **Properties** button to open the Properties view; dial open the **Old Film** settings by clicking the triangle next to Old Film.

9. Adjust the **Old Film** sliders to suit. Also, try changing the Wear Pattern menu from **Blotchy** to **Lite**.

10. Copy these adjustments over to the Old Film effect on the **Clouds.avi** clip.

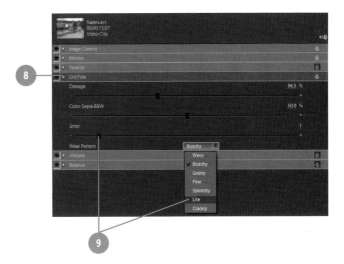

Adding Some "Flash" to the Clip

To customize the Old Film effect even more, you are going to add that flash of light that you often see in old movies. As movies age, the celluloid wears and weathers differently, allowing for bright spots as the projector bulb shines through with varying intensity at different points in the film. You can simulate this by animating the Brightness control so that it changes dramatically and suddenly at different points over time. To do this, you use the keyframes techniques you've picked up in previous chapters to adjust the Brightness levels over time, adding two bright flashes, one at 5 seconds, and another at 10 seconds.

Adjust the Brightness Over Time

1. Select the **Swans.avi** clip on the Background track on the Timeline.

2. If it is not already open, click the **Properties** button to open the Properties view.

3. In the Properties view, click the **Show Keyframes** button and expand the panel as needed to get a good view of the keyframes work area, as shown in the illustration.

    TIMESAVER *You'll be starting at the beginning of the clip, so press **Page Up** or **Home** on your keyboard to return the CTI to the start position of the track (the head of the clip) if it's not already there.*

4. With the CTI at the head of the clip, click the triangle for Image Control and then turn **Toggle Animation** on.

    NOTE *Premiere Elements has now automatically created a keyframe at the start of the clip for a Brightness value of 0.*

5. Move the **CTI** 5 seconds into the clip (**00;00;05;00**).

6. In the Properties panel, under Image Control, set the **Brightness** level to **60.0**.

    NOTE *Premiere Elements automatically places a keyframe at this spot.*

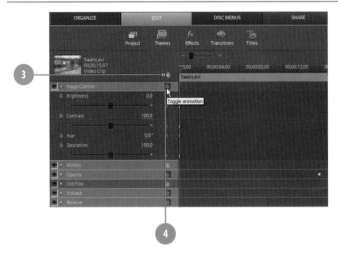

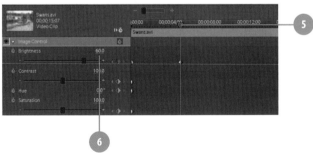

7 Move the **CTI** back 10 frames to **00;00;04;20** and reset the **Brightness** to **0.0**.

TIP *Press the left arrow 10 times to move the CTI back 10 frames.*

8 Move the **CTI** ahead to **00;00;05;10** and reset the **Brightness** to **0.0** here as well.

9 Using the mouse, drag a dotted square around these three newly created keyframes. When you release the mouse key, they should all be blue to indicate they are selected.

10 From the Edit menu, select **Copy** or press **Ctrl-C** on the keyboard.

11 Move the **CTI** to **00;00;10;00** and from the Edit menu, select **Paste** or press **Ctrl-V** on the keyboard. Three new keyframes identical to the ones you created in Steps 6, 7, and 8 should now have been created at that mark.

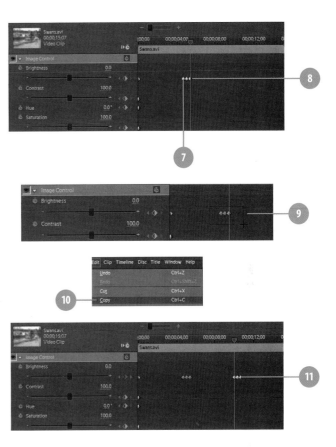

Simulate the Jumpiness of Old Films by Splitting Clips

The reason people seem to jump about in old films—where a person is standing in the middle of the room one second, and then suddenly, a second later, he or she is standing by the door—is because of the deterioration over time to which celluloid is prone, rather than to any latent vampiric talents! When film deteriorates, it eventually falls apart, and sections of it can no longer be run through the projector. When that happens, a film editor slices the film before and after the bad spot, and then tapes it back together in a process called *splicing*. You can simulate this effect using the Split Clip button. Just move the **CTI** to any point in the clip and click the **Split Clip** button. Again move the **CTI** a few frames or even a few seconds into the future and click **Split Clip** again. Depending on the length of the clip you are "deteriorating," you can create one or many such jump spots convincingly, and quickly age any clip.

6

Flying Solo: Adding Some Period Music

Now that you have developed an old style look for this project, the music no longer matches the visuals. Fly Solo now and delete the music on the Soundtrack track and then either import your own, or have a look in SmartSound to see if there is something suitable there.

Add Some Period Music to the Project

1 Delete the music track from the Soundtrack track (*Hint: select SmartSound > Underwater > Ascent.wav; press Delete*).

2 Do one of the following:

Search your hard drive for a suitable music track (*Hint: Import Music clips via the Organize tab*).

Open SmartSound and select a suitable music track (*Hint: SmartSound button; choose music; alter duration (00;00;15;05); select variation*).

TIP *Try the Piano Sonata in the Classical style—Variation: Solace.*

3 If you have added an mp3 or WAV file (or similar), add a fade out to the end of that clip (*Hint: Properties button for Music clip; Volume controls; Fade Out button*).

NOTE *SmartSound tracks generated inside Premiere Elements have their own natural fade out, so they do not generally require this step unless you alter the length of the track on the Timeline.*

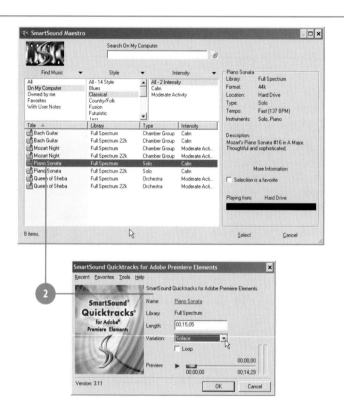

Flying Solo: Applying Some Camera Shake

As an optional extra to add a little more coolness and originality to the Old Film effect, try adding a little camera shake to simulate the camera being handheld. Fly Solo for this one using the skills you have learned in this chapter. Use your own settings for the Active Camera effect, but don't overdo it too much; you don't want your audience to feel ill!

Explore Custom Use of Active Camera

1. Select the **Swans.avi** media clip on the Background track.

2. Open the **Edit** workspace (*Hint: Edit tab*).

3. Open the **Effects** panel (*Hint: Effects button*).

4. Find the **Active Camera** effect (*Hint: type active in the text box*).

5. Add the **Active Camera** effect to the **Swans.avi** clip (*Hint: drag baby, drag*).

6. Open the **Properties** view if it is not already open (*Hint: Properties button*) and then open the **Active Camera** controls (*Hint: that little triangle again!*).

7. Alter the **Active Camera** settings to suit your own personal taste (*Hint: try reducing Jitter, Crop, and Rate first for a less extreme and stomach churning version of this effect*).

8. When you are happy with the effect, press **Ctrl-S** to save your work so far.

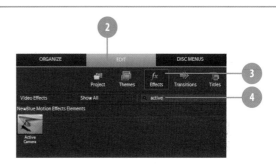

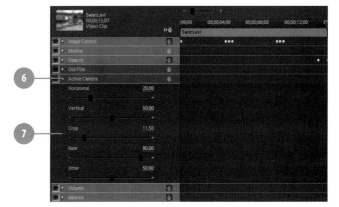

Making Adjustments, Rendering, and Exporting

When you have everything in place, press the **spacebar** on your keyboard to run through the clip and check that everything looks right. You may notice that things look a bit rough right now. To get a better sense of how the final version will look, press **Enter** to render your project.

Finish the Project

1. Once you have played back your project and made the necessary adjustments, press **Enter** on your keyboard to render your project.

2. Once you have made all of these adjustments, press **Ctrl-S** to make a final save of your project.

3. Finally, export your work as an AVI file (a standard Microsoft movie file) by selecting the Timeline, if it is not already selected, and then choosing **File > Export > Movie**.

4. When prompted, browse to the **Peachpit** folder and then **HSMovies_Final Renders** and save the exported file as **Chapter 6_ Old_Film_Effect.avi**.

    NOTE *This final render may be used again in Chapter 21.*

5. Exit or minimize Premiere Elements and browse to the **Peachpit** folder and then open **HSMovies_Final Renders**. Double-click the **Chapter 6_Old_Film_Effect.avi** file to play it in your default media player.

    TIP *Optionally, you can bring this clip into a larger project, show it on your computer, upload it to an Internet video sharing site, or burn it to a DVD.*

Hollywood Movie Looks:
Custom Building a Movie Look

MEDIA:

Chapter 2_With Music.prel

7

COMPLEXITY:	Simple	Moderate	Complex
SKILL LEVEL:	Easy	Intermediate	Advanced

Introduction

In the last chapter you saw how easy it is to create Movie Looks using presets in Premiere Elements 7, along with some imaginative tweaks. In this chapter you discover how to create your own custom built Movie Looks using just those tools available in Premiere Elements 7.

To get a handle on the potential available, you use the project you created in Chapter 2 to focus on just two Movie Looks: The '60s groovy look and the '70s home projector look.

If you have been following the chapters so far, many of the techniques you use in this chapter will seem familiar. With Premiere Elements 7, you can create endless variations on the Movie Looks with just a little effort and a dash of imagination.

What You'll Learn

Flying Solo: Preparing the Project

Creating a Cinematic '60s Movie Look

Copying Effects and Settings from One Clip to Another

Creating a Cinematic '70s Movie Look

Creating the Home Projector Look

Flying Solo: Adding Some Music

Making Adjustments, Rendering, and Exporting

Flying Solo:
Preparing the Project

In Chapter 2 you created a cool-looking title intro with a '60s feel; then in Chapter 3 you added some groovy music. In this section, you reload the project from Chapter 3 and prepare to give it a Movie Look makeover.

Load a Saved Project

1 Start Premiere Elements and open the project you modified in Chapter 3 (*Hint: Open Project [from the splash screen] or File > Open Project [if Premiere Elements is open]; File = Chapter 2 _With Music*).

TIP *You may need to click **Open** and browse to the **HSMovies_Chapter 2** file if the Chapter 2 project is not displayed.*

2 Create a working copy of this project (*Hint: File > Save As; Chapter 7_Movie Looks*).

NOTE *This is to ensure that your original project remains untouched and is available again should you need it.*

3 If you are in the **Sceneline**, switch to the **Timeline** (*Hint: Timeline button*).

4 Deselect audio tracks to see more of the Timeline (*Hint: right-click Track Header; deselect Show Audio Tracks*).

5 When your Timeline looks similar to the one in the screenshot opposite, press **Ctrl-S** to save your work so far.

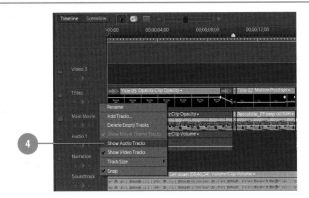

Creating a Cinematic '60s Movie Look

Although most Movie Look solutions involve expensive cameras and software as well as special filming techniques, you can create an acceptable approximation by using the Image Control settings to deliberately push the color and light levels outside the normal range. In this section you add some '60s brightness to the video, then sprinkle in a little noise to simulate the grainy appearance of '60s film.

Brighten the Clip

1 Move the CTI to the middle of the first **retro-footage_2.avi** segment on the Timeline and then click it once to select it.

2 If it is not already open, click the **Properties** button to see the Properties view and click the triangle next to **Image Control** to reveal the effect's controls.

3 Use the Image Control to create a more washed out '60s look. We suggest the following settings, but also try experimenting:

◆ Brightness: **20.0**

◆ Contrast: **80.0**

◆ Hue: **10.0°**

◆ Saturation: **200.0**

TIP *Scrub the* **CTI** *(current-time indicator) on the Timeline to a point in the clip past the black so that you can see the changes in the clip as you make them.*

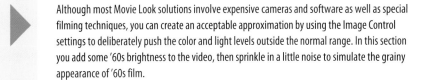

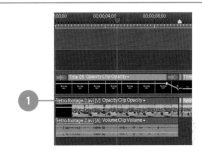

Add a Little Noise

1. If it is not already open, click the **Edit** tab to view the Edit workspace, then click the **Effects** button to switch to the Effects panel.

2. In the Effects panel, type **noise** in the text box.

3. Drag the **Noise** effect onto the first **retro-footage_2.avi** segment on the Timeline.

4. Open the Properties view by clicking the **Properties** button, and click the triangle next to **Noise** to reveal the effect's controls.

   TIP *You may need to close one of the other effects or scroll down the list of effects to find the Noise effect.*

5. Set the Amount of Noise to **12.0%**. Leave all other settings as is.

Did You Know?

You can switch the effect on and off. By toggling the eye symbol on and off you can see what effect, if any, the settings of your effect are having on the media clip. This can make it a little easier to judge the effect of an effect.

Copying Effects and Settings from One Clip to Another

Now that you have the first part of the movie set up, you could just enter the Image Control settings to the other two video segments on the Timeline and drag in the Noise effect as well. A more elegant, and less time consuming way of doing this is to copy and paste settings and effects from one video segment to another. In this section you do just that, by copying the Image Control settings and the Noise effect at the same time, and then pasting them both onto the second and then the third video segments on the Timeline.

Copy an Effect and Its Settings to Two Other Segments

1. Click the first segment on the Timeline to select it, then open the Properties view by clicking the **Properties** button.

2. Select the **Image Control** effect by clicking the actual text, then hold down the **Ctrl** key and select the **Noise** effect.

3. With both effects selected, right-click either one and select **Copy** from the contextual menu or press **Ctrl-C** on the keyboard.

4. Click the next video segment on the Timeline (not a freeze frame) and in a blank area of the Properties panel, right-click and select **Paste**.

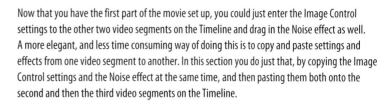

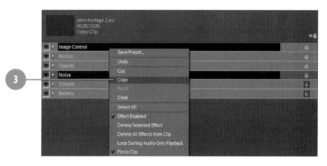

5 The **Noise** filter will be added to the clip, along with the correct value of 12%; the **Image Control** will adopt the settings copied from the first segment by the user in Step 3.

6 Repeat Steps 1–4 to copy and paste the Image Control settings and the Noise effect (plus settings) to the third video segment on the Timeline.

NOTE *If you want to see the effect of these changed and added effects, make sure the CTI is over the segment to which you are pasting.*

Creating a Cinematic '70s Movie Look

So far, in these last two chapters, you have created two looks: old time cinema and a '60s movie. Now in an attempt to embrace those wonder years you are going to attempt a '70s Super-8 camera look, complete with faded colors, scratch marks, and occasional blurring. For this you use many of the filters encountered so far, but in different and imaginative ways. In this longer-than-average section, you add and adjust the settings of multiple effects. It looks complex, but take it step by step and you should discover that it's easier than it looks.

Adjust the Existing Effects

1. Use **File > Save As** and save your project as **Chapter 2_ 70s movie look**.

    NOTE *This is to protect the previous version of your project while you create something new with this version.*

2. Select the first **retro-footage_2.avi** segment on the Timeline and, if it is not already open, click the **Properties** button to see the Properties view; then click the triangle next to **Image Control** to reveal the effect's controls.

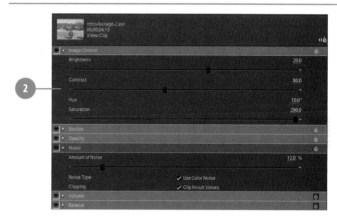

3. Try the following settings or set to suit:

    ◆ Brightness: **3.5**

    ◆ Contrast: **102.7**

    ◆ Hue: **10.0°**

    ◆ Saturation: **48.4**

    TIP *Scrub the **CTI** on the Timeline to a point in the clip past the black so that you can see the changes in the clip as you make them.*

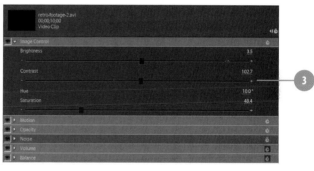

4. Close the **Image Control** settings and open the **Noise** settings:

    ◆ Amount of Noise: **8.0%**

    ◆ Noise Type: **Off**

    ◆ Clip Result Values: **On**

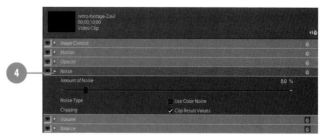

5 When you are happy with the effect, copy both the **Image Control** settings and the **Noise** settings to the other two segments using the copy and paste technique you learned in the "Copying Effects and Settings from One Clip to Another" section.

NOTE *When you copy and paste settings between different clips, Image Control, Motion, and Opacity will update and overwrite those settings already preset. If you copy and paste an "added" effect such as Noise, two instances of the effect will appear, their separate settings stacking in a cumulative fashion.*

Add and Adjust Some More Effects

1 If it is not already open, click the **Edit** tab to view the Edit workspace, then click the **Effects** button to switch to the Effects panel.

2 In the Effects panel, type **Old Film**.

3 Drag the **Old Film** effect onto the first **retro-footage_2.avi** segment on the Timeline.

4 Open the Properties view by clicking the **Properties** button and click the triangle next to **Old Film** to reveal the effect's controls.

TIP *You may need to close one of the other effects or scroll down the list of effects to find the Old Film effect.*

5 Set the Old Film effect's settings to these or adjust to suit:

◆ Damage: **54.3%**

◆ Color-Sepia-B&W: **0.0%**

◆ Jittter: **0**

◆ Wear Pattern: **Fine**

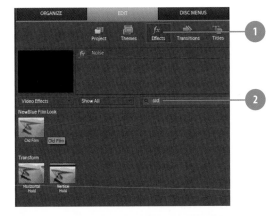

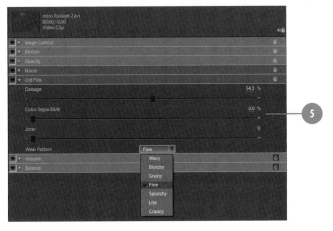

6 To further enhance the '70s look, repeat steps 1–4 to add the following two effects with their suggested settings, although you should also try your own variations.

Shadow/Highlight. Try these settings:

◆ Deselect **Auto Amounts**

◆ Shadow Amount: **75**

◆ Highlight Amount: **21**

◆ Blend with Original: **3.9%**

Lens Distortion (to create the illusion of a projector screen). Try these settings:

◆ Curvature: **3**

◆ Vertical Decentering: **-4** (negative)

◆ Horizontal Decentering: **0**

◆ Vertical Prism FX: **5**

◆ Horizontal Prism FX: **4**

◆ Fill Color: **White**

7 When you are happy with the effects, copy the **Old Film**, **Shadow and Highlight**, and **Lens Distortion** effects, including their settings, to the other two segments using the copy and paste technique you learned in the "Copying Effects and Settings from One Clip to Another" section earlier in this chapter.

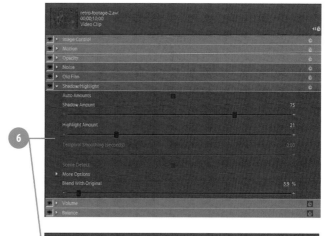

Did You Know?

You can copy all the effects from one clip to another with just two clicks. Once you have set up all the effects you want on one clip, right-click on that clip and select **Copy** from the contextual menu. Then right-click on the target clip and select **Paste Attributes**. All of the effects (Including Motion, Image Control, and any added effects) will be added to that target clip.

Creating the Home Projector Look

The '70s look is starting to shape up, but the effect you are looking for is that of a home movie being played back on a home clackety-clack projector. In this next section, you add some fast blur, keyframed to make it look as though the projector is falling in and out of focus (as they were likely to do), and a White Out effect, that simulates when the projector runs the film out of the frame and, for a moment, you see just the projector bulb and no picture. To create these effects, you use the Fast Blur and then a white Color Matte, both of which use a series of three keyframes to quickly bring the effect in and out. Remember, realism is not overdoing it!

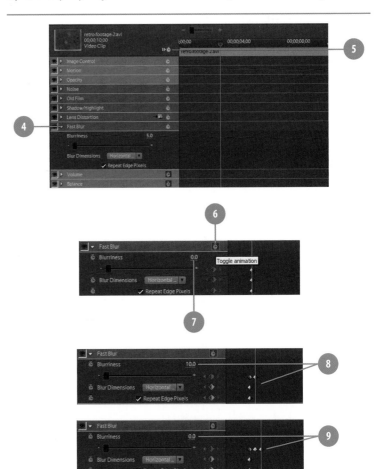

Add Some Keyframed Fast Blur

1. If it is not already open, click the **Edit** tab to view the Edit workspace, then click the **Effects** button to switch to the Effects panel.

2. In the Effects panel, type **Blur**.

3. Drag the **Fast Blur** effect onto the first **retro-footage_2.avi** segment on the Timeline.

4. Open the Properties panel by clicking the **Properties** button and click the triangle next to **Fast Blur** to reveal the effect's controls.

   TIP *You may need to close one of the other effects or scroll down the list of effects to find Fast Blur.*

5. Click the **Show Keyframes** button to open the Keyframes area.

6. Move the CTI to 00;00;01;10 and *then* set Toggle Animation to on for Fast Blur (not the other way around!).

   NOTE *Premiere Elements now creates a keyframe at the 01;10 point.*

7. Set Blurriness for this keyframe to **0.0**.

8. Move the CTI 10 keyframes forward (*Hint: use the right cursor key*) and set Blurriness to **10.0**.

9. Move the CTI 10 keyframes forward and set Blurriness to **0.0**.

10. When you are happy with the Fast Blur effect, copy the effect, including the settings, to the other two segments using the copy and paste technique you learned in the "Copying Effects and Settings from One Clip to Another" section earlier in this chapter.

Create a "White Out" Effect

1. If it is not already open, click the **Edit** tab to view the Edit workspace, then click the **Project** button to switch to the Media panel.

2. Click the **New Item** button and select **Color Matte** from the list.

3. Create a slightly off white Color Matte. Try this setting in the hex number # box: F7F5F5.

4. Drag the Color Matte onto the Video 3 above the first video segment, then drag the tail up the Timeline so that it matches the duration of the clip beneath.

    TIP *If you see a Videomerge message, click* **no** *because you won't be using that function in this section.*

5. If it is not already open, click the **Properties** button (with the Color Matte clip selected on the Timeline) to see the Properties view and click the triangle next to **Opacity** to reveal the effect's controls.

6. Click the **Show Keyframes** button if the Keyframes area is not already displayed.

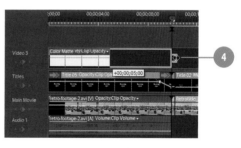

7 Move the **CTI** to 00;00;01;10 and alter the **Clip Opacity** to 8.4% and then set Toggle Animation to on to create an opacity keyframe at this point.

8 Move the **CTI** 10 frames forward (*Hint: use the right cursor key*) and set the opacity to **95%**.

9 Move the **CTI** 10 frames forward and set the opacity back to **8.4%**.

10 With the White Matte selected, press **Ctrl-C** on the keyboard, move the **CTI** to above the second video segment, and then press **Ctrl-V** to create a copy of the White Matte with its keyframing effect.

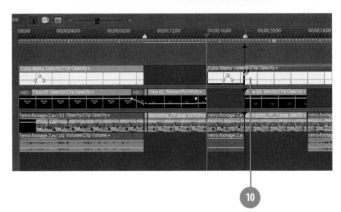

11 Drag the tail of the Color Matte to resize it to that of the second video segment.

12 Repeat Steps 10 and 11 to create a third White Matte, complete with opacity keyframes, above the third video segment on the Timeline. Don't forget to move the CTI before you press **Ctrl-V**.

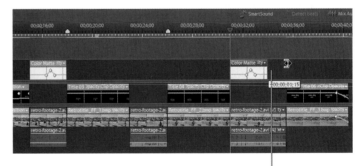

Did You Know?

You can create a favorite list of effects simply by right-clicking an effect and selecting Add to Favorites. You can then view all your selected favorites by switching the Video Effects menu to read Favorites. This can save a huge amount of searching for those effects you use on a regular basis.

Flying Solo: Adding Some Music

Now that you have developed a '70s style look to this project, the music doesn't really seem to match. Fly Solo now by deleting the music on the Soundtrack track and either importing your own, or having a look in SmartSound to see if there is something suitable that you feel matches the mood of your Movie Look.

Add Some Vintage Music to the Project

1 Delete the music track from the Soundtrack track (*Hint: select music; press Delete on the keyboard*).

2 Open SmartSound and select a suitable music track (*Hint: SmartSound button*).

TIP *Try the Blues To Go—Variation: "Too Cool." Alternatively, search through your hard drive and import a suitable music track.*

3 Add a fade out to the end of whichever music track you decide on (*Hint: Properties button; Volume; Fade Out button*), although if you are using SmartSound, you will probably not have to do this.

Making Adjustments, Rendering, and Exporting

When you have everything in place, press the **spacebar** on your keyboard to run through the clip and check that everything looks right. You may notice that things look a bit rough right now. To get a better sense of how the final version will look, press **Enter** to render your project.

Finish the Project

1. Once you have played back your project and made the necessary adjustments, press **Enter** on your keyboard to render your project.

2. Once you have made all of these adjustments, press **Ctrl-S** to make a final save of your project.

3. Finally, export your work as an AVI file (a standard Microsoft movie file) by selecting the **Timeline**, if it is not already selected, and then choosing **File > Export > Movie**.

4. When prompted, browse to the **Peachpit** folder and then **HSMovies_Final Renders** and save the exported file as **Chapter 7_70s-Projector.avi**.

   NOTE *This final render may be used again in Chapter 21.*

5. Exit or minimize Premiere Elements and browse to the **Peachpit** folder and then open the **HSMovies_Final Renders** folder. Double-click the **Chapter 7_70s-Projector. avi** file to play it in your default media player.

Hollywood Movie Time: The Passing of Time Effect

MEDIA:
Phone_Call.avi
Phone_Ring.wav
Phone_Beep.wav

8

COMPLEXITY:	Simple	Moderate	Complex
SKILL LEVEL:	Easy	Intermediate	Advanced

What You'll Learn

Flying Solo: Preparing the Project

Marking the Individual Scenes

Removing Time (Frames) from the Clip

Adding a Cross Dissolve Between Clips

Adjusting the Transitions

Adding Sound FX

Flying Solo: Using Titles and Fades

Adding the Music Track

Making Adjustments, Rendering, and Exporting

Introduction

Many times, when you're telling a story, you'd like to indicate a longer period of time passing. A man waits for an hour for an important phone call, the audience doesn't want to see the whole hour, but you, the film-maker, want them to know time has elapsed. You can create this illusion easily using the Passing of Time effect.

For this passage of time to be convincing, you really need to do two things. First, remove some time from the clip. But how? It sounds like you need magical powers, but actually you just delete segments of video (frames). For example, if someone crosses the room, you can leave the first and last part of the walk across the room, but delete all the frames in the middle of the clip. This way, the actor is first at one end of the room and then suddenly he appears at the opposite end. When you split the clip in two and apply a transition between the two new clips, the actor slowly vanishes (dissolves) from the left side of the room and simultaneously appears at the other end.

This effect works well in the example of a man waiting by the phone for an important phone call. He can be looking at the phone. Standing behind the couch. Off puttering around in the kitchen. And back sitting on the couch. By deleting all of the frames where he moves from location to location, and by adding a dissolve between clips, you can effectively communicate the sense of time passing without having your viewer witness every minute that passes!

Flying Solo: Preparing the Project

Setting up this project is very simple and something you should now be able to do with little effort. Below are some handy hints, but if you are at all lost, refer back to Chapters 1 and 2 for details on renaming tracks and importing media from the DVD.

Use Basic Timeline Preparation Skills

1 Create a new project called **Chapter 8_ Time_ Removed** (*Hint: File > New > Project*).

2 The Timeline should be set to the Timeline view (*Hint: Timeline button to the left of the interface*).

> **NOTE** *You need to switch to the **Timeline** because you will be working with multiple clips on multiple video tracks.*

3 Deselect the audio tracks for Video 2 and 3 (*Hint: deselect Show Audio Tracks*).

4 Rename (*Hint: right-click the header*) and change each track to the following:

- ◆ Video 1: **Main Video**

- ◆ Video 2: **Title**

5 Import the **Phone_Call.avi** and **Phone_ Ring.wav** media clips from the DVD (*Hint: Media Downloader; Show Audio; UnCheck All*).

> **TIP** *You can find complete instructions for importing media into Premiere Elements 7 in the Chapter 1 section "Adding Media to Your Project." Don't forget you need to uncheck all before you make your selection!*

> **NOTE** *The default settings of the Media Down-loader are set not to show audio media clips. To see any audio media clips you need to click the **Show Audio** button or press **Ctrl-U** on the keyboard while the Media Downloader is open. Watch out, Media Downloader rechecks all the files when you do this, so you need to uncheck them all again!*

Filming Tips

One of the first things you need to think about is framing. For a time frame removal to be successful, the camera should remain stationary and objects and people should move in and out of the audience's field of view, interacting with their imagination. So, you need to think about heads and toes: do they fit in your frame, do you need them in your frame, or maybe you only want the audience to see part of the body, the hands for example.

While setting up the framing, use a tripod and carefully place it where no one can knock it out of position. Once the framing is set, lock off all movement on the tripod and don't allow anyone near the camera during filming.

Once you've set this up, you are almost ready to film. Before you push the Record button, go through the routine a few times. Work out what is and is not possible. Now you are really ready to film. Once you press the Record button, don't go near the camera until the scene has completed. Don't allow anyone to turn off the camera, don't allow anyone to walk near the tripod, don't allow anyone to cast a shadow or block light to your scene.

While acting the part, avoid looking at the camera, keep breathing to a low level, and don't make any loud sounds off camera. For variation, try using a prop in one position— perhaps have it resting somewhere else in another position as a link between the frames. Oh, and don't forget to have fun.

6 Switch to the Edit workspace (*Hint: Edit tab*).

7 Drag the **Phone_Call.avi** to the Main Video track.

> **IMPORTANT** *Be sure to line up the head (start) of the **Phone_Call.avi** clip with the front of the Main Video track.*

8 Zoom in on the Timeline to show the clips (*Hint: use the Zoom slider above the Timeline*).

9 When your Timeline and Media panel look similar to the screenshots opposite, press **Ctrl-S** to save your work so far, then proceed to the next section.

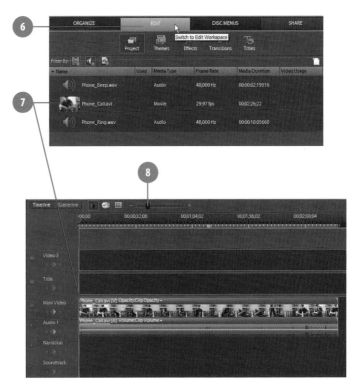

This is how your Timeline should look.

Marking the Individual Scenes

As it is, **Phone_Call.avi** is an odd scene, with the actor jumping around in a very unnatural fashion. You need to remove all the parts where the actor is moving and leave just those scenes where he is waiting for that call. Start by breaking this long clip into individual scenes. Once you have your scenes defined, you can work to make changes to each of the scenes so that they represent dramatic changes in time. To begin this process, you need to locate and then mark points of interest with a Numbered Timeline marker.

Place Numbered Markers on the Timeline

1 Switch to the Edit workspace if it is not already open (*Hint: Edit button*).

2 Move the **CTI** (current-time indicator) to 00;00;09;25 on the Timeline. This represents where the actor begins to move and gets into his next waiting position.

> **NOTE** *You'll need the My Project panel to be in the Timeline if it isn't already. To switch to the Timeline, click the **Timeline** button in the right corner of the My Project panel.*

3 At this point (00;00;09;25), right-click the actual **CTI** and select **Set Timeline Marker > Next Available Numbered** to place a marker with the number 0 at this point.

4 Move the **CTI** to 00;00;21;27. This represents the point at which the actor gets into his next waiting position.

5 At this point (00;00;21;27), right-click the actual **CTI** and select **Set Timeline Marker > Next Available Numbered** to place a marker with the number 1 at this point.

> **TIMESAVER** *You can optionally drag the **CTI** with your mouse (known as scrubbing), press the **spacebar** to play and pause the **CTI**, use the arrow keys on the keyboard, or type the timecode directly in the timecode area at the upper-left of the **Timeline**.*

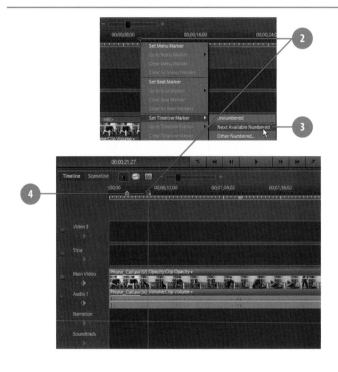

6 Repeat numbers 2–3 and add 10 additional markers, at these positions:

- ◆ **00;00;33;02** (marker number 2)
- ◆ **00;00;46;15** (marker number 3)
- ◆ **00;00;53;11** (marker number 4)
- ◆ **00;01;24;28** (marker number 5)
- ◆ **00;01;30;24** (marker number 6)
- ◆ **00;01;45;21** (marker number 7)
- ◆ **00;01;48;14** (marker number 8)
- ◆ **00;01;52;22** (marker number 9)
- ◆ **00;01;53;15** (marker number 10)
- ◆ **00;02;05;14** (marker number 11)

7 Stop when you have 12 numbered markers on your Timeline (0 to 11) as shown in the screenshot opposite.

NOTE *You may have more or fewer markers on your Timeline depending on how much or how little of the material you decided to keep.*

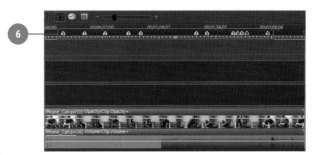

Twelve numbered markers on the Timeline

8

Removing Time (Frames) from the Clip

Now that you have the "bad" material marked out— those parts of the clips that you don't want to use—you need to remove the unwanted time (frames) by splitting the clip into smaller segments, then deleting the unwanted ones from the Timeline. What you have now is a series of *jump cuts*. A jump cut is created when you remove some or most of the middle of a clip, as you do in this task; this results in the actor (and even some of the objects) appearing to jump from their starting location at the beginning of the clip to their new location at the end of the clip.

Split the Clips

1. Press **Home** on your keyboard to return the CTI to the beginning of the **Phone_Call.avi** clip.

2. While holding down **Ctrl** on your keyboard, press the **right arrow** key to jump to the first marker; number 0.

3. Click the **Split Clip** button on the Monitor panel or press **Ctrl-K** on the keyboard to split the clip at this point (00;00;09;25).

4. Press **Ctrl-right arrow** again to jump to the next marker, number 1.

5. Repeat Step 3 and split the clip here: 00;00;21;27.

6. Press **Ctrl-right arrow** to jump to each of the remaining markers and split the clip using the **Split Clip** button or the keyboard short cut.

> **TIMESAVER** *You can use **Ctrl-Right arrow** and then **Ctrl-K** to accomplish this task in a few seconds without ever using the mouse.*

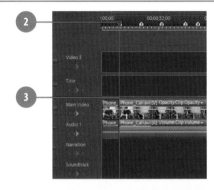

Cuts created at each of the 12 markers

Remove Time by Deleting Frames

1 Return the **CTI** to the beginning (head) of the clip by pressing **Home** on your keyboard.

2 Jump to the first marker (number 0) by pressing **Ctrl-right arrow** on your keyboard.

3 Select the second clip on the **Main Video** track by clicking it once.

4 Press **Shift-Delete** on your keyboard to delete the selected clip.

NOTE *If you press Delete without holding down the Shift key, the clips to the right of the deletion shuffle up and close the gap; this means all your markers are in the wrong position.*

5 You want to keep the next clip, so jump over it by pressing **Ctrl-right arrow** on your keyboard two times.

6 Once again, select the clip immediately to the right of the CTI line by clicking it once, then press **Shift-Delete** to delete it.

7 Repeat Steps 5 and 6 to leapfrog over the clip you want and delete the clip you don't want.

TIP *You may have to use the Timeline zoom slider to zoom in on the smaller clips before you can select them.*

Did You Know?

Let it rip(ple). Pressing **Shift-Delete** on the keyboard with a clip selected deletes the clip and leaves the gap "as is." You need to leave the gap at this point to use the markers you placed. If you want to use a "ripple delete" on a project, simply use the Delete key by itself. Using the **Delete** key deletes the clip and slides everything to the right of the deleted clip to fill the gap created by the deleted clip. This is known as a ripple edit because the clips "ripple" in to fill the space.

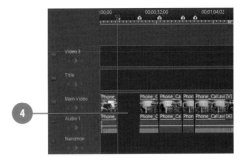

Use Shift-Delete to remove the clip.

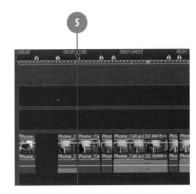

Delete the Gaps

1 Now that you've deleted the segments you don't need, it's time to close up the gaps you created in the process. Do this by right-clicking in the gap between the clips and select **Delete and Close Gap** from the contextual menu.

2 Repeat this until you've removed all the gaps.

3 To finish this section, right-click the **CTI** and select **Clear All Timeline Markers** to remove the numbered markers from the Timeline.

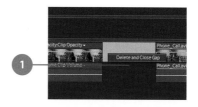

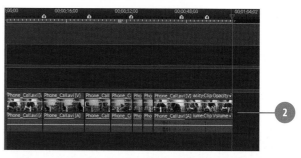

Disjointed Jumps

Disorienting Audiences Is Sometimes Deliberate

The jump cut can have a disconcerting effect. For you film history buffs, this sort of thing was once done deliberately in films as one part of a technique to deliberately remind the audience that they were watching a movie, thus not allowing them to enter the "world" the film was representing. The technique was known as *verfremdungseffekt* and has become known as the *V-effect* for short.

Adding a Cross Dissolve Between Clips

As of now, your clips show some startling and unnatural jumps in time. If this is the sort of effect you are looking for—promoting an edgy feel and heightening tension—then leave it as is. If, however, these jumps are a little too jumpy for you, follow the steps in this next section to add transitions between the cuts and a dream-like visualization to the passing of time.

Apply a Dissolve

1. If it is not already open, click the **Edit** tab to open the Edit workspace, then click the **Transitions** button to see the Transitions view.

2. In the text box in the Transitions view, type **cross**.

3. Drag the **Cross Dissolve** onto the Timeline between the first and second clips.

    TIP *If you hover the mouse over the transition in the Transition view you see a brief animation giving you some idea of what the transition does.*

    NOTE *A red line appears above the transition indicating that it needs rendering.*

4. Repeat Step 3 to add a **Cross Dissolve** transition between all the clips on the Timeline.

Did you know?

The Cross Dissolve transition is one of the more respected transitions and probably one of the only ones used in mainstream films. You can see the dissolve in many films; sometimes it is hidden away and lasts only a few frames and sometimes it is more deliberate and more dramatic—for instance, in *Aliens* when Sigourney Weaver's sleeping face is cross faded to a moon in the opening scene. Avoid, if you can, using any other transition unless you are making some kind of comedy or parody where a scene-jerking transition suits the mood of the film and isn't so important that you interrupt the audience's immersion levels!

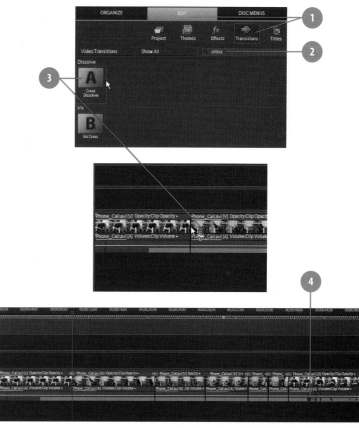

The Timeline with a transition between each clip

A transition midway between the first and second clip

Adjusting the Transitions

Once you have committed to the dreamlike Cross Dissolve effect, it becomes important to exaggerate the transitions between clips so that each lasts a little longer than the default (1 second). To alter this you use the Properties view for each of the transitions to control how the transitions behave. By extending all of the frames of the transitions to the first clip in each transition and increasing the duration of the dissolve, you can increase the dramatic effect to make it seem more dreamlike. The clips also overlap more obviously, and the actor in the scene appears to be in two places at once: dissolving out of one location while simultaneously appearing in another.

Change the Default Behavior for the Cross Dissolves

1. To access the Properties view for the transition, double-click the **Cross Dissolve** between the first and second clips on the Timeline.

2. In the Properties view for the transition, select the triangle on the Alignment menu and select **End at Cut**.

   NOTE *Selecting **End at Cut**, instead of the transition's default **Center at Cut** causes the Cross Dissolve transition to overlap all of the frames that use the first clip.*

3. Change the **Duration** of this transition to 7 seconds, or **00;00;07;00**, by clicking in the duration time field and entering the new time value.

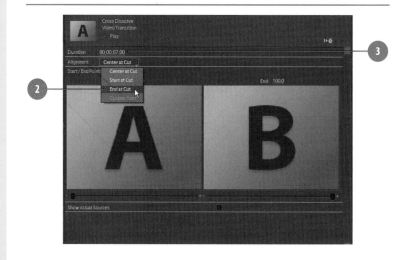

④ Repeat Steps 1–3 for all transitions on your Timeline, but alter the duration to suit the length of the clip; in other words, don't try to apply a 7-second transition to a 5-second clip, otherwise you will never fully see it.

⑤ Press **Ctrl-S** to save your work so far.

NOTE *If the Properties view for transitions is already open, you only need to click each transition in turn.*

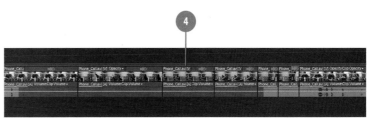

All transitions have now been modified.

Did You Know?

It takes just a second.... The default duration for transitions in Premiere Elements is 30 frames when using NTSC or 25 fps when using PAL, either way this is one second (shown in timecode format as 00;00;01;00). Because there are 30 (or 25 when using PAL) frames in each second, by default the Cross Dissolve fades out the last 15 frames on the first clip and fades in the first 15 frames on the second clip. However, you can change this duration to be any amount you want. To do so, select **Edit > Preferences > General**.

8

Adding Sound FX

Once you have finished adjusting transitions and making final adjustments to the clips, the visual aspect of this project is complete. If you play it back, clearly you can see it lacks the sound of the telephone ringing. The actor clearly reacts to it, but nothing is heard; you need to correct this now by adding the **Phone_Ring.wav** to the Timeline. Then you add the **Phone_Beep.wav** clip in two places: when the actor answers the phone and when he switches it off.

Add Two Sound FX to the Timeline

1. If it is not already open, click the **Edit** tab to switch to the Edit workspace.

2. Move the **CTI** to a few frames before the man reacts to the phone ringing—around 00;00;40;12 (*Hint: use the cursor keys to get the right position*).

3. Drag the **Phone_Ring.wav** file from the Media panel to the Narration track at the CTI location.

   TIP *If you don't have or plan to put in a Narration track for your movie, it makes a great place to place Sound FX media clips. If you do have a narration planned or in place, then you can use the audio tracks for any track above Video 1.*

4. Move the **CTI** to where the man pushes the button on the phone to answer it (around 00;00;44;12).

5. Click the **Phone_Ring.wav** to select it, then press **Ctrl-K** to split it at 00;00;44;12.

6. Click the right-hand section of the **Phone_Ring.wav** and press **Delete** on the keyboard to remove it from the Timeline.

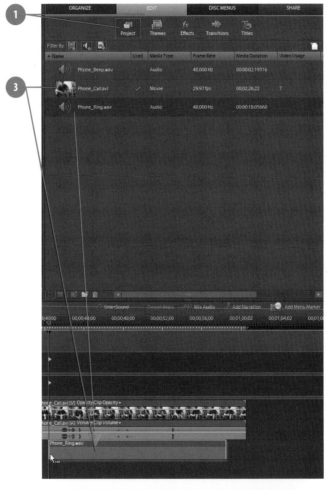

7. Drag the **Phone_Beep.wav** clip from the media panel to sit directly after the **Phone_Ring.wav** clip.

8. Press **Ctrl-S** to save your work so far.

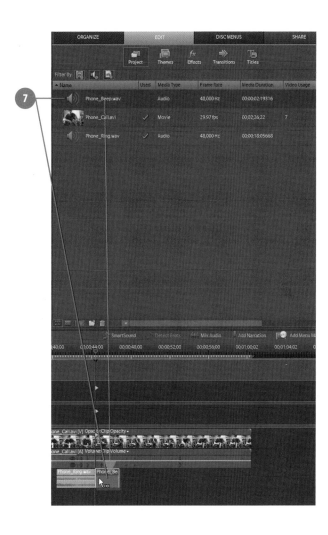

Trim the Phone_Beep.wav Clip

1 Zoom in on the Timeline so you can clearly see where the wave form of the Beep sound in the **Phone _Beep.wav** clip can be seen and move the **CTI** a few frames before it sounds.

> **NOTE** The visual effect of the Beep sound is the small wave form directly to the right of the CTI in the screenshot shown.

2 Select the clip and press **Ctrl-K** to split the clip at the CTI line.

3 Click the section to the left of the CTI (*not the right this time*) and press **Delete** on the keyboard to remove it from the Timeline.

> **TIMESAVER** Don't hold down the **Shift** key when you delete this clip to let Premiere Elements automatically close the gap between the two clips.

Copy and Paste the Phone_Beep.wav Clip

1 Right-click the **Phone_Beep.wav** file on the Timeline and select **Copy** from the contextual menu.

2 Move the **CTI** to approximately where the actor presses the button on the phone for the second time (00;00;50;27).

3 From the menu, select **Edit > Paste**.

4 The **Phone_Beep.wav** should now be duplicated on the Narration track at the CTI line.

> **NOTE** Times given are approximate and you should move the **CTI** through the Timeline with the cursor keys to find your ideal insertion point.

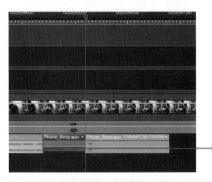

The CTI positioned a few frames before the Beep sounds

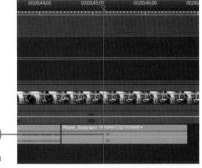

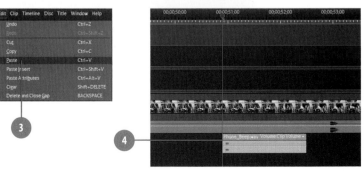

Flying Solo: Using Titles and Fades

The project is nearly complete—a true mini movie lasting just over 60 seconds. The optimal YouTube length! But it needs some final polish before you show it to the world. In this next section, you Fly Solo to add that polish. Using the skills you have learned so far in this book, you add a fade in and a fade out to the beginning and end of this movie. Next you add a simple and brief opening and closing title. Hints and tips are available in the following text, and if you get very lost, go back to the relevant chapter and look up the skill details again.

Fade In and Fade Out

1 Switch to the Edit workspace (*Hint: Edit tab*).

2 Right-click the first clip in the Timeline and select **Fade In Audio and Video** from the contextual menu.

3 Right-click the last clip in the Timeline and select **Fade Out Audio and Video** from the contextual menu.

TIMESAVER *This is an alternative method for adding a fade in and fade out to your Timeline clips. If the Properties view is not open, then it's the most efficient way to create a fade with the fewest mouse clicks.*

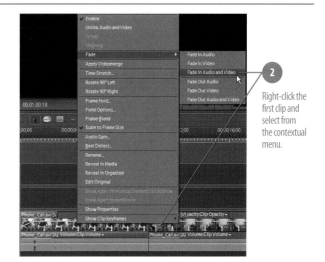

Right-click the first clip and select from the contextual menu.

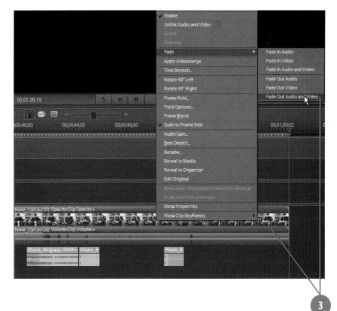

Add an Opening and Closing Title

1. Switch to the Edit workspace (*Hint: Edit tab*).

2. Send the **CTI** back to the start of the Timeline (*Hint: Home key*).

3. Open the **Titler** (*Hint: Add Default Text button*).

4. Replace the **Add Text** with **Waiting for a Phone Call** (or similar text—hey it's your movie!).

5. Choose **Font** and **Font Size** (*Hint: center the text*).

6. Exit the **Titler** (*Hint: use the Done button or click anywhere on the Timeline*).

7. Create a fade in and fade out for this title (*Hint: right-click the clip and select Fade In / Fade Out*).

8. Move the **CTI** to around 5 seconds before the end of the movie.

9. Create a closing title (*Hint: repeat Steps 3–7, but use "The End?" as the text, or again, something similar*).

Adding the Music Track

To give this project a little more atmosphere, you add SmartSound music—something soft and melodic that you cut off suddenly when the actor answers the phone. You then add a second copy to the Timeline to play as the actor continues to wait.

Select and Trim the Music

1 Switch to the Edit workspace (*Hint: Edit tab*).

2 Move the **CTI** to the start of the Timeline and then open the **SmartSound interface** (*Hint: Home key; SmartSound button*).

3 Open the **SmartSound Maestro** box (*Hint: Click here to select music! hyperlink*).

4 Select **On My Computer**, **New Age/Easy**, **Underwater**.

5 Click **Select** to close the SmartSound Maestro box.

6 Enter a duration that takes you a few seconds past when the telephone starts to ring (around 00;00;44;00).

7 Select **Ascent** (*Hint: Variation list*).

8 Select **Loop**.

9 Click **OK** and save the file to a location on your hard drive.

10 Premiere Elements adds this to your Timeline.

11 Move the **CTI** to just where the phone rings, then with the SmartSound clip selected, split the music clip at this point (*Hint: Ctrl-K; Shift-Delete*).

> **NOTE** Don't forget to hold down the **Shift** key when you delete this section of the music, otherwise all your other clips move out of position!

12 As a final touch, drag the **SmartSound tune** from the Media panel and add it just after the point where the actor hangs up the phone. Trim the music back so that it plays on for a few seconds longer than the end credit, but not too long.

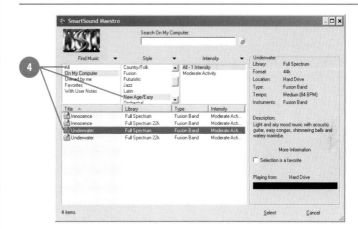

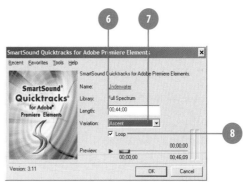

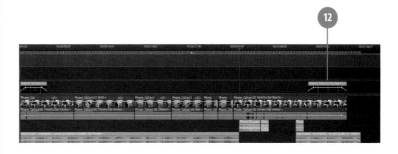

The final Timeline complete with fades on all video, audio, and title tracks

Making Adjustments, Rendering, and Exporting

Well, you've done it: another special effects production completed! Test your production by pressing the **spacebar** to see how it all fits together. If it's not quite right, tweak things a bit, such as the timing of the dissolves or the relative loudness or softness of the music track, until they're to your liking. Then, press **Enter** on your keyboard to render (apply all effects and transitions to the clips) your project and you're ready to export the finished movie for all to see!

Finishing the Project

1. Once you have played back your project and made the necessary adjustments, press **Enter** on your keyboard to render your project.

2. Once you have made all of these adjustments, press **Ctrl-S** to make a final save of your project.

3. Finally, export your work as an **AVI** file (a standard Microsoft movie file) by selecting the **Timeline**, if it is not already selected, and then choosing **File > Export > Movie**.

4. When prompted, browse to the **Peachpit** folder and then the **HSMovies_Final Renders** and save the exported file as **Chapter 8_Phone Call.avi**.

   NOTE *This final render may be used again in Chapter 21.*

5. Exit or minimize Premiere Elements and browse to the **Peachpit** folder and then open the **HSMovies_Final Renders** folder. Double-click the **Chapter 8_Phone Call.avi** file to play it in your default media player.

The finished movie, playing in Windows Media player

Hollywood Movie Time: Fast Times

MEDIA:
manypeople.avi
oneperson.avi
moreanimated.wav

9

COMPLEXITY:	Simple	Moderate	Complex
SKILL LEVEL:	Easy	Intermediate	Advanced

What You'll Learn

Flying Solo: Preparing the Project

Adding the Foreground Video Clips

Flying Solo: Increasing the Speed of the Crowd

Matching the Appearance of the Two Clips

Flying Solo: Adding the Soundtrack

Making Adjustments, Rendering, and Exporting

Introduction

If you want to show the world rushing by your subject as he or she moves sedately through normal time, the Fast Time effect is perfect. By using this effect, you can communicate a world of information about the character and the story. This effect if very popular in Pop videos, for example. The dramatic effect of everyone else in the world moving at high speed emphasizes the deeper emotions of the slower-moving actor.

You can also use the Fast Times effect whenever you need your main character to move with superhuman speed. In this case, keep your Background clip at normal speed, speed up the clip of the main character filmed in normal speed to super speed, and overlay this clip on top of the normal-moving background. Think Dash from *The Incredibles*.

In addition to using the Fast Times effect, you can play with time by experimenting with the Time Stretch function in Premiere Elements. This can yield a range of results that may be useful in different projects. Keep in mind that although the effect can be very dramatic (as demonstrated in this chapter), you can also use it subtly. For example, in a normal scene you could use the Time Stretch function in reverse for just a second or two as two people pass each other on a crowded city street and have an internal moment of "haven't we met before, maybe in another lifetime...?" And then the scene returns to full speed. For the most part, you are only limited by your imagination in how you can apply this effect.

Flying Solo: Preparing the Project

The first steps you take when you're creating this effect are the same basic steps you use for virtually all of the projects in this book: you begin a project, name the tracks, and import your media clips. For this project, the required media clips are **manypeople.avi**, **oneperson.avi**, and **moreanimated.wav**. In Chapter 1, you learned the necessary techniques to do all of the tasks on this page, so Fly Solo now and see how much you can remember. Hints and tips are listed here in this section to help you out, but if you get really lost, take a peek back at Chapter 1 for more detailed instructions.

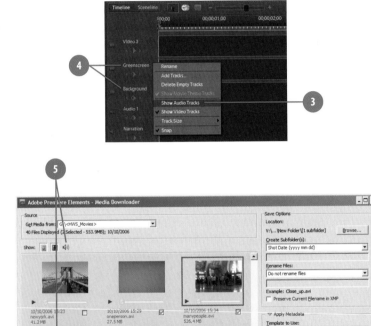

Start a Project, Customize the Timeline, and Get Some Media

1 Start Premiere Elements and create a **New Project** called **Chapter 9 –Fast_Times** (*Hint: use the New Project at the Splash screen or File > New > Project if Premiere Elements is already open; save in the Peachpit folder created in Chapter 1*).

NOTE *You should use the sample files on the DVD on an NTSC Timeline. If your default Project Settings are not NTSC, change them now by clicking the **Change Settings** button and selecting: **NTSC > DV > Standard 48kHz**.*

2 If the Timeline is set to the **Sceneline**, switch it back to the **Timeline** (*Hint: Timeline button!*).

NOTE *You need to switch to the **Timeline** because, for this project, you are working with multiple clips on multiple video tracks.*

3 Deselect audio tracks 2 and 3 (*Hint: right-click Track Header; deselect Show Audio Tracks*).

4 Rename tracks 1 and 2 to the following (*Hint: Right-click the track name; select Rename*):

- ◆ Video 1: **Background**

- ◆ Video 2: **Greenscreen**

5 Import the **manypeople.avi**, **oneperson.avi**, and **moreanimated.wav** media clips from the DVD (*Hint: Get Media; DVD [Camcorder or PC DVD Drive] button; Advanced button; select DVD drive; UnCheck All*).

TIP *You can find complete instructions for importing media into Premiere Elements 7 in the Chapter 1 section "Adding Media to Your Project."*

6 Once the clip appears in the panel, switch to the Edit workspace (*Hint: Edit tab; Project button*).

7 Drag the **manypeople.avi** clip to the Background track on the Timeline.

> **TIP** *Make sure the start of the media clip is at the head of the track.*

8 Use the **Zoom In** or **Out** controls so the **manypeople.avi** clip occupies around two-thirds of the Timeline. Move onto the next section when your Timeline looks similar to the one shown here.

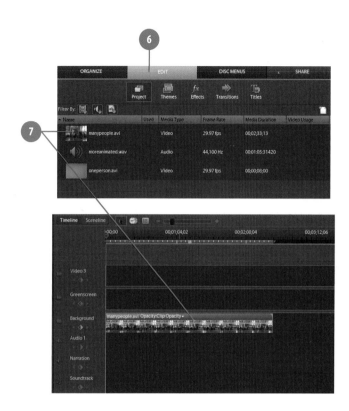

Adding the Foreground Video Clips

In this project, you are using two clips. One, **manypeople.avi**, is the "rest of the world" clip, which should already be on the Main Movie Timeline track; the other, **oneperson.avi**, is the main subject of the piece, the actor who is moving in real time. This clip has been shot in front of a green screen, and as you add it to the Timeline, Premiere Elements attempts to remove much of the green using Videomerge. All you need to do is tweak the Videomerge settings to create a "cleaner" key (by removing the green from around the actor).

Add the Foreground Clip to the Timeline

1. If it is not already selected, click the **Edit** tab to select the Edit workspace and then click the **Project** button to view the Media panel.

2. Drag the **oneperson.avi** clip from the Media panel and onto the Timeline in the Greenscreen track. Again, be sure to line up the head of the **oneperson.avi** clip with the beginning of the track.

3. When you drag the clip onto the track, Premiere Elements asks you if you want to add Videomerge. Select **Yes** and the green screen should vanish from view.

   NOTE *If you don't see this prompt, right-click on the clip on the Timeline and select Apply Videomerge.*

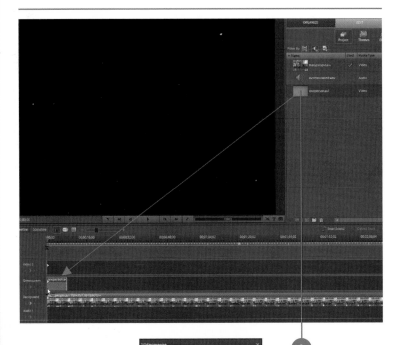

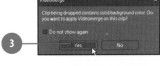

The Greenscreen clip with the Videomerge removing almost all the green

Adjust Videomerge for a Cleaner Key

1 With the **oneperson.avi** clip selected, click the **Properties** button to open the Properties view and dial down the **Videomerge** controls by clicking the triangle.

2 Adjust the **Tolerance** to 0.60.

TIP *Move the CTI to around 00;00;04;00 to clearly see the effect of adjusting the Videomerge controls. You can also experiment with the Select Color controls, but as it stands, a small tweak to the Tolerance levels with all other settings at default is enough to achieve a clean key with this clip and remove all the green screen.*

3 Press **Ctrl-S** to save your work so far.

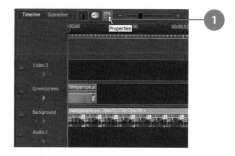

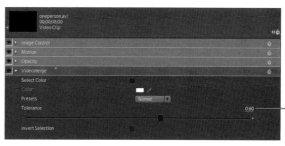

Before adjusting the Videomerge tolerance level. Note the traces of green around the body.

After adjusting the Videomerge tolerance level to 0.60. Note the traces of green are gone.

9

Acquiring a Green Screen for Your Projects

Web Sources for Green Screens

After you've mastered this technique, you'll want to use it with your own clips. Creating green screen clips requires a green screen (or blue screen) for the background. Although any solid green surface works for a green screen or a blue screen, such as a sheet, for best results get an industry-approved green screen. If you search for "green screen" using your favorite Web search engine, you'll find a lot of different makes and models to choose from. Throughout this book, we've been using green screens, stands, and other equipment from **www.chroma-key.com**. They supply a variety of blue and green screens, portable and studio stands, and even green screen paint.

Flying Solo: Increasing the Speed of the Crowd

In this task, you super speed the clip of the crowd to achieve the effect of time rushing past. To speed up the background clip, you need to apply the Time Stretch function, something you have used before in Chapter 4 where you added frames to a title to slow it down. Here you do the reverse and remove frames to speed it up. Fly Solo now and use Time Stretch to speed up and condense 3 minutes of meandering into 10 seconds of purposeful action. Then add and adjust an Opacity fade out to the **manypeople.avi** clip. Hints and tips are available here should you need them.

Time Stretch the Crowd

① Access the Time Stretch feature for the **manypeople.avi** clip (*Hint: right-click the clip; select Time Stretch from the contextual menu*).

② Set the **Speed** to 1700.00%.

> **NOTE** *Three minutes of real time lasts a mere 9 seconds. This is something to bear in mind if you come to film this effect yourself.*

③ Click **OK** to close the Time Stretch dialog and apply the effect.

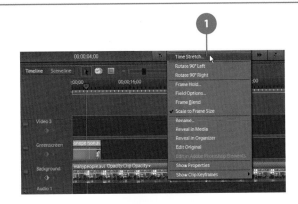

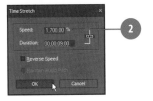

Did You Know?

Increasing a clip's speed shortens its duration (and vice versa). You can use the Time Stretch dialog to change the speed of a clip, which simultaneously affects its duration (how long the clip plays). Making the clip play faster decreases its duration (by playing faster, it finishes sooner). The inverse is true, as well. Making a clip slower increases its duration (it plays slower, so it takes longer to finish). In other words, as non-intuitive as it may seem at first, when adjusting a clip's speed, up is down and down is up. For example, increasing the **Speed** of a clip to 200 percent reduces the clip to half its normal duration, and decreasing the **Speed** to 50 percent increases the clip to twice its normal duration.

Add a Fade Out and Adjust the Timing of the Fade

1 Zoom the Timeline so that both clips occupy about two-thirds of the Timeline (*Hint: Use the zoom control or keyboard shortcuts "-" and "+"*).

2 Select the **manypeople.avi** clip and open the **Properties** view (*Hint: Properties button*).

3 Open the **Opacity** controls (*Hint: click the triangle*).

4 Add a fade out to the end of the clip (*Hint: Fade Out button*).

> **NOTE** *Using the contextual (right-click) menu to add a fade out adds the fade at an unexpected place because Time Stretch is being used. Adding the fade out via the Properties view does not show this problem.*

5 Adjust the fade (because this clip is accelerated) so the fade out keyframe starts just under the end of the **oneperson.avi** clip (*Hint: drag the first keyframe toward the oneperson.avi clip—00;00;08;00*).

> **TIP** *The yellow box shows you the timecode as you move the keyframe. Just watch as the number decreases and approaches 00;00;08;00, and stop when it reaches that number.*

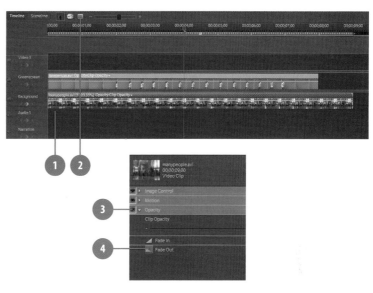

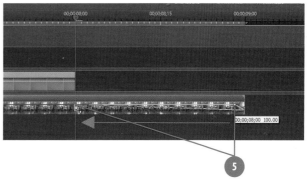

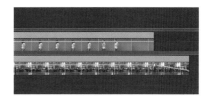

The adjusted opacity keyframe on the Background clip. The green screen actor moves out of frame before the end of the clip, so she does not need a fade out.

9

Matching the Appearance of the Two Clips

The two sample video clips for this project, **oneperson.avi** and **manypeople.avi**, were filmed at different locations, at different times of day, and under uniquely different lighting conditions. When you are using your own clips—or perhaps a royalty-free clip as the background—you may run into similar color and lighting mismatches, either great or small. Fortunately, these are usually fairly easy to fix with some minimal tweaking using the various color correction tools available to you in Premiere Elements. In this section, you add the Color Balance (RGB) effect to warm up the actor's skin a little.

Adjust the Image Control Settings

① Click the **Effects** button to display the Effects panel and enter **RGB** in the text field.

② Drag the Color Balance (RGB) effect to the **oneperson.avi** clip.

③ Click the **Property** button to open the Properties view, then make the following adjustments to the Color Balance (RGB) controls:

- ◆ Red: **105**

- ◆ Green: **96**

- ◆ Blue: **93**

TIP *Make sure the CTI is over a part of the clip where the actor is visible before you start making RGB corrections.*

Did You Know?

All clips are different, at least to some degree. Keep in mind that the settings in Step 3 are specifically for the two clips you use in this project. When you are working on your next green screen project, look at how the clips are working together on the screen and make adjustments as necessary—use your own judgment. Maybe the Hue needs to be +1.0°. Maybe the Saturation needs to be increased and the Contrast decreased. Experiment until you like what you see. For this task, it's a little bit art, and a little bit science.

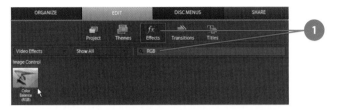

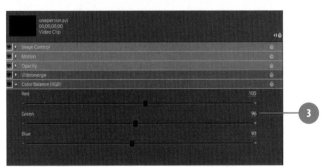

Before RGB corrections

After RGB corrections. Note the warmer flesh tones and that the clothes and hair are less washed out.

Flying Solo: Adding the Soundtrack

Music sets the mood, as you have seen plenty of times in this book. Fly Solo now to either add the **moreanimated.wav** clip to the Timeline, which provides a rock and roll beat and some ironic lyrics to the scene, or use **SmartSound** to come up with your own custom-built music track.

Use the WAV File

1. Switch to the Media panel (*Hint: Edit tab; Project button*).

2. Add the **moreanimated.wav** clip to the **Soundtrack** track (*Hint: drag!*).

   TIP *Be sure to line up the start (head) of the* **moreanimated.wav** *clip with the beginning of the* **Soundtrack** *track.*

3. Move the **CTI** to 00;00;09;00 and select the **moreanimated.wav** clip by clicking it once.

4. Split the **moreanimated.wav** clip at the CTI and delete the right-hand segment (*Hint: Ctrl-K or click the Split Clip button [the scissors icon at the bottom of the Monitor panel]; press Delete on the keyboard*).

   TIMESAVER *You may want to use the zoom controls to view all of the clips on the Timeline in full.*

5 Add a volume fade out to the **moreanimated.wav** clip (*Hint: right-click the clip; Fade > Fade Out Audio*).

Use SmartSound

1 Switch to the **Media** panel (*Hint: Edit tab; Project button*).

2 Move the **CTI** to the start of the Timeline (*Hint: Page Up*).

3 Open the **SmartSound** Quicktracks box (*Hint: SmartSound button*).

4 Access the **SmartSound Maestro** interface (*Hint: Click here to Select Music!*).

5 Make your choices and click **Select** (*Hint: double-click a track to preview it; we suggest "Synergy"*).

6 Change the **Duration** to match the Timeline duration and select the **Variation** you want (*Hint: 00;09;00; we suggest "Insight"*).

TIMESAVER *SmartSound adds your choice to the Soundtrack track on the Timeline. SmartSound tracks have a built-in fade out, so you won't need to adjust the volume level on this track.*

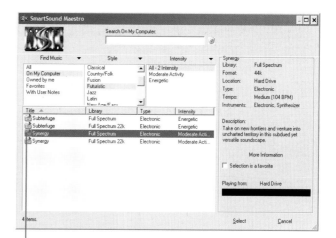

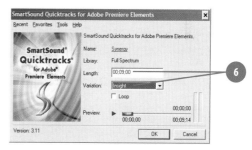

Making Adjustments, Rendering, and Exporting

Before you call this project finished, you may want to make some final adjustments to the clips as needed, based on your own personal style. After this, you're ready to save, render, and make your movie.

Finish the Project

1. Once you have played back your project and made the necessary adjustments, press **Enter** on your keyboard to render your project.

2. Once you have made all of these adjustments, press **Ctrl-S** to make a final save of your project.

3. Finally, export your work as an AVI file (a standard Microsoft movie file) by selecting the **Timeline**, if it is not already selected, and then choosing **File > Export > Movie**.

4. When prompted, browse to the **Peachpit** folder and then the **HSMovies_Final Renders** folder and save the exported file as **Chapter 9_Fast_Timesl.avi**.

   NOTE *This final render may be used again in Chapter 21.*

5. Exit or minimize Premiere Elements and browse to the **Peachpit** folder and then open the **HSMovies_Final Renders** folder. Double-click the **Chapter 9_Fast_Timesl. avi**. file to play it in your default media player.

   TIP *You can optionally bring this clip into a larger project, show it on your computer, upload it to an Internet video sharing site, or burn it to a DVD.*

The finished project running in Windows Media Player

Hollywood Movie Time: The Power of the Force—Reversing Time

MEDIA:

Long_shot.avi
Close_up.avi
Background.jpg
Floor_Background.jpg

10

COMPLEXITY:	Simple	Moderate	Complex
SKILL LEVEL:	Easy	Intermediate	Advanced

Introduction

The Reverse Action effect is one of the easiest and quickest effects to accomplish in Premiere Elements. You can apply the effect in less time than it took you to read that last sentence, yet it has the potential to be one of the most powerful and dramatic visual effects in your video-editing arsenal.

In this chapter you use it in a scene where a Jedi, having carelessly left his light saber on the floor, uses The Force to pull it back to him. You will also learn how to insert a clip into the Timeline to help *sell*, or convince, the audience that what is happening on screen *isn't* a special effect. Suspension of disbelief only takes you so far. With a modern audience, you need to work a little harder; this is why you use the **Close_up.avi** selling shot in this chapter!

You can use the Reverse Action effect for dramatic and comic purposes, and you can apply it to virtually any clip with interesting results. You're probably familiar with the Jedi "power of the force"; another example you may be familiar with is the Bionic woman leaping up great heights (again, what you're seeing is the stunt person leaping down, played in reverse—when they are not using wires, that is).

You can use this effect, too, to show your son leap out of a pool, your daughter slide up the slide, or a friend extract a candy bar out of his mouth and reassemble it back into its wrapper. Because this effect is found on the Time Stretch dialog (which is used to speed up and slow down clips), reversing clips and at the same time changing their speed or duration are natural effect companions.

What You'll Learn

Flying Solo: Preparing the Project

Adding a Jedi to the Timeline and Removing the Garbage

Creating a Clean Key

Working with Green Screen Footage

At Last! Selecting Reverse

Adding a Selling Shot

Flying Solo: Removing the Green Screen from the Inserted Clips

Adjusting the Jedi's Scale

Making Adjustments, Rendering, and Exporting

Flying Solo: Preparing the Project

The first steps in creating this effect are the same as the ones for virtually all of the projects in this book: begin a project, name the tracks, and import your media clips. For this project, you require four media clips, two AVIs and two JPGs. In Chapter 1, you learned the necessary techniques to perform all these tasks, so Fly Solo now and see how much you can remember. Hints and tips are listed in the following steps to help you out, but if you get really lost, take a peek back at the Chapter 1 section "Preparing the Project" for more detailed instructions.

Start a Project, Customize the Timeline, and Import Some Media

1 Start **Premiere Elements** and create a **New Project** called **Chapter_10_Reverse Time** (*Hint: use the New Project at the splash screen or File > New > Project if Premiere Elements is already open; save in the Peachpit folder created in Chapter 1*).

> **NOTE** *The sample files supplied on the DVD are for use on an NTSC Timeline. If your default Project Settings are not NTSC, change them now by clicking the* ***Change Settings*** *button and selecting* ***NTSC > DV > Standard 48kHz***.

2 If the Timeline is set to the **Sceneline**, switch to the **Timeline** (*Hint: Timeline button*).

> **NOTE** *You need to switch to the* ***Timeline*** *because for this project you are working with multiple clips on multiple video tracks.*

3 Deselect the audio tracks 2 and 3 (*Hint: right-click Track Header; deselect Show Audio Tracks*).

4 Rename tracks 1 and 2 to the following (*Hint: Right-click the track name; select Rename*):

◆ Video 1: **Background**

◆ Video 2: **Movie**

5 Import the **Long_shot.avi, Close_up.avi, Background.jpg**, and **Floor_Background.jpg** media clips from the DVD (*Hint: Get Media; DVD [Camcorder or PC DVD Drive] button; Advanced button; select DVD drive; UnCheck All; check the required media clips*).

> **TIP** *You can find complete instructions for grabbing media into Premiere Elements 7 in the Chapter 1 section "Adding Media to Your Project."*

Filming Tips

You don't need to have your actor standing in front of a green screen to make this work. The green screen is only necessary if you are going to remove the background at a later stage. However, you do need to be aware that when you reverse time, everything in the background also goes backward! So again, when you set up your shot, it is essential that you think about what is in the frame (known as blocking a shot) and then lock down your camera and tripod, even before an actor makes it onto the stage area.

Once you are set to shoot, get the actor to run through the moves a few times. The actor needs to move fluidly, and he should be aware that he is acting the scene in reverse. Dropping the object later becomes picking up the object. This skill can be hard to master and requires time and patience...and a lot of DV cassettes!

TIP Keep the camera running during rehearsals and practice sessions because you never know if a good take will end up being there, and not in the actual real takes.

6 Once the clips appear in the panel, switch to the **Edit** workspace (*Hint: Edit tab; Project button*).

7 Drag the **Background.jpg** media clip to the Background track on the **Timeline** and then zoom in using the zoom slider. Move on to the next section when your Timeline looks similar to the one in the screenshot.

TIP *Make sure the start of the media clip is at the head of the track.*

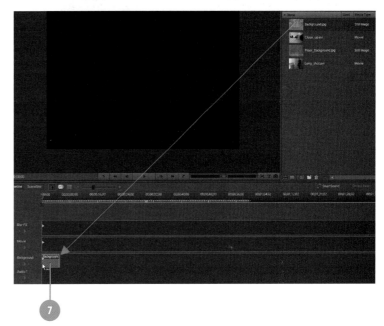

Adding a Jedi to the Timeline and Removing the Garbage

On the DVD supplied with this book, we provide you with a sample clip, **Long_shot.avi**. This is the core shot that you reverse in this chapter. The shot was taken in front of a green screen, which obviously needs to be removed, but it is surrounded by a lot of unwanted background and foreground garbage that you need to clean away. In this section, you add the clip to the Timeline, then you use one of the garbage mattes to clean away the "garbage" to prepare for the next section, where you remove the green screen background.

Add a Clip to the Movie

1. If it is not already displayed, click the **Edit** tab to show the Edit workspace and then click the **Project** button to show the Media panel.

2. Select the **Long_shot.avi** clip for this project and drag it to the Movie track on the Timeline. Make sure the head of the clip lands at the very start (or head) of the Timeline.

   TIP *For this project, you need to be in the Timeline because you are working with multiple clips on multiple video tracks. If you are in Sceneline, click the* **Timeline** *button to switch.*

3. Drag the **Background.jpg** clip out so that it stretches the length of the **Long_shot.avi**.

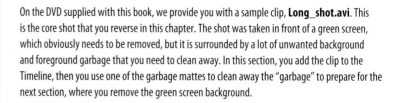

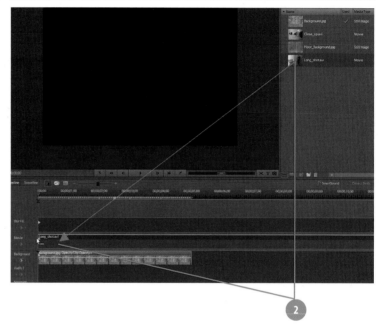

Remove the Garbage from the Movie

1. If it is not already displayed, click the **Edit** tab to show the Edit workspace and then the **Effects** button to show the Effects panel.

2. Type **gar** into the text field to reveal the garbage effects available in Premiere Elements.

3. Drag the **Eight-Point Garbage Matte** onto the **Long_shot.avi** clip.

4. If it is not already selected (shown by a dark purple band running the top length of the clip), click the clip once to select it.

5. Click the **Properties** button to open the Properties view, then dial down the **Eight-Point Garbage Matte** controls by clicking the triangle.

6. Click the actual title, **Eight-Point Garbage Matte**, to highlight all eight points in the Monitor panel.

7. If some of those points are outside your field of view, right-click inside the Monitor panel area and choose **Magnification > 100%** or lower.

NOTE *Before you move any of the garbage matte points, move the **CTI** to 00;00;06;21 on the Timeline. This is where our fearless Jedi extends his elbow right to the very edge of the green screen, and you need to make sure your garbage matte doesn't cut part of his arm off at this time frame.*

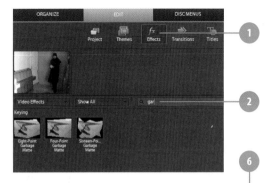

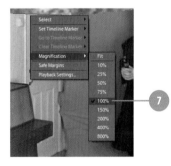

10

8 One by one, drag the points across the Monitor panel to remove the garbage and show only the green screen. When you have finished, your Monitor panel should look something like that in the screenshot.

The Eight-Point Garbage Matte with all the points in the optimal position

Did You Know?

The more time you spend with the Garbage Matte effect the less time you have to spend trying to remove the green screen background. This is because the Green Screen Key (like other Chroma tools) only has to work on the visible areas of the clip, anything that is not obscured by the garbage matte. Using the garbage matte cleverly can save a badly filmed green screen clip from never being used.

Understanding Aspect Ratio and Garbage Mattes

The unfortunately named set of mattes known collectively as **garbage mattes** serve an important purpose within Premiere Elements: they let you hide stuff you don't want, basically the garbage.

For the purposes of this project, you use the Eight-Point Garbage Matte to crop the footage and get rid of anything that is not the green screen. Premiere Elements also has a Four-Point Garbage Matte and a Sixteen-Point Garbage Matte available for lesser- or finer-detailed situations.

The Coordinates on the Screen

The standard video signal in North America and Japan—that is, the non-letterbox, not high definition signal—is 480 by 720. This is known as the *aspect ratio*.

You use these numbers when you're positioning items on the screen as coordinates. Specifically, the location of any item on the screen can be defined by its *x* (horizontal) and *y* (vertical) coordinates. For an NTSC signal (the television standard in the United States and elsewhere in the world), the horizontal length (left and right) is 720, and the vertical length (up and down) is 480. In Cartesian terms (*x,y*), the four corners of the television screen (as well as the Premiere Elements Monitor panel) for an NTSC signal are expressed as *0,0* for the upper-left corner; *720,0* for the upper-right; *0,480* for the lower-left; and *720,480* for the lower-right.

Creating a Clean Key

In video making, removing the background, whether it is blue or green, is called *creating a clean key*. In this context, *clean* means that the audience can see none of the green screen, either in the background or as a green halo surrounding the actor. In this section, you attempt to remove as much of the green as possible using a variety of different effects, including the Auto Color and Auto Contrast effects as well as the Green Screen Key effect. When all these effects are used together on a green screen clip, they should help create a clean key and reveal the Science Fiction background beneath! As a final step, you use the Non Red Key effect to defringe (remove green around the actor's fingers).

Apply the Auto Color and Auto Contrast Effects

1. If it is not already open, click the **Edit** tab to switch to the Edit workspace and click the **Effects** button to switch to the Effects panel.

2. In the text box on the Effects view of the Media panel, type **auto**.

3. Select the **Auto Color** effect and drag it onto the **Long_shot.avi** clip on the Movie track.

4. Leave the Auto Color settings at the defaults.

5. Select the **Auto Contrast** effect and drag it onto the **Long_shot.avi** clip on the Background track.

6. Leave the Auto Contrast settings at the defaults.

> ### Did You Know?
>
> **It's a study in contrasts.** When you use a green or blue screen effect in your future projects, apply the **Auto Color** and **Auto Contrast** effects to give the picture an instant "light level" improvement. You will be surprised at the difference this can make.

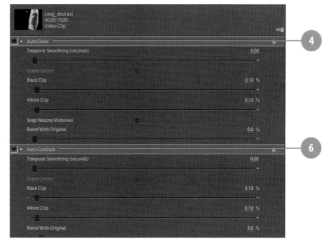

10

Add the Green Screen Key Effect

1. If it is not already open, click the **Edit** tab to switch to the Edit workspace and click the **Effects** button to switch to the Effects panel.

2. In the text box on the Effects view of the Media window, type **green**.

3. Select the **Green Screen Key** effect and drag it onto the **Long_shot.avi** clip on the Movie track.

4. Adjust the effect as follows:

   ◆ Threshold: **31.0%**

   ◆ Cutoff: **30.0%**

   ◆ Smoothing: **High**

Before...

...and after adding the garbage matte, Auto Color and Auto Contrast, and the Green Screen key

Defringe the Green Screen Clip

1. Play the clip forward to about **00;00;09;26**. Study the fingers and the face of the actor. You should just be able to see green fringe surrounding those body parts.

2. To remove it, open the **Effects** panel and in the text box, type **Non**.

3. Select the **Non Red Key** effect and drag it onto the **Long_shot.avi** clip on the Movie track.

4. Adjust the effect as follows:

   ◆ Threshold: **100.0%**

   ◆ Cutoff: **35.0%**

   ◆ Defringing: **Green**

   ◆ Smoothing: **High**

5. After these adjustments, the **Long_shot.avi** clip should look something like that in the screenshot.

   TIP *If you are having trouble removing all the green, review the placement of your garbage matte and move some of the points to see if you can reduce the number of adjustments and/or Chroma Key effects you need to use.*

   NOTE *You can find more advice on trouble-shooting the removal of a green screen background in the sidebar "How Two Controls Help the Green Screen Key Filter Out the Green," later in this chapter.*

10

Working with Green Screen Footage

When you first apply the Green Screen key to a clip, you rarely get a perfect result. What you typically see is the first layer of green removed from the background of the green screen clip, revealing the hazy background behind the clip. The background itself is revealed as if behind a curtain. As you tweak the two key settings for the Green Screen key—Threshold and Cutoff—you'll gradually see the background emerge and the foreground become brighter and more pronounced. Tweaking too far causes the figure in the foreground to deteriorate, allowing some of the background to bleed through. Typically, the Threshold and Cutoff settings are the same, and when you find the right settings for the clip, the scene looks natural, with little, if any, evidence that a green screen was used.

Troubleshooting a Green Screen Project

Sometimes, no matter how well you thought you set up your green screen backdrop, or how well you thought you had the backdrop and your subject lit, when you get your clip into Premiere Elements and apply the Green Screen key, what you see is mud. All you know is that the thing doesn't look like it's supposed to. Perhaps it's the color of your background. Maybe it's your lights (or lack of them). Maybe it's the fact that your green screen material has gotten a bit too wrinkled or you didn't quite stretch it (or iron it) enough this time. But no matter what the problem, there's a fix right in Premiere Elements.

Chroma Key to the Rescue

With the Chroma key, you can choose the color by either selecting it from the background using an eyedropper tool or by picking it from a color swatch.

After you've applied the key, go to the Properties view, click the triangle next to the Chroma key, and then select the eyedropper tool. With the eyedropper tool, click a color in the background of the clip in the Monitor panel. The color swatch next to the eyedropper tool is now the same color as the color you selected.

Clicking the color swatch next to the eyedropper tool brings up the Color Picker dialog. This is an alternative way to select your starting color for the Chroma key. From the Color Picker dialog, you can either select a color by clicking it or you can enter a numeric value.

Adjust the Chroma Key to Eliminate the Green

As you may notice the first time you use this effect, at first the Chroma key does a rough cut, a kind of wide sweep, and removes a certain amount of the background. In order for you to remove the rest, you need to tweak the Chroma key's controls. On the Properties view, you can adjust the Similarity setting for the Chroma key by dragging your mouse across the setting (or by typing in a value) until as much as possible of the background disappears.

You can also tweak the controls to adjust the key until, hopefully, all of the background has been eliminated. Controls for the Chroma key include Blend (how and to what degree it merges with the background), Threshold (the amount of shadows included in the selected color), and Cutoff (how dark or light the shadows are). (The green disappears and reappears as you make adjustments.) Keep in mind that you can apply the **Chroma** key as many times as necessary to completely eliminate all of the background color or colors in the clip.

Non Red Is the Right "Non" Color

Premiere Elements has another key that you can use to eliminate any final vestiges of green, especially the nefarious green "fringe" that sometimes remains around an actor after the green background has been removed. When you need to rid yourself of this pesky fringe, try the Non Red Key effect. In the Properties view, click the **Defringing** menu and choose **Green**. This should, in most cases, remove the green fringe. By the way, if your actor has a blue fringe from a blue background, select **Blue** instead.

At Last! Selecting Reverse

At last, after all that preparation, you now finally come to the point where you apply the Reverse effect to the entire **Long_shot.avi** clip. This is accomplished with a couple of mouse clicks and the Premiere Elements 7 Time Stretch feature.

Switch to Reverse Using Time Stretch

① Right-click the **Long_shot.avi** clip to bring up the Long contextual menu.

② There are many choices here, but you are after **Time Stretch**, which appears near the middle of this list. Click it once to bring up the Time Stretch dialog.

③ Leave all other settings as they are, but place a check in the **Reverse Speed** box.

④ Click **OK** and the Reverse effect is applied to this clip.

⑤ Playback the Timeline to see the Jedi use The Force to pick up his weapon of choice.

Right-click the **Long_shot.avi** clip on the Timeline to bring up this contextual menu.

Did You Know?

You can keep the sound moving forward. One problem with reversing action (or adjusting speed) is that the sound also gets modified. If you choose to leave the sound unaltered using the Maintain Audio Pitch check box, keep in mind that doing so puts lip movement out of sync with speech. Also, if you choose to speed up your footage but keep the soundtrack normal, the video of the clip finishes before the audio, thereby clipping the audio. For example, a child saying, "Dad, watch me slide down the slide!" in the unaltered clip may become, "Dad, watch...!" in the altered version. Or, for that matter (in reverse), "!...hctaw ,daD".

10

Adding a Selling Shot

So far you have created the illusion of the Jedi picking up his weapon with just the power of his mind. Cool. But it all seems to be over very quickly and the saber itself isn't very clear until the last second. What you need is a selling shot! In this section, you open the **Close_up.avi** clip in the Preview window. Define a section that you want to use, then insert it into the Timeline at a predefined location. Then you need to trim the **Long_shot.avi** clip to make it match the inserted clip. Finish this section by defining and inserting the **Floor_Background.jpg** beneath the **Close_up.avi** clip.

Define a Section of the Close-up.avi Clip

1. If it is not already displayed, click the **Edit** tab to show the Edit workspace and then the **Project** button to show the Media panel.

2. Double-click the **Close_up.avi** clip to open it in the Preview window.

3. Move the **CTI** in the Preview window just as the hand is entering the field of view (00;00;01;09).

4. Click the **Set In** button to set this as the point where you would like the clip to start.

5. Move the **CTI** (using the right arrow key) to around 00;00;02;00.

6. Click the **Set Out** button to set this as the point where you would like the clip to end. Leave the Preview window open and move to the next section.

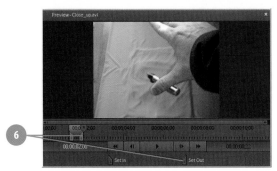

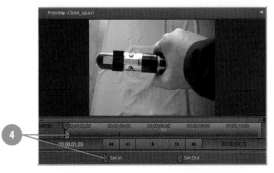

7 Right-click inside the Preview window area and select **Time Stretch** from the contextual menu.

> **TIP** *You must apply Time Stretch after the in and out clips are defined, otherwise the in and out points are transferred to an inverse point on the Preview window's Timeline.*

8 Leave all the other settings as they are, but place a check in the **Reverse Speed** box.

9 Close the **Preview** window by clicking the X in the top-right corner.

Insert the Section to the Timeline

1 Move the Timeline **CTI** to where the handle of the saber just begins to move (00;00;08;23).

2 Right-click the **Close_up.avi** clip in the Media panel and choose **Insert To Timeline** from the contextual menu.

3 On the Timeline, the **Long_shot.avi** and **Background.jpg** clips are split at the insertion point. Unfortunately, when you're using the **Insert** command, the default track is Video 1, or in this case, the Background track.

4 Drag the **Close_up.avi** clip up to the Movie track on the Timeline to correct this.

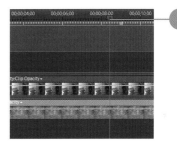

10

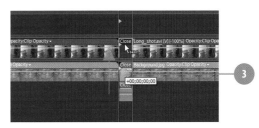

Trim the Long_shot.avi Clip

1 Move the **CTI** to 00;00;9;22, approximately where the Jedi grabs the light saber handle.

2 Using the mouse, grab the head of the **Long_shot.avi** clip and drag it toward the CTI.

3 Now grab the right-hand instance of the **Background.jpg** clip on the Timeline and drag it up the Timeline so that the head of the **Background.jpg** clip is level with the head of the second instance of the **Long_shot.avi** clip.

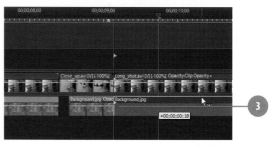

NOTE *When you trim the background clip after trimming the long_shot, the long_shot clip may "ripple" to the left, overlapping part of the close-up. Holding the Shift key and selecting both clips and trimming them simultaneously rather than one at a time will resolve this problem.*

4 If necessary, trim the tail end of the **Background.jpg** clip to be the same length as the **Long_shot.avi** clip.

Define a Section of the Floor_Background.jpg Clip

1 Hover the mouse over the **Close_up.avi** clip on the Timeline. The pop-up bubble displays the start and end point of the clip and also, more importantly, the Duration! In this case it is 22 frames (00;00;00;22) long. If yours is different, jot that figure down now.

2 If it is not already displayed, click the **Edit** tab to show the Edit workspace and then the **Project** button to show the Media panel.

3 Double-click the **Floor_Background.jpg** clip to open it in the Preview window.

4 Drag the **Set Out** marker down the Preview Timeline while keeping an eye on the Duration field. Stop when the duration is 00;00;00;22 (or the duration you wrote down in Step 1).

5 Exit the **Preview** window and then move the **CTI** to the start of the **Close_up.avi** inserted clip using Page Up or Page Down.

6 Hold down **Ctrl**, and drag the **Floor_Background.jpg** clip from the Media panel to the CTI on the Timeline, then drop it into the gap on the Background track.

NOTE *If you don't hold **Ctrl** down, all the clips to the right of the **Floor_Background.jpg** clip jump out of position.*

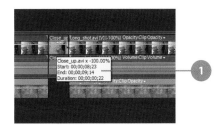

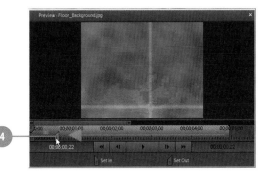

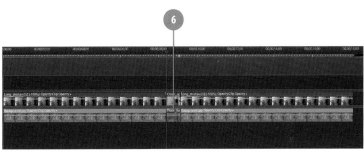

Make sure you hold down **Ctrl** while dragging the **Floor_Background.jpg** clip from the Media panel to the gap in the Timeline to avoid the other clips jumping out of position.

10

Flying Solo: Removing the Green Screen from the Inserted Clips

Now that you have the inserted clips in place, you need to see the **Floor_Background.jpg** clip to finish the effect. Fly Solo now and use the **garbage matte**, the **Green Screen Key** effect, and the **Non Red Key** effect if you think you need to create a clean key for the **Close_up.avi** clip. You will find hints and tips in this section and if you get totally lost, refer back to the instructions earlier in this chapter.

Create a Clean Key

1. Add a **Four-** or **Eight-Point Garbage Matte** to the **Close_up.avi** clip (*Hint: Effects panel; type garbage; drag*).

2. Adjust the **garbage matte** so that it gets rid of any unwanted background but doesn't clip the moving "saber" handle (*Hint: Properties view; select the effect name; adjust points*).

3. Add the **Auto Contrast** and **Auto Color** effects to the **Close_up.avi** clip.

4. Add the **Green Screen Key** from the Effects panel and adjust the sliders to remove as much green as possible (*Hint: Threshold=30.1%; Cutoff=30.7%*).

5. Add the **Non Red Key** effect from the Effects panel and adjust to suit your own personal taste (*Hint: Threshold 100%; Cuttoff 45.9%; Defringing green*).

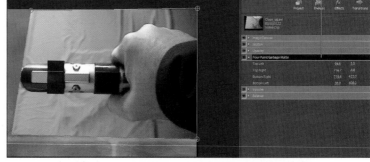

The resulting clean key!

Adjusting the Jedi's Scale

The project is almost complete and is ready to be exported as an AVI so that you can use it in Chapter 17 where you add a laser to the Jedi's laser sword! However, the Jedi is a little close to the camera for the full laser to be seen, so in this section you adjust the scale on both the first and second **Long_shot.avi** clips on the Timeline.

Reduce the Scale of the Long_shot.avi

1. Click once on the first instance of the **Long_shot.avi** clip on the Timeline to select it.

2. Click the **Properties** button to open the Properties view and click the triangle next to Motion to dial down the Motion controls.

3. Reduce the **Scale** to 75%.

4. Click once on the second instance of the **Long_shot.avi** clip on the Timeline to select it.

5. The Properties view should already be open, if it is not, open it by clicking the **Properties** button and dial open the **Motion** controls.

6. Reduce the **Scale** to 75%.

7. Press **Ctrl-S** to save your work so far.

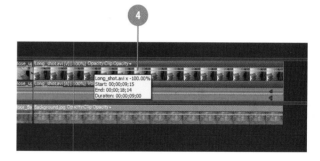

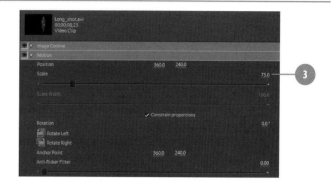

Before...

...and after the rescale of the Jedi!

Making Adjustments, Rendering, and Exporting

Render your project by pressing **Enter** to see if everything is working as you expect it to. If it doesn't, you need to make adjustments and tweaks as needed. Once you're ready, you can export your clip as an AVI. In Chapter 17 you take this AVI and add a light saber visual and audio sound effect to it.

Finish the Project

1. Once you have played back your project and made the necessary adjustments, press **Enter** on your keyboard to render your project.

2. Once you have made all of these adjustments, press **Ctrl-S** to make a final save of your project.

   TIP *Make sure you remember where you saved this project (the **Peachpit** folder is a good bet) because you will revisit it in Chapter 17 where you will add a Visual and Audio sound effect to the light saber.*

3. Finally, export your work as an AVI file. To export the clip, select **File > Export > Movie,** then browse to a local hard drive and the folder called **HSMovies_Final Renders** that you should have created in chapter 1. Save the file here as **Chapter_10_Reverse Time.avi**.

   TIP *This final render may be used again in Chapter 21, as will many of your other final renders from the exercises in this book.*

The completed movie playing in the Windows Media Player

Hollywood Movie Effects:
The Hidden Identity Effect

MEDIA:

The_Interview.avi

11

COMPLEXITY:	Simple	Moderate	Complex
SKILL LEVEL:	Easy	Intermediate	Advanced

Introduction

The Hidden Identity effect is one of everyone's favorite effects simply because it has so many uses, and because it is one of those universally recognizable effects used in everyday TV.

This effect has been burned into our collective consciousness because it's used on such shows as *60 Minutes*, *Nightline*, and of course, *COPS* (what you gonna do, what you gonna do when they come for you? There, I hummed it for you!).

The effect has obvious comical applications. For instance, parents and children can comment on each other with their identities kept well "hidden"; this can be used in birthday, graduation, or wedding videos. You can also use this type of effect with friends, relatives, and co-workers; they can comment "anonymously" at special occasions, such as promotions, award ceremonies, and retirement dinners.

Although we are applying the effect to a face in this chapter—the most well-known use of this effect—you can also use this effect to hide a poster on a wall, a license plate on a car, a hand gesture in a crowd, or a logo on a T-shirt; without this effect a great clip might be unusable.

Just pixelize the problem away, and save that clip!

Flying Solo:
Preparing the Project

Prepare the Timeline

1 Start Premiere Elements and create a new project called **Chapter 11 - Hidden_Identity**.

2 The Timeline should be set to the Timeline view (*Hint: Timeline button to the left of the interface*).

> **NOTE** *You need to switch to the Timeline because you are working with multiple clips on multiple video tracks.*

3 Deselect the audio tracks for Video 2 and 3 (*Hint: deselect Show Audio Tracks*).

4 Rename (*Hint: right-click the header*) and change each track to the following:

◆ Video 1: **Interview**

◆ Video 2: **Blurred**

◆ Video 3: **Mask**

5 Import the **The_Interview.avi** media clip from the DVD (*Hint: Media Downloader; UnCheck All*).

> **TIP** *Full instructions on importing media can be found in the Chapter 1 section "Preparing the Project."*

6 Switch to the Edit workspace (*Hint: Edit tab*).

7 Drag the **The_Interview.avi** clip to the Interview track.

> **IMPORTANT** *Be sure to line up the head (start) of the media clip with the start of the Interview track.*

8 Use the zoom slider so that your Timeline looks similar to the screenshot opposite (*Hint: The zoom slider is between the Timeline and the Monitor panel*).

Setting up a project like this is very easy, so Fly Solo now and create a new project, rename the tracks as detailed here, and bring in the media clips you require to complete the project, in this case, **The_Interview.avi**. Then add the clip to the Timeline.

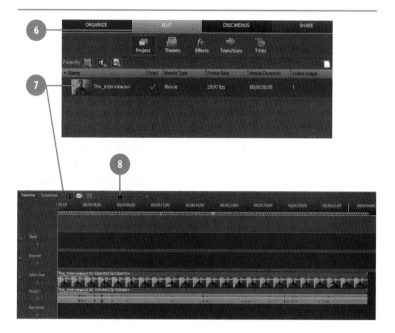

Filming Tips

You can try to use this Hidden Identity effect with any shot, but when you start to create your first test file to use with this effect, it might pay to make life easy and follow the filming tips on this page.

Use a tripod when filming your subject. Request that they move as little as possible. If you are trying to blur out a car license plate, try to film the car approaching directly towards the camera in a linear fashion. Remember, Premiere Elements doesn't support motion tracking, so all blurred out masks will need to be animated by hand using, in some cases, many, many keyframes.

In the example used in this chapter, the subject is sitting in a chair, in front of a green screen, talking directly to the camera or to an unseen person just off camera. This is probably the easiest Hidden Identity effect you will work on, but it's a good place to learn this important skill.

Adding the_Interview.avi Clip to the Timeline— Again!

This project uses just a single clip, **The_Interview.avi**, to create the Hidden Identity effect. However, you need to use this clip twice to achieve the proper effect. You open the first clip, then open the second clip, blur everything in it, and then poke a hole (or create a mask) in the first clip to let the blurred second clip show through.

Add Your Clip—Again

1. If it is not already open, click the **Edit** tab to switch to the Edit workspace and click the **Project** button to display the Media panel.

2. Drag the **The_Interview.avi** clip to the Timeline for a second time, but this time, drop the clip on the Blurred track, with the clip at the very beginning of the track, as shown in the illustration.

3. If you receive a message inviting you to apply the **Videomerge** effect, select **No**.

   INFORMATION *Premiere Elements 7 is very good at using the same clip in a single project, multiple times. However, the more times you use the same clip in a single project, the more processing power your computer needs.*

4. Press **Ctrl-S** to save your work so far.

   IMPORTANT *Be sure to line up each clip so that the head of the clip is at the front of the track, as shown in the illustration.*

Did You Know?

You have four video track display options. Use the **Set Video Track Display Style** button to change how video clips look on a given track. Clips display on a track in one of four ways. First, a clip can display as a series of frames that run the full length of the clip. Second, a clip can display with just a single frame at the head and another at the tail of the clip. Third, a clip can display with just a single video frame at the start (head) of the clip. And finally, a clip can display with no frames at all.

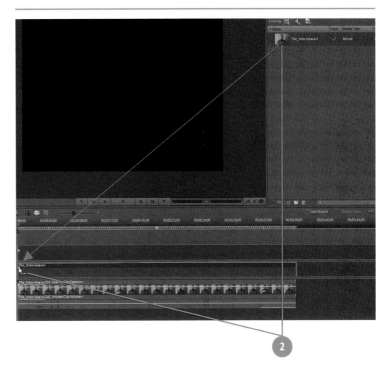

The Timeline showing **The_Interview.avi** on the Interview track and the Blurred track

Creating a Hider Object to Hide the Face

Now that your two clips are set in place, you create the initial object you'll use to blur, or hide, the identity of the actor. Once you've mastered this technique, you can use it to hide anyone or any object. The easiest way to create an object in Premiere Elements 7 is to use the Titler and its ability to create geometric objects as well as text. Since a circle (actually, an ellipse) naturally matches the shape of a face, you'll use that. In future projects, use a shape that matches the object being disguised.

Hide the Face

1 Click the **Add Default Text** button at the bottom of the Monitor panel.

> **TIP** *Safe margins should automatically appear. If they don't, you can turn them on yourself by clicking the **More** button in the upper-right corner of the Monitor panel. Then, click **Safe Title Margin**.*

2 Once the text editor opens, the Add Text box should appear with both words already selected. Press **Delete** on your keyboard to delete this text. You won't use the Titler to add text but rather to add an object to the screen in the next step.

> **NOTE** *If the text is not selected, drag the mouse over it while holding down the left mouse button or press **Ctrl-A** on the keyboard.*

3 Select the **Ellipse Tool** button from the toolbar and drag an ellipse in the general area of the actor's face.

> **TIP** *You want to err on the side of making this ellipse a little too big, rather than too small; the blur you add a bit later can cause the object to shrink slightly.*

The ellipse shape should just cover the outer edges of the actor's face.

4 With the ellipse selected, click the **Color Properties** button and make sure that the ellipse is perfectly white. To ensure that it is, each of the Red, Green, and Blue (RGB) settings must be at 255. Adjust them as necessary.

5 Click **OK** to close the Color Properties box and then click anywhere on the Timeline to exit the Titler and return to Edit mode and the Edit workspace.

6 Resize the **Title 01** clip by grabbing the tail end of the clip and pulling it back so that it lines up with the two **The_Interview.avi** clips.

Did You Know?

Let the arrows be your guide. If you have **Snap** turned on (**Timeline > Snap**), when you stretch the **Hider** clip to match the other two clips in the Timeline, Premiere Elements shows you that you've reached the right spot by using black arrows as indicators (as shown in the illustration). It's a useful visual clue to let you know that your clip is exactly the right length.

11

Synchronizing the Hider Object to the Action

Now you need to adjust the movement of the Hider object so that it synchronizes with the movement of the man's face. To do so, use keyframes in the Movement controls to enable the ellipse to track backward and forward in time with the head movement. Again, this is probably the easiest piece of keyframing you will ever do, so enjoy it while you can!

Enable Motion (Animation) for the Ellipse

1 Select the **Title 01** clip on the Mask track if it's not already selected.

2 Click the **Properties** button to open the Properties view and dial down the **Motion** controls by clicking the triangle.

3 Click **Show Keyframes** and expand this panel.

4 Click the **Toggle Animation** button to enable motion effects.

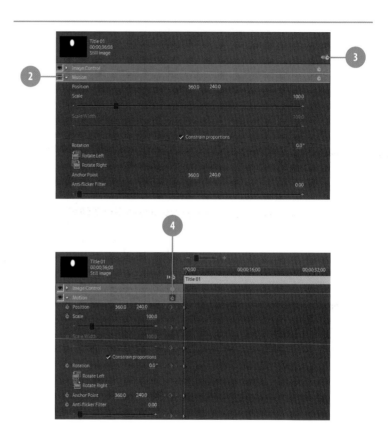

Did You Know?

All the Motion settings have individual Toggle Animation buttons. Premiere Elements enables you to make large and small adjustments as you need to for every possible motion-related setting. These include Position, Scale, Scale Width, Rotation, and Anchor Point. You can even control the Anti-Flicker setting frame-by-frame.

Insert Motion Keyframes

1 Scrub the **CTI** through the clip. Most of the movement occurs at 00;00;28;08 where the man turns to his left and back again, so move the **CTI** to 00;00;28;29 using the mouse or by directly entering this time into the CTI read out.

2 Click the **ellipse** in the Monitor panel directly and drag it with your mouse to better cover the actor's face (in this case, slightly to your left).

> **NOTE** *This also adds a slow movement from the very start of the clip to the very end. Where possible, avoid moving the mast around the screen in a jerky fashion.*

3 Move the **CTI** to 00;00;27;15, and in the Monitor panel drag the **ellipse** toward your right and slightly upward to cover the actor looking off stage and up.

4 Move the **CTI** a few frames further along (where the actor looks back toward the long-suffering interviewee) and drag the **ellipse** back toward your left and down slightly.

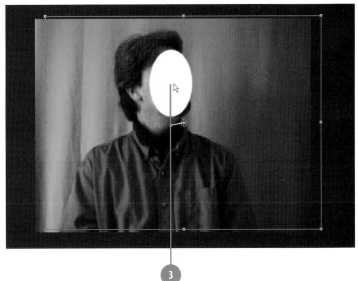

11

5 Move through the Timeline dragging the ellipse about the Monitor panel and adding more keyframes where you think you need them. Use the zoom slider above the Effects keyframe area to expand this area. If you prefer a challenge, resize the ellipse to a smaller one that requires much more movement.

TIMESAVER *Because you changed the location of the object, Premiere Elements automatically inserts a keyframe for Position at this point.*

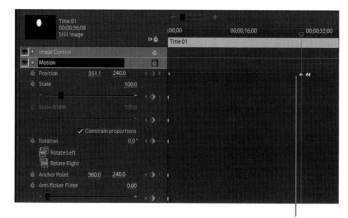

The keyframes created during Steps 2–4

Did You Know?

You don't need to have a keyframe for every frame. This is because Premiere Elements does all of the "tweening," that is, filling in the points between the keyframes that you set. However, you do need to manually step through each frame to make sure the effect is lining up.

Did You Know?

You can use the Opacity control to keep an eye on things. You can set the **Opacity** for the Hider clip (Title 01) down to around 70 or 80 percent while you're working. This helps you more precisely locate the Hider object for situations where, for example, multiple people are walking down the street together or are seated together on a couch and you need to see the action a little more clearly. Remember to reset **Opacity** back to 100 percent when you have finished setting all of your keyframes.

Flying Solo: Applying the Mosaic Effect to the Second Clip

With the Hider object now tracking perfectly, you are ready to finish this effect. Fly Solo to add the **Mosaic** effect to **The Interview.avi** clip on the Blurred track (*not* on the Interview track). You follow this up (in the next set of steps) with the Track Matte effect to hide everything in the clip except the ellipse.

Apply the Mosaic Video Effect

① Find the Mosaic effect in the Effects panel (*Hint: type mosaic in the text box on the Effects panel*).

> **TIP** *If the Media panel is not in the Effects panel, click the* **Effects** *button to switch to that panel.*

② Drag the **Mosaic** video effect onto the clip on the Blurred track.

③ Open the **Mosaic** settings (*Hint: Properties view*) and make the following adjustments:

◆ Horizontal Blocks: **25**

◆ Vertical Blocks: **25**

◆ Sharp Colors: **Leave unchecked**

> **TIP** *Make these blocks a bit larger or a bit smaller as you prefer. Keep in mind that too large of a block will lose all facial definition, and too small of a block will end up revealing the identity that's supposed to be hidden.*

Did You Know?

You can browse through the list of effects to find the effect you're looking for. You could have navigated to this effect by selecting the triangle next to Video Effects in the Effects panel to reveal the available effects. You would then click the Keying triangle to see the available keys and then select the **Track Matte Key** effect.

11

Applying the Track Matte Key Effect

Now you need to find a way to hide everything in the Blurred track except that small portion that you want to show through the ellipse. To do this, apply the ubiquitous **Track Matte Key** effect to the clip in the Blurred track and select the **Mask** track as the "target."

Apply the Track Matte Key Effect

1. If it is not already open, click the **Edit** tab to switch to the Edit workspace and click the **Effects** button and type **Track** in the text box.

2. Select the **Track Matte Key** effect and drag it onto the **The_Interview.avi** clip in the Blurred track (*not* on the Interview track).

3. Click the **Properties** button to open the Properties view for the **The_Interview.avi** clip on the Blurred track and click the triangle next to **Track Matte Key** to reveal the effect's controls.

4. Set up the **Track Matte Key** effect using the following settings:

   ◆ Matte: **Mask**

   ◆ Composite Using: **Matte Alpha**

   ◆ Reverse: **Leave unchecked**

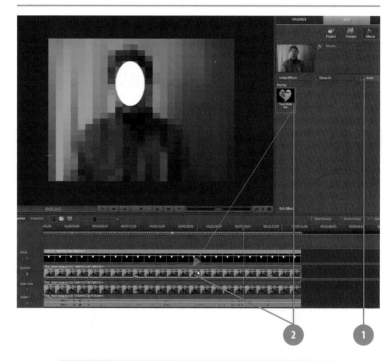

> ### Did You Know?
>
> **Track Matte Keys work best in black and white.** When you use track mattes for other projects, remember that you want to be sure that you are always using pure black (R: 0, G: 0, B: 0) and pure white (R: 255. G: 255, B: 255). Shades of gray will cause you shades of problems.

Applying a Blur Effect to the Image

The effect looks pretty good, but the disadvantage of using the Ellipse tool is the hard line around the edges of the shape. By applying a subtle blurring effect to the title, you can soften this hard edge, although it may decrease (meaning more keyframes) or increase the size of the ellipse. This step is very straightforward and involves applying the **Gaussian Blur** video effect and tweaking the settings a bit.

Apply a Blur

1. If it is not already open, click the **Edit** tab to switch to the Edit workspace and click the **Effects** button on the Media panel to switch to the Effects panel.

2. Type **blur** in the text box on the Effects panel.

3. Select the **Gaussian Blur** and drag it onto the Title 01 clip on the Blurred track on the Timeline.

4. Click the **Properties** button to open the Properties view for the Title 02 clip and click the triangle next to Gaussian Blur to view the controls.

5. Adjust the **Gaussian Blur** to these settings:

   ◆ Increase the **Blurriness** amount to **40.0**.

   ◆ Leave the **Blur Dimensions** as they are (Horizontal and Vertical).

11

Making Adjustments, Rendering, and Exporting

Finish the Project

1. Once you have played back your project and made the necessary adjustments, press **Enter** on your keyboard to render your project.

2. Use **Ctrl-S** to save a final version of your project, complete with render files.

3. Finally, export your work as an AVI file. To export the clip, select **File > Export > Movie**, then browse to a local hard drive and to the **HSMovies_Final Renders** folder you created in Chapter 1, and save the file as **Chapter 11_hidden_ID.avi**.

You will use this rendered AVI in the next chapter (Chapter 12), where you add some bleeps to obscure the poor actor's name and the swear word he let slip!

> **NOTE** *This final render will also be used again in Chapter 21, as will many of your other final renders from the exercises in this book.*

Press the **spacebar** on your keyboard to run your clip and check out your effect. Now is the time to make a few small adjustments. If the hidden identity isn't hiding so well, go back and tweak the tracking path by adding a few more keyframes or adjusting the location of the ellipse to your liking. Are the blocks in the Mosaic effect too big or too small? You can easily adjust this. And if it turns out that you created your Hider object a little too big or too small as well, just double-click the **Title 01** clip in the Timeline to bring up the Titler. Adjust the size of the object again in the Titler to suit your needs.

The finished result playing back in the Windows Media Player. In the next chapter, you use this AVI to bleep out errant words.

Hollywood Movie Sound: #$% Word Removal—The Bleeping Effect

MEDIA:

Chapter 11_Hidden_ID.AVI
(on your hard drive)
airhorn.wav
airwrench.wav
carhorn.wav
jalopyhorn.wav

12

COMPLEXITY:	Simple	Moderate	Complex
SKILL LEVEL:	Easy	Intermediate	Advanced

Introduction

You've no doubt seen, or more accurately heard, that slip of the tongue, that inadvertent expletive, or someone's name mentioned when it shouldn't have been. Unfortunate or "bad" audio moments like this can render a scene useless for a variety of reasons, but what do you do if you really need the scene? What if the funniest or the most "memory worthy" moment happened just as someone was reacting to pain or embarrassment (or, yes, joy) with a bad word? Well, don't fret, this is very fixable, thanks to the sound capabilities of Premiere Elements and to the fascinating world of sound effects.

In Chapter 11 you created a blurred ellipse to hide the identity of the actor. In this chapter, you take that concept one step further by bleeping out words such as the actor's name (which would, of course, also identify him) and the bad word he says.

You can use this effect to salvage clips that might otherwise be unusable (or at least in cases where the audio is unusable). You can also use it on any clip to add a comical effect to anyone's dialogue, whether or not they are actually cursing a blue streak.

What You'll Learn

Flying Solo: Preparing the Project

Finding and Marking Bad Audio Moments

Removing the Audio at Each Bad Audio Moment

Flying Solo: Adding Sound Effects to Each Bad Audio Moment

Making Adjustments, Rendering, and Exporting

Flying Solo: Preparing the Project

Preparing the project in this chapter is very simple. You create a new project, rename two tracks, and import several media clips. These tasks should all be very familiar because you've performed them at least 11 times prior to this chapter. Fly Solo now to accomplish these tasks before you move on to the next section. As always, we've offered you some handy hints.

Create a New Project and Import Files

1 Start Premiere Elements and from the splash screen create a New Project called **Chapter 12_Word_removal**. If Premiere Elements is already open, create a new project via the **File** menu (*Hint: File > New Project*).

2 Import the following media files from the DVD: **Chapter 11_Hidden_ID.avi, airhorn. wav, airwrench.wav, carhorn.wav, jalopyhorn.wav** (*Hint: Media Downloader; Show Audio; UnCheck All*).

TIP *You can find complete instructions for importing media into Premiere Elements 7 in the Chapter 1 section "Adding Media to Your Project." Don't forget you need to uncheck all before you make your selection!*

NOTE *The default settings of the Media Down-loader are set not to show Audio media clips. To see any Audio media clips, you need to click the **Show Audio** button or press **Ctrl-U** on the keyboard while the Media Downloader is open. Watch out, Media Downloader rechecks all the files when you do this and you need to uncheck them all again!*

3 Deselect the audio tracks for Video 2 and 3 (*Hint: deselect Show Audio Tracks*).

4 Rename (*Hint: right-click the header*) two tracks to the following:

- ◆ Video 1: **Chap 11 Video**

- ◆ Narration: **Bleeping**

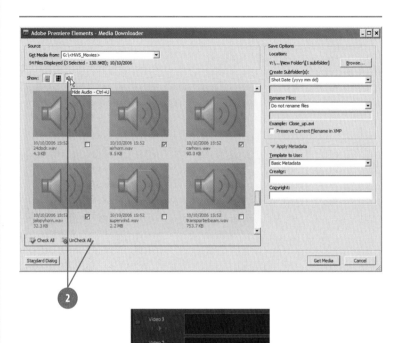

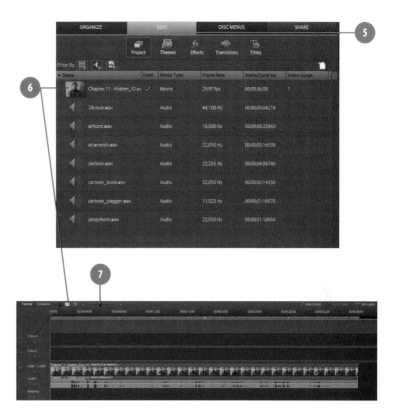

5 Switch to the Edit workspace (*Hint: Edit tab*).

6 Add the **Chapter 11 _ Hidden_ID.avi** to the **Chap 11 Video** track.

7 Zoom in using the Zoom slider to see the whole AVI on the Timeline (*Hint: click the "+" symbol next to the zoom slider*).

8 When your Timeline and Media panel look similar to the screenshots shown here, press **Ctrl-S** to save your work so far, then proceed to the next section.

Did You Know?

You can drag clips into Premiere Elements right from Windows Explorer. You don't need to use the tools that Premiere Elements provides; you can alternatively drag any supported media (including entire folders of media) directly from Windows into Premiere Elements. Use whichever system best suits your working style.

12

Finding and Marking Bad Audio Moments

In this section, you listen to the entire clip once to find the sections of the video where the actor's name is mentioned (twice) and where he drops a swear word. Next, you play it again with your finger poised over the spacebar on your keyboard. As you reach each bad place, press the **spacebar**, place a marker, and press the **spacebar** again to move on. The marker lets you jump to each bad place and allows you to take positive action in the next section!

Go on the Offensive

1. If it isn't already displayed, switch to the **Timeline** by clicking the **Timeline** button just below the Monitor panel.

2. Press the **spacebar** and listen carefully.

3. The first bleepable moment occurs at 00;00;06;07 (6 seconds and 7 frames in). Press the **spacebar** to pause here.

   TIP *If you press the **spacebar** a little late, use the **left arrow** key to rewind a few frames. You can hear audio even when you're moving backward through the Timeline.*

4. Right-click the **CTI** in the Timeline, and select **Set Timeline Marker > Next Available Numbered**. A marker with the number 0 should appear under the CTI.

5. Repeat Steps the 2–4 to place markers at the following Timeline points:

   ◆ **00;00;16;15** (16 seconds and 15 frames)

   ◆ **00;00;27;05** (27 seconds and 5 frames)

   TIP *Don't forget to use the **left** and **right arrow** keys on the keyboard to find the exact spots to place each marker.*

6. Press **Ctrl-S** to save your work so far.

The three numbered markers indicating where each bad audio moment begins

Did You Know?

You can add comments to markers. By double-clicking a marker, you access the Marker dialog. Here you can add comments, such as describing why you placed this marker. You can also add a URL link and frame information; create chapter links to use with Adobe Encore; change the duration of the marker; jump to the previous or next marker; or delete just the marker.

Removing the Audio at Each Bad Audio Moment

In this section, you add keyframes to the clip volume line on the audio track in the Timeline so that you can lower the volume where the bad audio moment occurs. You have already placed markers at each of the three points in the clip where you found bad audio moments, so finding where the first keyframe should go isn't a problem. Adding a keyframe at the beginning and end of each word or phrase can seem complex, but if you do it once, you'll be a fan for life.

Add Keyframe Sets at Each Bad Audio Moment

1 If it is not already displayed, click the **Edit** tab to switch to the Edit workspace and send the **CTI** to the start (or head) of the Timeline by pressing **Home** on the keyboard.

> **TIP** *You must be in the Timeline to work through this next section. Click the **Timeline** button if you are in the Sceneline.*

2 Select the **Chapter 11_Hidden_ID.avi** on the Chap 11 Video track. It should now be highlighted and show as a deep purple color.

3 Jump to the first marker by right-clicking in the time ruler and from the contextual menu select **Go To Timeline Marker > Numbered**.

4 When the **Go to Numbered Marker** panel appears, select the **0** marker (at 00;00;06;07) and click **OK**. The CTI should now jump to that position.

5 With the CTI at this marker point (00;00;06;07), add a keyframe to the Audio 1 track by clicking the **Add/Remove Keyframe** button in the Track Header area of the Timeline.

> **TIP** *You must select the clip or the **Add/ Remove Keyframe** button won't work. This makes sense because without a clip selected, the keyframe won't know which clip on a track you want to mark.*

6 Repeat the keyframe procedure again at the end of this bleepable phrase by first moving the **CTI** to the end of the phrase (use your **right arrow** key). The phrase ends at about 00;00;07;00.

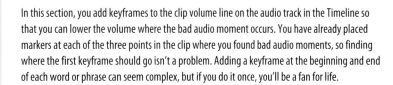

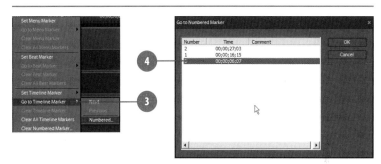

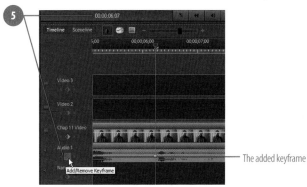

The added keyframe

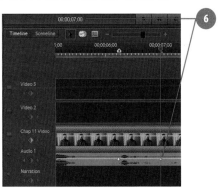

12

(7) You don't want to remove the audio for the whole clip, just the second between these two keyframes. To do this, you need two more keyframes, one right next to the start keyframe and one right next to the end keyframe. Add these keyframes now.

◆ Click the **Add/Remove Keyframe** button at **00;00;07;01**.

◆ Click the **Add/Remove Keyframe** button at **00;00;06;06**.

(8) Jump to marker **1** and repeat the above procedure to add keyframes at the following points:

◆ **00;00;16;15**

◆ **00;00;16;16**

◆ **00;00;16;26**

◆ **00;00;16;27**

(9) Jump to marker **2** and repeat the above procedure to add keyframes at the following points:

◆ **00;00;27;04**

◆ **00;00;27;05**

◆ **00;00;27;18**

◆ **00;00;27;19**

TIMESAVER *Zoom in sufficiently to see what you're doing, otherwise you'll be looking at just a clump of keyframes on the screen.*

Did You Know?

Arrows are a quick way to jump to a marker. The easiest way to move from marker to marker along the Timeline is to use the arrow keys again. This time, however, you use them in conjunction with the **Ctrl** key on your keyboard. To move to the next marker in the Timeline, press **Ctrl-right arrow**. To move to the previous marker, press **Ctrl-left arrow**.

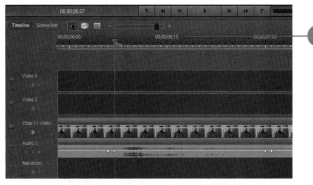

The four keyframes added to the Audio 1 volume level

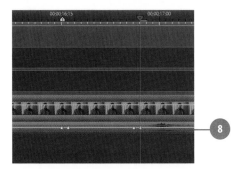

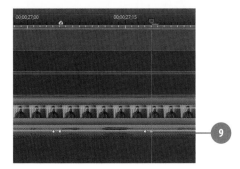

Lower the Sound for Each of the Bad Audio Moments

Now that you have all the keyframes in position, you can start to lower the sound levels of each bad audio moment. This creates an audio "hole" of silence at each of these points, but don't worry; you'll correct this with an audio special effect in this next section.

1. If it is not already displayed, click the **Edit** tab to switch to the Edit workspace and send the **CTI** to the start (or head) of the Timeline by pressing **Home** on the keyboard.

2. Use the alternative method of moving to the next numbered marker by pressing **Ctrl-right arrow** on the keyboard.

3. With the Timeline zoom slider, expand the Timeline so that you can clearly see the four keyframes you placed at marker 0.

4. Place the mouse pointer between these keyframes and over the Clip Audio line. A Volume indicator is added next to the mouse pointer.

5. With this indicator displayed, hold down the left mouse button and drag the **yellow audio line** to the bottom of the Audio 1 track, as shown in the illustration. This silences this portion of the clip.

   NOTE *The yellow audio line will turn blue when being dragged as shown in the screenshot on this page.*

   TIP *Lowering the sound level under each bad audio moment ensures that, after you have applied the sound effects, you will never be able to hear any of the offensive words under the chosen sound effect.*

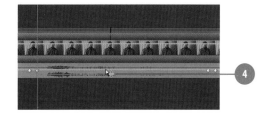

12

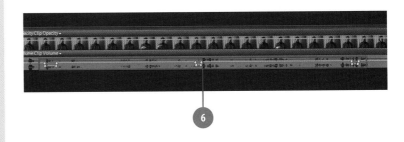

6 Repeat Steps 2–5 and reduce the volume at markers 1 and 2.

TIMESAVER *You may want to zoom out while you navigate along the Timeline; then zoom back in while you adjust the Volume levels.*

7 Zoom out so that your Timeline looks similar to the screenshot opposite, then press **Ctrl-S** on the keyboard to save your work so far.

Did You Know?

You can zoom in and out using your keyboard. No doubt, you already know how to zoom in and out on the Timeline using the zoom buttons and the slider. However, there's an even easier way to do this. Simply press the equal sign (=) on your keyboard to zoom in, or the minus sign/dash (-) next to it to zoom back out. (The minus sign on the numeric keypad won't work.)

Flying Solo: Adding Sound Effects to Each Bad Audio Moment

It's now time to add some "blooper" sounds at each of the "silent sections" that you created using the keyframes. Fortunately, these are easy to spot and overlay with your sound effects, thanks to the obvious dips in the volume you created in the last task. This really is a matter of just dragging, with a little trimming on the side, so Fly Solo now and finish off this project with a little style.

Add a Sound Effect at Each Marker

1 Switch to the **Edit** workspace and access the **Media** panel (*Hint: Edit tab; Project button*).

> **TIP** *You must be in the Timeline to work through this next section. Click the **Timeline** button if you are in the Sceneline.*

2 Select the **Timeline** and return the CTI to the start (*Hint: click anywhere in the Timeline; press Home on the keyboard*).

3 Add the **airwrench.wav** to the Bleeping track and position it directly below the first silent spot, that is, the first dip in the yellow audio band (*Hint: drag from Media panel to 00;00;06;07*).

4 Repeat Step 3 and add two more sound effects of your choice to the Bleeping track under the second and third bad audio moments (*Hint: If the sound effect is too long, trim the tail back so that the whole clip fits inside the dipped audio area. If the sound effect is too short, add it to the Timeline twice!*).

> **TIP** *To preview a sound file, double-click it in the Media panel and it appears in its own preview window.*

Did you Know?

We've supplied a number of sound effects files on the book's DVD. You can also use other sound effects, if you have them. Feel free to find plenty more on the Internet, as well; see Chapter 16 for details.

The completed Timeline with three audio clips and three replacement sound effects

---

Changing the Voice as Well as the Face

If the clip you're using lends itself to this, you can also try using Premiere Elements' built-in voice modulator effects to alter the sound of the person's voice a bit. This makes it exceedingly difficult to identify the person in the clip, if that's your goal. From the Effects panel, go to the **Audio Effects** selections and drag the **PitchShifter** effect to the audio track for the clip. From the Properties view, try using one of the preset effects, such as **Female becomes secret agent**, **Cartoon Mouse**, or **Sore Throat**. Or use the **PitchShifter** knobs to make your own custom changes to the voice.

The PitchShifter has plenty of fun options for changing the sound of anyone's voice.

12

Making Adjustments, Rendering, and Exporting

Your audio surgery is complete and—unless you have altered the audio track in some way, for example, using the **PitchShifter**—you shouldn't be seeing any red render bars at all. To preview your work, use the **spacebar** on your keyboard or click the **Play** button in the Monitor panel. For a truer TV-like experience, use the **Play Full Screen** button on the Monitor panel, or press **Alt-Enter** on your keyboard.

Finish the Project

1. Once you have played back your project and made the necessary adjustments, press **Enter** on your keyboard to render your project if necessary.

2. Once you have made all of your final adjustments, press **Ctrl-S** on the keyboard to save your project.

3. Export the **Timeline** by first making sure the Timeline is selected (click anywhere in the Timeline to accomplish this) then choose **File > Export > Movie** and browse to the **HSMovies_Final Renders** folder you created in Chapter 1.

4. Save the file as **Chapter 12_Word_removal.avi**.

   NOTE *This final render may be used again in Chapter 21, as will many of your other final renders from the exercises in this book.*

The finished project playing in Windows Media player

Hollywood Movie Effects:
The Night Vision Effect

MEDIA:
bond.mp3
Swans.avi
Watcher.avi

13

COMPLEXITY:	Simple	Moderate	Complex
SKILL LEVEL:	Easy	Intermediate	Advanced

Introduction

If you are a student creating a spy film or a sci-fi epic, you don't need to film your nighttime scenes at night or invest in expensive night vision equipment. Instead, use the Night Vision and Night Light effects to enhance the shots just like the pros do. The Night Vision effect is a much-requested effect because of its many applications, especially in amateur filmmaking. You can use it to simulate the point of view of someone using night vision equipment or to suggest a darkened room at night with low visibility.

In this chapter you create circle cutouts to simulate a night vision scope; you can also use this technique in other projects to simulate the view through a telescope, a camera lens, or even a keyhole. You also learn how to add a colorcast to an outdoor scene, suggesting to the audience that it was shot at night. However, it won't fool anyone who knows how to do this technique, and once you know, you'll be surprised how many times you see it being used in film or on TV.

The effect is great for spy flicks, as already mentioned, and you can use it very effectively for thrillers and horror films as well. For example, if you're creating a spy film, you can just videotape the view out your window; have your friends sit in a car across the street and act as if they are staking you out. Or for a horror film, do the same thing, but instead of sitting in a car, have your friends act like zombies moving slowly (but inexorably!) down the street. Next, film your hero picking up special night vision-equipped scopes (also known as ordinary binoculars) to look out the window. In post production, cut in the zombie or stakeout footage, alter it with the Night Vision effect, and then cut to footage of your hero reacting. The entire scene will be instantly believable. So, let your imagination soar as you follow your vision—your *night* vision, that is.

What You'll Learn

Flying Solo: Preparing the Project

Start this project just as you have all the projects in this book: load Premiere Elements, create a new project, and bring in your media clips. Fly Solo now to set up the Timeline and import the **Watcher.avi** and **Swans.avi** media clips by following the hints and tips here.

Set Up the Timeline and Get the Media

1 Start Premiere Elements and create a new project called **Chapter 13-Night_Vision**.

2 The Timeline should be set to Timeline view (*Hint: Timeline button to the left of the interface*).

NOTE *You need to switch to the **Timeline** because you are working with multiple clips on multiple video tracks.*

3 Deselect the audio tracks for Video 2 and 3 (*Hint: deselect Show Audio Tracks*).

4 Rename (*Hint: right-click the header*) and change each track to the following:

◆ Video 1: **Main Video**

◆ Video 2: **Goggles**

5 Import the **Watcher.avi** and **Swans.avi** media clips from the DVD (*Hint: Media Downloader; UnCheck All*).

TIP *You can find complete instructions for importing media into Premiere Elements 7 in the Chapter 1 section "Adding Media to Your Project." Don't forget you need to uncheck all before you make your selection!*

6 Switch to the **Edit** workspace (*Hint: The Edit tab!*).

7 Drag the **Swans.avi** clip to the Main Video track.

IMPORTANT *Be sure to line up the head (start) of the media clip with the start (the head) of the Main Video track.*

8 Zoom the Timeline in or out to view the whole clip (*Hint: Use the zoom slider above the Timeline*).

Creating a new chapter. Note that you need to use the NTSC-DV-Standard 48kHz preset to use the material on the DVD without extra rendering.

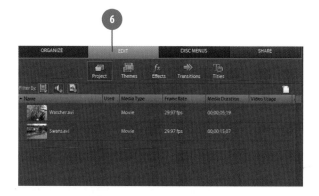

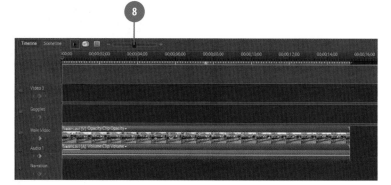

Removing the Existing Colors from the Clip

In order to effectively add the "night vision green" to your clip, you first need to remove the existing full-color palette from the clip. If you don't, the tinting process only colorizes the clip, leaving a variety of shades of the original colors still showing through. To convert a color clip to a clip with no colors is simple with Premiere Elements: all you do is drag the **Black & White** video effect onto the clip you want to change and the effect is instantaneous.

Start with a Blank Palette

1 If it is not already open, click the **Edit** tab to switch to the Edit workspace and click the **Effects** button to display the Effects panel.

2 Type **black** in the text box in the Effects panel.

3 Select the **Black & White** video effect and drag it onto the **Swans.avi** clip on the Main Video track on the Timeline.

4 In the Monitor panel, view how your clip has changed from color to black and white.

TIP *In general, the more of the name of the effect you are looking for you type in the text box in the Effects panel, the more you'll narrow your search, and the less scrolling through the search results you'll need to do.*

Adding the Green of Night Vision Using the Tint Effect

Most people (correctly) associate the look of a night vision scope with a dark green color. To capitalize on this association, in this section you tint your clip a deep green—the next step in creating the illusion that your clip is filmed under night vision circumstances. To produce this greenness, first apply Premiere Elements' **Tint** video effect to the clip. Then tweak the color to achieve an acceptable night vision green.

Tint the Clip Green

1. In the text box on the Effects panel, type **Tint**.

2. Select the **Tint** effect and drag it onto the **Swans.avi** clip on the Main Video track.

3. Select the **Swans.avi** clip on the Timeline, click the **Properties** button to open the Properties view, and then (if it is not already open) dial down the controls for the Tint effect by clicking the triangle.

4. Adjust the **Black** color value by clicking the black color swatch next to Map Black To and entering the following values in the Color Picker dialog.

   ◆ H: **150**

   ◆ S: **100**

   ◆ B: **30**

5. Click **OK** to close the Color Picker dialog.

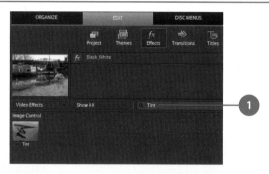

6 Adjust the **White** color value by clicking the white color swatch next to Map White To and entering the following values in the Color Picker dialog:

◆ H: **120**

◆ S: **80**

◆ B: **60**

7 Click **OK** to close the Color Picker dialog.

8 Back on the Properties view, set the **Amount To Tint** to **85%**.

The result of using the Tint effect

Flying Solo: Adding Noise to Simulate the Graininess of Night Vision

Because of the low-to-no light available at night (and the need for night vision technology), the images in the night vision scope are typically grainy. Fly Solo now to simulate this graininess by applying the **Noise** effect and adjusting it to suit. Hints and tips are given here, but by now, finding, adding, and altering the parameters of an effect should be second nature.

Add Noise to the Night

1 Return to the **Effects** panel and find the **Noise** effect (*Hint: Effects button; Type "Noise"*).

NOTE *The Noise effect appears in the **Stylize** folder in the Video Effects section of the Effects panel—you may need to scroll down to find it.*

2 Add the **Noise** effect to the **Swans.avi** clip on the Main Video track.

3 Adjust the **Noise** level to suit (*Hint: Properties button; open Noise effect; adjust noise amount; try 18%*).

NOTE *Leave the Noise Type and Clipping check boxes as they are.*

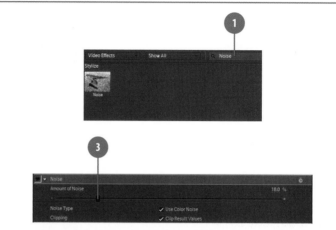

Adding noise gives a greater nightscope illusion.

Adding Darkness to the Nighttime Clip

To make the clip look like it is really happening in the dark of night, you need to darken it. By making a simple adjustment to the **Opacity** setting for the clip, you can bring any clip, even one shot in the bright summer sunshine, into near total darkness—a darkness penetrated only by night vision goggles!

Adjust Opacity to Bring On the Night

1 Select the **Swans.avi** clip on the Main Video track.

2 Click the **Properties** button to open the Properties view, and then click the triangle next to Opacity to reveal the effect's controls.

3 Adjust the **Clip Opacity** to **80%**.

Did You Know?

More noise means less volume! When you use this technique on your own clips, remember that things are just quieter at night. After you've darkened a clip to make it more like night, you may also need to dampen the volume level of the clip. To do so, simply select the clip, and in the Properties view go to the Volume setting. Click the triangle to display the controls, and then drag your mouse across the **Clip Volume** number to soften the volume. If you do this while the clip is playing, you'll get real-time feedback on the clip's volume while you adjust it.

Adding an Overlay to Simulate Night Vision Goggles

For this task, you use the Titler to create a simple binoculars-like shape using two identical, overlapping circles. The purpose of creating this cutout shape is to create an opening that gives your audience the POV (movie-speak for point of view) of someone wearing the night vision goggles usually worn by Special Forces personnel. A bit later in this chapter, you add a couple of special effects to these circles to bring out their goggleness and to add to the realism of this effect.

Add the First Cutout Goggle Shape

1 Press **Home** on your keyboard to return the CTI to the start of the tracks.

2 Click the **Add Default Text** button on the Monitor panel.

3 Use **Delete** on your keyboard to remove the **Add Text** from the display.

> **NOTE** *If the Add Text text box is not selected (all letters are highlighted when it is), drag your mouse cursor over the letters or use **Ctrl-A** to select all the letters.*

4 You won't be using the Titler to add text; instead, you'll use it to add an object to the screen, so click the **Ellipse** tool.

5 Drag a circle on the Monitor panel so that it fills the upper-left quadrant while staying within the Safe Title Margin, as shown in the illustration.

> **TIMESAVER** *Press **Shift** on your keyboard and you'll draw a perfect circle. Let go of the left mouse button before you let go of the Shift key.*

6 Click the **Color Properties** button.

7 In the Color Properties dialog, check that the RGB values are set to the following:

- ◆ R: **255**
- ◆ G: **255**
- ◆ B: **255**

8 Click **OK**.

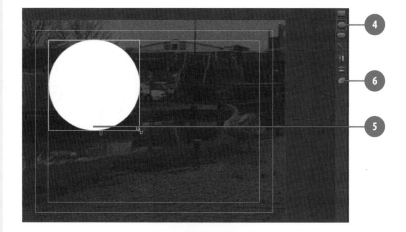

Delete this text.

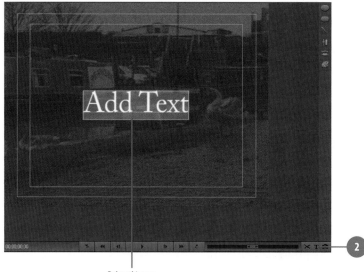

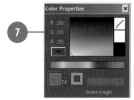

Add the Second Cutout Goggle Shape

1 Without leaving the Titler and with the circle you just created still selected (click it once if it is not), press **Ctrl-C** to copy it, and then **Ctrl-V** to paste the copy.

2 Drag the new copy of the circle right across the screen until the two circles are just overlapping, as shown.

3 Hold down **Shift** on your keyboard and click the other circle so that both circles are selected.

TIP *If you find **Shift-click** doesn't select the circle, check that you have the Selection tool active.*

4 Center your goggles on the screen by first clicking the **Vertical Center** button and then the **Horizontal Center** button.

5 Finally, you want the goggles to appear for the full length of the **Swans.avi** clip, so exit the Titler by clicking anywhere on the Timeline, then grab the tail end of the **Title 01** clip (the goggles) on the **Goggles** track and drag it to the right until it lines up with the end of the **Swans.avi** clip in the **Main Video** track.

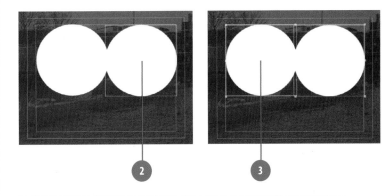

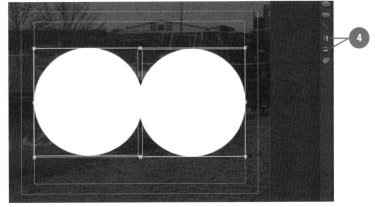

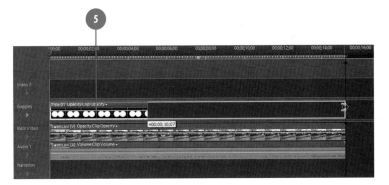

Turning the Little White Circles into True Goggles

Now that the "goggles" are in place, it's time to turn your two, white, intersecting circles into actual goggles, while at the same time hiding everything but what the goggles see. This is easily achieved by applying our old friend the **Track Matte Key** to the **Swans.avi** video clip on the Main Video track and pointing the **Track Matte Key** at the Title 01 clip in the Goggles track.

Apply the Track Matte Key Effect

1 Return to the Effects panel and find the **Track Matte Key** effect (*Hint: Effects button; Type "track"*).

2 Drag the **Track Matte Key** effect onto the **Swans.avi** clip on the Main Video track.

3 Click the **Properties** button to open the Properties view and dial open the **Track Matte** controls (if they are not already open) by clicking the triangle.

4 From the Matte menu, select **Goggles**. Note that in the Monitor panel, your night vision goggles are working! They've gone from opaque white discs to realistic night vision goggles with just a click of the mouse.

IMPORTANT *Leave the other* **Track Matte Key** *options as set.*

The goggles in all their glory!

Did You Know?

You can track a matte. One of the purposes of the Track Matte Key is to create this "peephole" effect to show another track through it. Typically, it's used to superimpose one image over another, such as a bride and groom in a heart shape, superimposed on a clip of the chapel. You can also use it to show the state champion (soccer or spelling) "super'ed" within a star shape. But in this portion of the chapter, you are using the technique a little differently. You don't want another clip showing through; you just want to use the **Track Matte Key** to hide most of the nighttime track and to use the key as the point of view for your audience.

Adding Blurriness to the Goggles for Additional Realism

Well, you've created night vision goggles, but there's still a problem. The goggles have very sharp, unrealistic looking edges and still look a little like two overlapping circles—which is, of course, what they are. To achieve a more realistic look, you need to blur those sharp edges. Fly Solo now to add and adjust the **Gaussian Blur** to the Title 01 on the Goggles track. Use the hints if you get stuck.

Add the Gaussian Blur Effect to Remove the Sharp Edges of the Goggles

1. Switch to the **Effects** panel (*Hint: Effects button*).

2. Find the **Gaussian Blur** effect (*Hint: type "blur"*).

3. Add the **Gaussian Blur** to your goggles (*Hint: drag to the Title 01 clip*).

    TIP *Make sure the Gaussian Blur lands on the **Title 01** clip and not the **Swans.avi** clip.*

4. Open the controls for the Gaussian Blur (*Hint: Title 01 clip selected; Properties button; click the triangle*).

5. Set the **Blurriness** to **50%** or adjust the slider to suit.

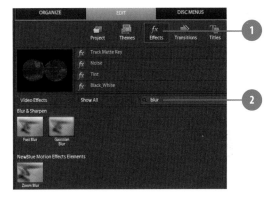

The goggles with a less defined border

Adding the Setup Scene

To sell an effect, you need more than just a cool way to create visuals, although this definitely helps. To really enhance a scene you also need to introduce a little visual prompting, usually by way of a setup scene—a short scene that appears before the special effect, reinforcing to the audience the probability of what the man is about to see through his binoculars. In this case, you add a watcher, a man with binoculars, to the start of the scene.

Add the Watcher.avi to Sell the Effect

1. Click the **Edit** tab to return to the Edit workspace and click the **Project** button to view the Media panel.

2. Send the **CTI** to the start of the Timeline by pressing **Home** on the keyboard.

3. Right-click the **Watcher.avi** in the Media panel and select **Insert to Timeline** from the contextual menu. All the existing clips jump down the Timeline and the **Watcher.avi** clip appears in the Main Video track at the head of the Timeline.

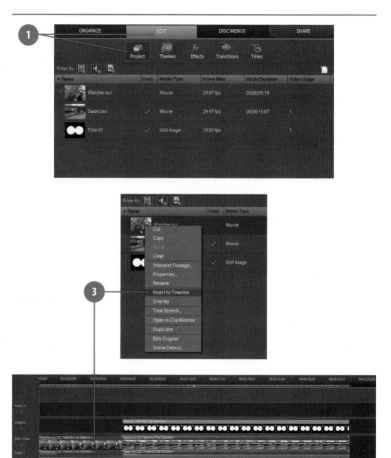

Flying Solo: Turning the Setup Scene to Night

Now when you play back the Timeline, the movie makes a lot more sense. The watcher is watching the swans, the swans are being watched through goggles. OK! But the watcher appears in daytime and our swans are supposed to be viewed at night. You can provide a simple fix using a technique and an effect you used earlier in this chapter. Fly Solo now to remove the colors from the **Watcher.avi** with the **Black & White** effect and then add a blue colorcast to the scene using the **Tint** effect.

Add the Nighttime Effect

1. Open the **Effects** panel and locate the Black & White effect (*Hint: Effects button; type Black*).

2. Add the **Black & White** effect to the **Watcher.avi**.

3. In the Effects panel, locate the **Tint** effect (*Hint: type Tint*).

4. Add the **Tint** effect to the **Watcher.avi** on the Main Video track.

5. Open the **Properties** view for the **Watcher.avi** and then open the **Tint** controls (*Hint: Properties button; click the triangle next to Tint*).

6. Adjust the **Black** color value by entering the following values in the Color Picker dialog, then close the **Color Picker** dialog.

   ◆ H: **226**

   ◆ S: **89**

   ◆ B: **34**

   INFORMATION *Most people associate a nighttime look as being dark with a little moonlight. In fact, unless there's some form of ambient lighting, night is just black. But this would be uninteresting from a visual point of view so the accepted movie compromise is to use a blue tint for nighttime shots. Strange but true.*

7. Adjust the **White** color value by entering the following values in the **Color Picker** dialog, then close the **Color Picker** dialog.

   ◆ H: **207**

   ◆ S: **64**

   ◆ B: **55**

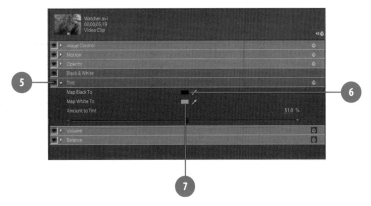

8 Back on the Properties view; set the **Amount to Tint** to **51%**.

9 Dial open the **Opacity** settings for the **Watcher.avi** and reduce the opacity to **75%**.

NOTE *If this still isn't dark enough for you, open the image controls and play with the three sliders there to create your optimal illusion of darkness.*

10 As always, play with these settings until you see something like the screenshot shown, then press **Ctrl-S** to save your work so far.

Did You Know?

Included on the DVD is the bond.mp3 track courtesy of the folks at UniqueTracks. For a sinister musical touch, try adding this music to your project. UniqueTracks is a great source for original, royalty-free music. They have hundreds of music clips available in a variety of formats that you can download or order on CD. These are high-quality, multitrack clips in styles that include Filmscapes, Spies, Cafe Metro, Cafe UK, The Martini Sessions, and more. The UniqueTracks web site (**www.uniquetracks.com**) is a place to explore and learn about different musical styles. They have a newsletter about music, downloadable software, and links to other interesting sites—all of which make a visit to their site well worth the time.

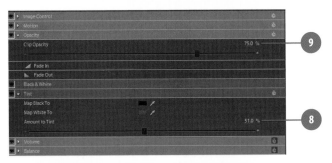

The resulting "fake" night shot

Making Adjustments, Rendering, and Exporting

13

Press the **spacebar** on your keyboard or click the **Play** button on the Monitor panel to test your project and see that everything is working as you expect it to. Remember, all of your clips are still in preview mode. If you want a better idea of how the whole thing will look when finished, press **Enter** on your keyboard to render the project first. Make any final tweaks, as needed—for example, you might want to fade out both the goggles (the Title 01 clip) and the **Swans.avi** clips—and you'll be ready to export your project to a movie file.

Finish the Project

1 Once you have played back your project and made the necessary adjustments, press **Enter** on the keyboard to render your project.

2 Once you have made all of your final adjustments, press **Ctrl-S** on the keyboard to save your project.

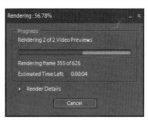

Pressing **Enter** shows the rendering progress box.

3 Finally, export your work as an AVI file. To export the clip, select **File > Export > Movie**, and then browse to a local hard drive and to the **HSMovies_Final Renders** folder you created in Chapter 1, and save the file as **Chapter 13-Night_Vision.avi**.

NOTE *This final render may be used again in Chapter 21, as will many of your other final renders from the exercises in this book.*

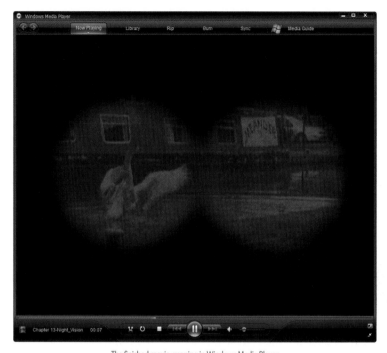

The finished movie, running in Windows Media Player

Hollywood Movie Effects:
The Beam Me Up Effect

MEDIA:
transporterbackground.avi
transporterbeam.avi
transporterbeam.wav
transporterman.avi

14

COMPLEXITY:	Simple	Moderate	Complex
SKILL LEVEL:	Easy	Intermediate	Advanced

Introduction

"Beam me up, Scotty" has become a part of the American vernacular. We're all familiar with the expression, and we all know (despite Kirk only actually saying it in one film) what it refers to: the transporter on the starship *Enterprise* from *Star Trek* and its ability to deconstruct a person down to the subatomic level, transport them through space, and reconstruct them again in another location. We are all familiar with the transporter sound and the transporter sparkles. Re-creating this effect, then, requires some faithfulness to the original idea used on the *Star Trek* television show for it to work.

What is surprising about this effect is that to create it, you don't need a green screen or any additional software beyond Premiere Elements 7. Basically, in this version, you place the transporter beam in front of the person you are transporting while you dissolve them into the scene (by adjusting the Opacity on the top clip of two nearly identical clips). An additional flash of light adds a nice dramatic effect.

What You'll Learn

Flying Solo: Preparing the Project

Adding the Transported Man and Creating the Freeze Frame

Adding the Transporter Beam to the Timeline

Creating a White Matte

Applying the Track Matte Key to the White Matte

Location, Location, Location: Adjusting the Transporter Beam

Adjusting the Opacity of the Transported Man

Adding a Bright Flash to the Transported Man as He Rematerializes

Flying Solo: Applying the Transporter Sound

Making Adjustments, Rendering, and Exporting

Flying Solo: Preparing the Project

Establish Basic Timeline Preparation Skills

1 Create a new project called **Chapter 14 - Beammeup** (*Hint: File > New > Project*).

2 The Timeline should be set to Timeline View (*Hint: Timeline button to the left of the interface*).

> **NOTE** *You need to switch to the **Timeline** because you will be working with multiple clips on multiple video tracks.*

3 Deselect the audio tracks for Video 2 and 3 (*Hint: deselect Show Audio Tracks*).

4 Add a new video track to the Timeline (*Hint: right-click the header; add Tracks; Video=1/ Audio=0*).

5 Rename (*Hint: right-click the header*), and change each track to the following:

- ◆ Video 1: **Background**
- ◆ Video 2: **Man**
- ◆ Video 3: **White Matte**
- ◆ Video 4: **Beam**

Setting up this project is very simple and something you should now be able to do with little effort. Below are hints on how to accomplish this, and if you are at all lost, refer back to Chapters 1 and 2 for details on track renaming and grabbing media from the DVD. This effect uses four clips we have supplied on the DVD and a still image that you'll be creating later in this chapter. The actor needs somewhere to beam into, so finish this section by adding the **transporterbackground.avi** clip to the Timeline.

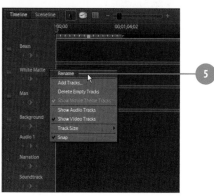

6 Import the **transporterbackground.avi, transporterbeam.avi, transporterbeam. wav,** and **transporterman.avi** media clips from the DVD (*Hint: Media Downloader; Show Audio; UnCheck All*).

TIP *You can find complete instructions for importing media into Premiere Elements 7 in the Chapter 1 section "Adding Media to Your Project." Don't forget you need to uncheck all before you make your selection!*

NOTE *The default settings of the Media Downloader are set not to show Audio media clips. To see any Audio media clips you need to click the* **Show Audio** *button or press* **Ctrl-U** *on the keyboard while the Media Downloader is open. Watch out, Media Downloader re-checks all the files when you do this and you will need to uncheck all of them again!*

INFORMATION *You can use the* **transporterbeam. avi** *and* **transporterbeam.wav** *clips in your own projects to transport whomever you wish using the technique you'll learn in this chapter.*

7 Switch to the **Edit** workspace (*Hint: Edit tab*).

8 Drag the **transporterbackground.avi** to the Background track.

IMPORTANT *Be sure to line up the head (start) of the* **transporterbackground.avi** *clip with the front of the Background track.*

9 Zoom the Timeline to show the clips as in the screenshot shown (*Hint: Zoom slider*).

10 When your Timeline and Media panel look similar to those in the screenshot, press **Ctrl-S** to save your work so far, then proceed to the next section.

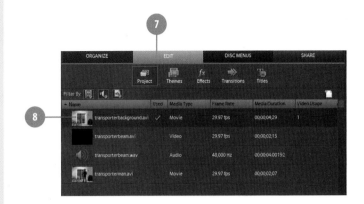

Filming Tips

A tripod is the essential ingredient in this movie; without it, the effect is unsellable to anyone, including your great aunt with her poor vision. You also need to avoid a background with any movement. Fast moving traffic is a non-starter, as are tree branches swaying in the breeze. All of these point the fickle finger of fake at the special effect you are trying to re-create. You can film these situations and re-create the special effect in "difficult" conditions, as seen in various Trek episodes, but you'll need some serious money to do it. Be good to your wallet, choose a background that is relatively static.

Once you have the background, you need an actor who doesn't move around too much during the beam-in stage. This lets you avoid blurring, another telltale sign an experienced audience is unconsciously looking for.

Now you really are ready to film. As with many of the other special effects in this book, once you press the Record button, don't go near the camera until after the scene completes. Don't allow anyone to turn the camera off, don't allow anyone to walk near the tripod, and don't allow anyone to cast a shadow or block light onto your scene.

While acting the part of beaming in (or out) of the scene, avoid looking at the camera, keep breathing to a quiet level, and don't make any loud sounds off camera. Oh, and don't forget to have fun.

Adding the Transported Man and Creating the Freeze Frame

The **transporterman.avi** clip shows a few seconds of an actor standing in place for a brief moment before he walks away. In this chapter, you take this very basic clip (which is exactly the kind of clip that you should shoot to use the Beam Me Up effect with your own friends and family) and transform it into a science fiction masterpiece. First, you add the actor to the Timeline, and then you take a snapshot of him standing in place. When you fade the actor in (using the Opacity settings over time), since the actor is the only thing different in this scene and the background scene, he appears to fade in, even though, actually, the entire clip is gradually fading in, not just the actor.

Drag the Clip and Add a Still

1. Drag the **transporterman.avi** clip onto the **Man** track on the Timeline so that the head (front) of the clip is at the very beginning of the track.

   NOTE *If you receive a message about Video-merge, click* **No** *because you won't be using that feature in this project.*

2. With the **CTI** (current-time indicator) at the beginning of the Background track, click the **Freeze Frame** button on the Monitor panel.

   TIP *To send the* **CTI** *to the first frame of the Timeline, press* **Home** *on your keyboard.*

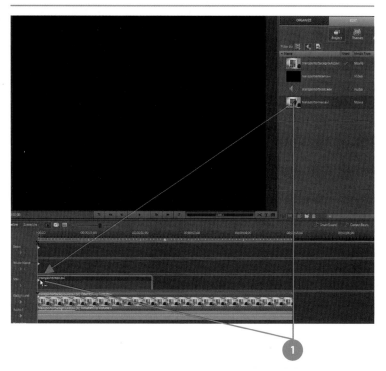

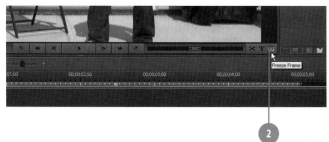

3 Click the **Insert In Movie** button on the **Freeze Frame** dialog.

4 By default, the freeze frame is added to the **Background** (Video 1) track and both the **transporterman.avi** and the **transporter background.avi** clips move up the Timeline. Correct this by selecting the freeze frame and then dragging it to the Man track.

5 Now select the **transporterbackground.avi** clip and drag that down the Timeline so it is directly under the freeze frame. When you have finished, your Timeline should look something like that in the Screenshot.

TIP *The default for the freeze frame image is 5 seconds. If you have set this to be anything other than 5 seconds, reset it back now.*

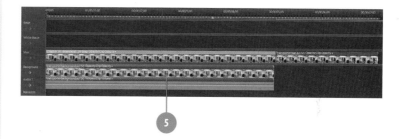

14

Adding the Transporter Beam to the Timeline

Now that the inter-dimensional traveler and the place he's traveling to are both on the Timeline, it's time to add the transporter beam to the Timeline to get him to his destination. The transporter beam is just an animated lighting effect that appears to move slightly down from above. It has no sound yet; you add that critical component in a later task.

Turn the Transporter On!

1. You need to have the transporter beam appearing about two seconds into the scene, so first move the **CTI** to the 00;00;02;00 mark.

2. Drag the **transporterbeam.avi** clip to the Beam track on the Timeline so that the head (front) of the clip lines up with the CTI. If you receive a message about Videomerge, click **No** because you won't be using this feature in this project.

3. Press **Ctrl-S** to save your work so far.

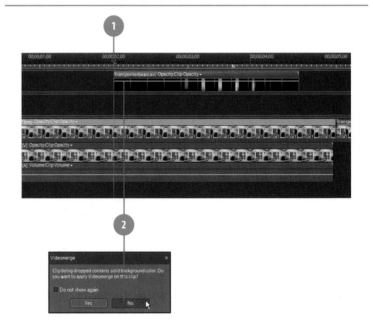

Creating a White Matte

Creating a color matte now serves two purposes. First, it colors your transporter beam a bright white, which gives it a bright light look. Second, once you apply the Track Matte Key effect in the next task, this matte acts as a color matte and allows the transport beam to show through on top of the still image by making all of the black in the **transporterbeam.avi** clip act as a transparent color. Once you have created the white matte, it shuffles your clips around in an unhelpful manner, which you will also need to correct.

Create a Matte and Color It White

1. Press Page Down on the keyboard until the CTI reaches the end of the last clip on the Timeline. If it is not already displayed, click the **Edit** button to view the Edit workspace and click the **Project** button to view the Media panel.

2. Click the **New Item** button at the top-right of the Media panel.

3. Select **Color Matte**.

4. In the **Color Picker** dialog, drag the color picker circle all the way down to the lower-left corner of the window.

   TIP You want absolute white, so as an alternative you can type **FFFFFF** in the hexadecimal area (labeled "#") or **255, 255, 255** as the **RGB** values.

5. Click **OK**.

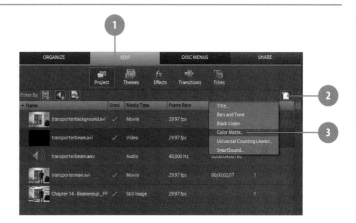

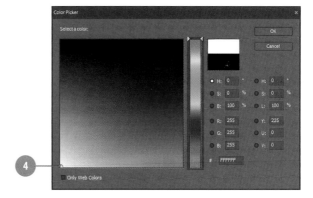

Adjust the Timeline Position of Two Clips

1 Zoom out of the Timeline so that you can see the **transporterman.avi** clip's new position using the zoom slider above the Timeline.

2 Select **Color Matte** on the Timeline and drag it up to the White Matte track.

> **NOTE** Align the front of the **White Matte** clip with the front of the **transporterbeam.avi** clip.

3 Grab the tail end of the **White Matte** clip and drag it back until it exactly lines up with the end of the **transporterbeam.avi** clip. This makes the duration of the two clips exactly the same.

4 Right-click inside the gap between the freeze frame and the **transporterman.avi** media clip and select **Delete And Close Gap**.

5 Once your Timeline looks something like that in the screenshot, press **Ctrl-S** to save your work so far, and then move on to the next section.

Did You Know?

You can color a matte any color you want. For this project, the chosen color of the matte is white because it works well for the effect you're going for (a beam of white containing a flash of white). However, you may think differently. Once you've learned and practiced this effect, you might decide that you'd prefer a green transporter beam. Or a magenta one. Or one that's grape-colored. It makes no difference, technically speaking, what color you make the beam, so go ahead and design the transporter beam to be whatever color you choose. Perhaps you'll decide that humans and animals have different colored beams. Or, for your projects, perhaps men have blue beams and women have purple beams. Or maybe beams that beam you up are a different color than the beams that beam you down. Endless fun to be had…

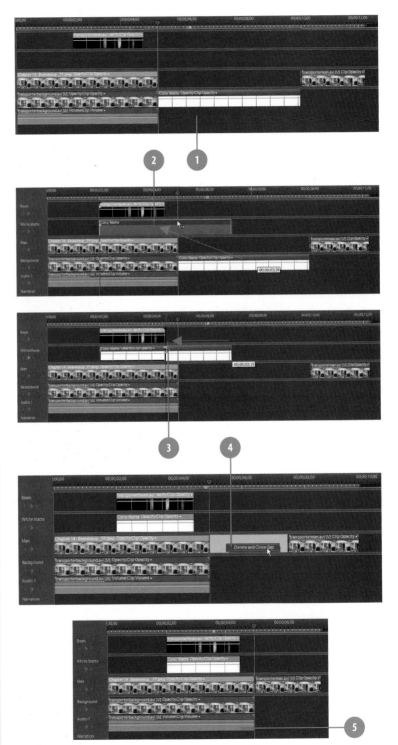

How your Timeline should look at the end of this section

Applying the Track Matte Key to the White Matte

At the moment, if you scrub through the Timeline, all you see is a fading transporter beam and not much else. Disappointing, but worry not, you are about to add the secret ingredient—the Track Matte Key! In order for the transporter beam to actually appear superimposed on the still image, you need to apply the **Track Matte Key** to the white matte and then point it at the track holding the **transporterbeam.avi** clip. Don't worry, this is easier than it sounds. In fact, you did something similar way back in Chapter 1.

Apply the Track Matte Key

1 If it is not already displayed, click the **Edit** button to view the Edit workspace and click the **Effects** button to switch to the Effects panel.

2 In the text box on the Effects panel, type **Track**.

3 Drag the **Track Matte Key** to the Color Matte clip on the White Matte track.

4 Click the **Properties** button to open the Properties view for the **White Matte** clip, click the triangle next to the Track Matte Key to see the effect's controls.

5 From the Matte menu, select **Beam**.

6 Still nothing? Oh, then don't forget to alter the **Composite Using** menu to show **Matte Luma** (by default it is set to Matte Alpha).

Location, Location, Location: Adjusting the Transporter Beam

By default, the transporter beam is positioned on the left side of the screen. The transporter man is standing just to the right of center. In order for this illusion to work, you need the transporter beam to overlay exactly on top of the actor. To do so, you drag the **transporterbeam.avi** clip across the screen until it lines up correctly. When you use the transporter beam in future projects, use the same technique to relocate it as needed.

Relocate the Beam

① Move the **CTI** across the length of the **transporterbeam.avi** clip until you can see the beam fairly well in the Monitor panel (around 00;00;03;10).

② Click the **transporterbeam.avi** clip on the Beam track on the Timeline to select it.

③ Click the **Properties** button to open the Properties view for the **transporterbeam. avi** clip, then click the actual **Motion** text label to both highlight the text and select it in the Monitor panel.

TIP *The name of the Motion effect should reverse (highlight in black) as shown in the illustration if you've selected it correctly. In addition, handles should appear around the clip in the Monitor panel.*

④ Click the **transporterbeam.avi** clip in the Monitor panel and drag the clip across the screen until the transporter beam overlays directly on top of the actor, as shown in the screenshot (*Hint: position should be around 586 – 240*).

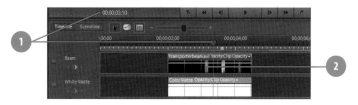

The header on the clip is dark purple when selected.

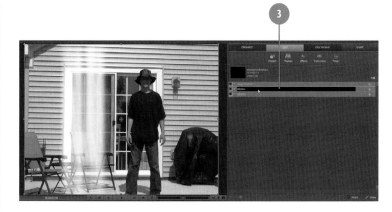

The beam in its new location

Adjusting the Opacity of the Transported Man

So far so good. You have the beam dissolving nicely over the actor, now you need your intergalactic traveler from another dimension to appear to dissolve into the scene. To do this you adjust his opacity from 0 percent (invisible) to 100 percent (fully visible) over time. You accomplish this using keyframes in the Opacity settings area.

Set the Opacity to Increase Over Time

1. If it is not already displayed, click the **Edit** button to view the Edit workspace and the **Project** button to switch to the Media panel.

2. Select the freeze frame still image on the **Man** track on the Timeline.

3. Click the **Properties** button to open the Properties view for the freeze frame and click the **Show Keyframes** button to reveal the keyframe area, then dial down the controls for Opacity.

    TIP *The* ***Show Keyframes*** *button, once clicked, becomes the* ***Hide Keyframes*** *button and its function changes to match.*

    TIMESAVER *Adjust the horizontal size of the* ***Properties*** *view as needed so that you can work most effectively with keyframes. To expand the keyframe area of the Properties view, drag the left side of the panel to the left. You want to see as much of the Properties view Timeline as possible.*

4. Move the **CTI** to 00;00;03;00 entering **03;00** in the CTI read out (just as the beam is reaching its peak).

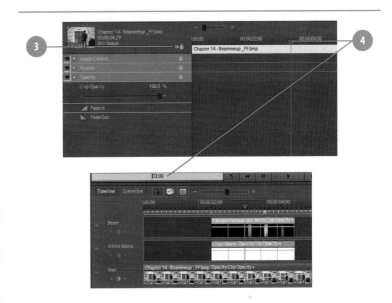

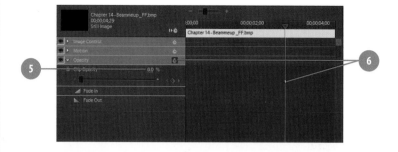

⑤ In the Properties view, set the **Clip Opacity** to 0% (zero) so that the actor vanishes from the Monitor panel.

⑥ Click the **Toggle Animation** button to turn on the animation functionality of Premiere Elements.

TIP *Premiere Elements automatically inserts a keyframe at this point.*

⑦ Move the **CTI** to the end of the clip by pressing **Page Down** twice.

TIP *You need to press **Page Down** twice because the first time you press it, the **CTI** jumps to the end of the **White Matte** clip.*

⑧ Set the **Clip Opacity** to 100% to make the actor wholly visibly again.

TIP *Premiere Elements automatically inserts a keyframe at this point.*

Did You Know?

Opacity is the opposite of transparency. Opacity shares the same root word as opaque (to be non-transparent; a wall is opaque, but a window is transparent). It refers to the degree to which an image allows the images behind (below) it to show through; in other words, how see-through the image is. An opacity setting of 100 percent means that the clip is completely opaque. An opacity setting of 0 percent means that the clip is completely transparent.

Adding a Bright Flash to the Transported Man as He Rematerializes

What gives your effect a convincing "punch"—or the cherry on top, if you prefer—is the addition of a bright flash just as the actor rematerializes. The flash of light seems to imply the power of the transportation and gives it the look of science fiction convention as understood and accepted by sci-fi fans and geeks, such as the authors of this book!

Add a Lens Flare

1 Move the **CTI** to 00;00;04;00.

2 If it is not already displayed, click the **Edit** button to view the Edit workspace and the **Effects** button to switch to the Effects panel.

3 In the text box on the Effects panel, type **Lens**.

4 Drag the **Lens Flare** from the Effects panel onto the freeze frame clip, **BeamMeUp_transporterman_FF.bmp**, on the Man track in the Timeline.

5 Click the **Properties** button to open the Properties view for the still image, and open the **Lens Flare** settings using the small triangle.

6 Click the actual words **Lens Flare** and a small circle appears in the main screen. Click and hold the mouse button with the pointer inside this circle and drag it to the middle of the actor, at about chest height.

TIMESAVER *You can also access the Lens Flare Settings dialog from the Properties view. Click the **Setup** button for Lens Flare to do so.*

7 Set the **Brightness** for the lens flare to **250**.

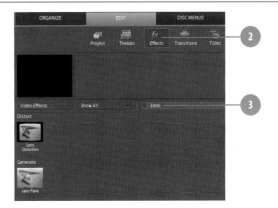

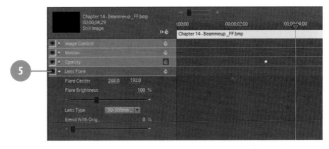

Create the Appearance of the Lens Flare Flashing

1. Open the keyframe area if it's not already open by clicking the **Show Keyframes** button.

2. Click the **Toggle Animation** button to turn on the animation functionality of Premiere Elements.

    TIP *Premiere Elements automatically places keyframes at this point for the Center X, Center Y, and Brightness controls.*

3. Move the **CTI** to 00;00;02;00.

4. Set the **Brightness** to 10%.

    TIP *Premiere Elements automatically places a keyframe at this point.*

5. Move the **CTI** to 00;00;04;14.

6. Set the **Brightness** here at the end of the clip to 10% as well.

7. Press **Page Down** to move to the end of the clip and set **Brightness** here to 0%.

    TIP *Once again, Premiere Elements places a keyframe at this point.*

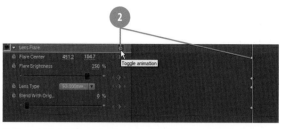

Keyframes for the set values are automatically added when Toggle Animation is pressed.

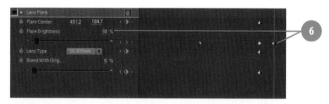

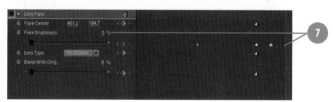

Flying Solo: Applying the Transporter Sound

Without the sound of the transporter, the effect is somewhat lifeless and certainly less geeky than it could be. Fly Solo now for the final task in this project—add the **transporterbeam.wav** sound file to your project and then use the Audio Mixer to adjust the level of sound to suit. Hints and tips abound.

Add the Transporter Noise Sound FX

1 Drag the **transporterbeam.wav** sound file to the Soundtrack track (*Hint: Edit workspace; Media panel; drag*).

2 Correctly position the clip (*Hint: tail end lines up with the tail end of the still image clip*).

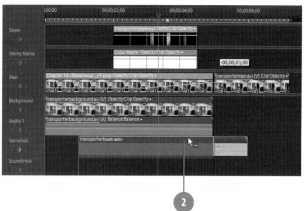

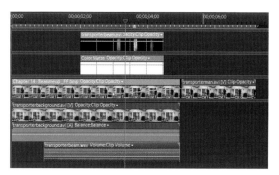

The tail of the sound file should line up with the tail of the **transporterbackground.avi** clip and the freeze frame above.

3 Open the Audio Mixer controls and reduce or increase the sound over the life of the sound file to suit your own taste (*Hint: Mix Audio button; move CTI or press spacebar; add keyframes with slider*).

TIP *To use the Audio Mixer, the clip must be selected and the CTI must be somewhere over that selected clip. Otherwise no alterations to the volume take place, no matter how frantically you slide the slider!*

NOTE *The Audio Mixer will raise or lower the level for the entire clip when the CTI is stationary. But, if the Audio Mixer is adjusted while the CTI is moving, it will add keyframes to lower the audio level at the point where the slider is moved.*

The clip must be selected *and* the CTI must be over that clip; otherwise the slider in the Audio Mixer has no effect!

Did You Know?

You can use sounds creatively for effect. You may have noticed that the **transporterbeam.wav** file is quite a bit longer in duration than the **transporterbeam.avi** file that it's supposed to be associated with. The reason this is the case is because you want to hear the transporter working before you actually see it. You also want to continue to hear the transporter fading away, even after the visual image of the transporter is no longer on screen. Working with sound is an art in itself, and the more you use it, the more you'll see that sometimes you want sounds to fade in or fade out at different times other than when you might intuitively or logically expect them to. It's not unusual for a film editor to let viewers hear a sound first before showing them a visual, such as the sound of a train whistle at the end of a scene of two people talking indoors. It's not until the next scene that you see the train.

Creating a Man-Shaped Beam-In

As it stands, this is a pretty cool-looking project, but as a bonus, and if you want to take it further, you can also create a man-shaped beam by adding the Eight-Point Garbage Matte (and a Gaussian blur to take the edge off the matte) to the white matte. You can find a full description of how to use the garbage matte in Chapter 10.

Use the Eight-Point Garbage Matte and the Gaussian Blur effect on the Color Matte to create a man-shaped beam. The more points you use, the better the shape!

Making Adjustments, Rendering, and Exporting

Now that you have completed all of the tasks for this project, you're ready to "share" the movie, or incorporate it into a bigger project. You can burn a DVD or a VCD or share the clip on a video sharing web site. It's up to you, and you can accomplish all of these tasks from within Premiere Elements 7 (see Adobe Help for more details on these features). But always make sure you save, save, save whenever you are working on a video editing project. You can, and should, render while you work and you render one more time here, now that you have reached the end of your project.

Finish the Project

1. Once you have played back your project and made the necessary adjustments, press **Enter** on your keyboard to render your project.

2. Once you have made all of your final adjustments, press **Ctrl-S** on the keyboard to save your project.

3. Finally, export your work as an AVI file. To export the clip, select **File > Export > Movie**, then browse to a local hard drive and to the **HSMovies_Final Renders** folder you created in Chapter 1, and save the file as **Chapter 14 - Beammeup.avi**.

    TIP *This final render will be used again in Chapter 21, as will many of your other final renders from the exercises in this book.*

The Beammeup clip, playing in the Windows Media player

Hollywood Movie Effects:
The Sinister Ghost Effect

MEDIA:
Ghost.avi
No_Ghost.avi
DarkCity30.mp3

15

COMPLEXITY:	Simple	Moderate	Complex
SKILL LEVEL:	Easy	Intermediate	Advanced

Introduction

The Ghost effect, despite the specificity of its name, is more of an all-purpose supernatural effect than it is simply a ghost maker. In addition to making ghosts, you can use this technique (with minor variations) to produce the "incredible vanishing boy" (or girl)—you've probably seen this effect in old science fiction or horror films as the main character holds his hand up to his face and stares in disbelief at his own disintegrating flesh.

A version of this effect was used in the last chapter to create a beam down effect by increasing opacity over time, and if you looked at the sidebar at the end of the chapter, you learned that you could add a garbage matte around the man to shape the beam.

In this chapter, using keyframes, you create a ghostly visitor who gradually becomes more solid as it enters our Earthly dimension and then you animate the garbage matte to allow the ghost to be part of its surroundings. Once you have mastered this technique, you'll no doubt invent some of your own applications for this supernatural effect.

In addition to the opacity controls used to produce the Ghost effect, believe it or not, Premiere Elements provides an additional effect called "Ghosting." This effect creates a residual copy of the actor's movements in the clip and adds an eerie look to an already otherworldly scene.

In this chapter, you also add some music, sound effects, and a little Gaussian blur, all by using keyframes in one way or another.

It's a packed chapter, but don't forget to have fun with this one: this is an easy-to-do effect that's a huge hit with younger audiences and you can use it over and over in your own horror movies or horror comedies ("*horror*dies"?—Ouch!).

What You'll Learn

Flying Solo: Preparing the Project

Adding the Ghost to the Timeline

Creating the Mask

Animating the Mask

Refining the Mask and the Ghost

Understanding Opacity: How Opacity Works

Flying Solo: Polishing the Project

Making Adjustments, Rendering, and Exporting

Flying Solo: Preparing the Project

Establish Basic Timeline Preparation Skills

1 Create a new project called **Chapter 15_ The_Ghost** (*Hint: File > New > Project*).

2 The Timeline should be set to Timeline View (*Hint: Timeline button to the left of the interface*).

NOTE *You need to switch to the **Timeline** because you are working with multiple clips on multiple video tracks.*

3 Deselect the audio tracks for Video 2 and 3 (*Hint: deselect Show Audio Tracks*).

4 Rename (*Hint: right-click the header*) and change each track to the following:

◆ Video 1: **Person**

◆ Video 2: **Ghost**

◆ Video 3: **Mask**

Setting up this project is something you should now be able to do with your eyes closed. If you are struggling, use the wealth of hints in the text and if you get totally lost, refer back to Chapters 1 and 2 for details on track renaming and importing media from the DVD.

This project uses two video clips (**Ghost.avi, No_Ghost.avi**) and it also uses a sound file (**DarkCity30.mp3**) we supplied on the DVD. To start with, you need to create the project, rename two tracks, and import your media clips. You'll finish this section by adding the **No_Ghost.avi** clip to the Timeline.

Filming Tips

Assuming you don't have access to a ghost—one that can turn up on time, work within budget constraints, and not eat all of the production supplied lunch—then you need your trusty tripod again.

Before you set up, think carefully about light, specifically from which direction it is coming and how it interacts with the actors. While framing this shot, look at what is in the background. Anything in motion, even plants, can kill this effect stone dead. Also look out for reflective surfaces that might show things you would rather they didn't.

Now you are ready to film. As with many of the other special effects in this book, once you press the Record button, don't go near the camera until after the scene completes. Don't allow anyone to turn off the camera, don't allow anyone to walk near the tripod, and don't allow anyone to cast a shadow or block light onto your scene.

While acting the part of a ghost, or a haunted person, make sure your actors avoid looking at the camera, that they keep their breathing to a quiet level, and that no one, including yourself, makes any loud sounds off camera (don't laugh for example!).

Oh, and don't forget to have fun.

5 Import the **Ghost.avi, No_Ghost.avi,** and **DarkCity30.mp3** media clips from the DVD (*Hint: Media Downloader; Show Audio; UnCheck All*).

TIP *You can find complete instructions for importing media into Premiere Elements 7 in the Chapter 1 section, "Adding Media to Your Project." Don't forget you need to uncheck all before you make your selection!*

NOTE *The default settings of the Media Downloader are set not to show Audio media clips. To see any Audio media clips, you need to click the* **Show Audio** *button or press* **Ctrl-U** *on the keyboard while the Media Downloader is open. Watch out, Media Downloader rechecks all the files when you do this and you will need to uncheck them all again.*

6 Switch to the **Edit** workspace (*Hint: Edit tab*).

7 Drag the **No_Ghost.avi** to the Person track.

IMPORTANT *Be sure to line up the head (start) of the* **No_Ghost.avi** *clip with the front of the Background track.*

8 Zoom the Timeline to show the clip as in the screenshot shown (*Hint: use the zoom slider*).

9 When your Timeline and Media panel look similar to that in the screenshots, press **Ctrl-S** to save your work so far, then proceed to the next section.

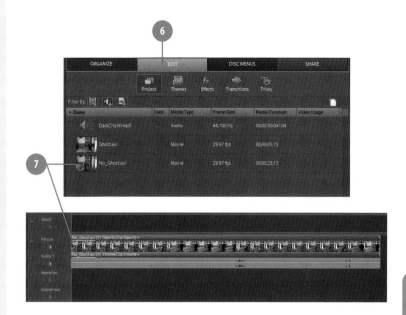

15

Adding the Ghost to the Timeline

Now that you have your Timeline set up with the haunted location in place, it's time to add your visitor from beyond the grave. In this next step, you add the clip to the Timeline, but this time, you use Insert To Timeline instead of dragging to demonstrate an alternative Premiere Elements 7 workflow.

Insert the Ghost to the Timeline

1. If it is not already displayed, click the **Edit** tab to switch to the Edit workspace and click the **Project** button to view the Media panel.

2. If you have moved the CTI, press **End** on the keyboard to move the **CTI** to the end of the **No_Ghost.avi** clip.

3. Right-click the **Ghost.avi** clip on the Media panel and select **Insert To Timeline**. The clip then appears on the Person track. This is the renamed Video 1 track.

   NOTE *All video added to the Timeline via Insert To Timeline appears at the CTI position on the Video 1 track.*

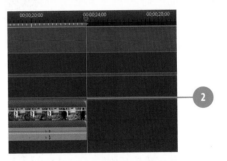

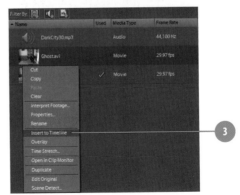

4. Move the **CTI** five seconds (00;00;05;00) into the video.

5. Drag the second clip, **Ghost.avi**, onto the Ghost track. Position the clip directly against the CTI so the clip starts at 00;00;05;00.

6. Finish this section by dragging the tail of the **No_Ghost.avi** clip toward the tail of the **Ghost.avi** media clip.

After the Insert To Timeline, the **Ghost.avi** clip appears on the Person track (default Video 1).

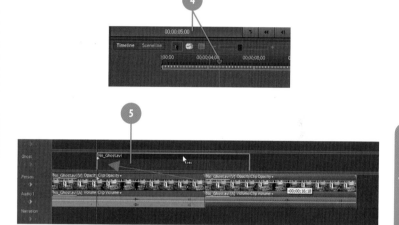

After you trim the tail of the **No_Ghost.avi** clip, your Timeline should look like this.

15

Creating a Mask

In this next section, you begin by creating a mask for the **Ghost.avi** media clip using a white matte on the Timeline. This is the first stage in creating a mask through which your ghost appears. Once you create the mask, you then move it to the correct position, add a Track Matte Key effect to activate the mask, and then finally, add an animated Sixteen-Point Garbage Matte to prepare for creating an animated matte that flows around the shape of the ghost. For more information on why you need to create a mask, see the sidebar entitled "**Masks: What Are They Good For?**" later in this chapter.

Create a Mask Step 1: Add a White Matte

① If it is not already displayed, click the **Edit** tab to switch to the Edit workspace and click the **Project** button to view the Media panel.

② Use **Page Down** to move the **CTI** to the end of the No_Ghost.avi clip.

③ Click the **New Item** button at the top right of the Media panel.

④ Select **Color Matte**.

⑤ On the **Color Picker** dialog, drag the color picker circle all the way down to the lower-left corner of the window.

> **TIP** *You want absolute white, so as an alternative, you can type FFFFFF in the hexadecimal area (labeled "#") or 255, 255, 255 for the RGB values.*

Press **Home** on the keyboard to send the CTI to the end of the last clip.

6 Click **OK**.

7 The Color Matte clip appears on the Person track. Drag it over the top of the **Ghost.avi** media clip on the Mask track.

8 Drag the tail of the White Matte clip up the Timeline so that it is the same length as the **Ghost.avi** clip.

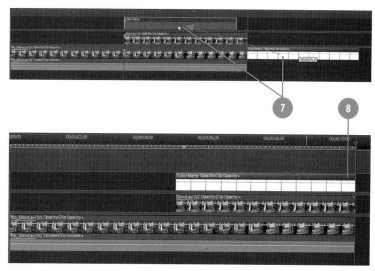

After you drag the tail of the White Matte clip up the Timeline, your Timeline should look like this.

Create a Mask Step 2: Add a Track Matte Key

1 Click the **Effects** button to switch to the Effects panel and type **track** into the text field.

2 Drag the **Track Matte Key** effect onto the **Ghost.avi** media clip on the Ghost track.

3 If it is not already selected, click the **Ghost.avi** media clip to select it, and then click the **Properties** button to display the Properties view.

4 Open the controls for the Track Matte Key by clicking the small triangle.

5 Change the **Matte** control to Mask. Leave the other settings as they are.

15

Create a Mask Step 3:
Add a Garbage Matte

1. Click the **Effects** button to switch to the Effects panel and type **matte** into the text field.

2. Drag the **Sixteen-Point Garbage Matte** onto the White Matte clip on the Mask track.

3. Click the **Properties** button to open the Properties view for the White Matte clip, and click the **Sixteen-Point Garbage Matte** so the title is highlighted and the various handles appear in the Monitor panel.

   NOTE *You need to move the CTI over the White Matte clip before you can see the Sixteen-Point Garbage Matte handles.*

   TIP *The Sixteen-Point Garbage Matte allows the man shape to have greater detail, whereas the Eight-Point Garbage Matte is less time consuming to set up.*

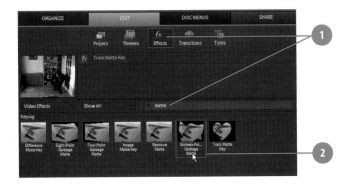

Masks: What Are They Good For?

In the preceding section, instead of adding a Sixteen-Point Garbage Matte to the **No_Ghost.avi** clip, you first created a White Matte clip, then added a Track Matte Key effect so you could see the underlying tracks through the White Matte clip, and finally, you added the Sixteen-Point Garbage Matte.

Why?

If you had added the garbage matte to the clip, you would have created a mask, but one with a clear border that would have been very easy for the audience to see. This is because of small differences in lighting, often the result of different objects, in this case the actors, being introduced into the scene. In other video editing applications, the Feather function allows you to soften this border, but unfortunately this version of Premiere Elements does not have this feature.

To overcome the lack of a Feather feature, and to cancel out this border problem, you can just add a Gaussian blur to the **No_Ghost.avi** clip and ramp up the blurring until the border is diffused. But doing this also blurs the ghost, and this might not be the effect you are looking for.

Instead, by adding the garbage matte to the white matte and adding a track matte to the Person layer, you are effectively creating a mask layer that is independent of the video it affects.

Now you can add the blur to *feather*, or soften, the mask's border without affecting the video in any way. In this case, the white matte is effectively made transparent by the track matte and it becomes nothing more than a convenient place to park your garbage and blur effects as you're creating this mask.

This solution is a little more time consuming, but it does create a fantastic looking movie effect.

Without any added blur, the edges of the mask are easy to spot.

When you use the Mask method detailed in this chapter, you can add the blur effect to reduce the edges of the mask.

15

Animating the Mask

Now that you have the mask in place, it's worth moving the **CTI** up and down the Timeline to see which parts of the **Ghost.avi** clip you need to mask away. At first, the mask is fairly simple and is only there to separate the ghost from the background, enabling you to use opacity in a later step to make your ghost all ghostly. But as the man on the sofa reacts, gets up, and stands in front of the ghost, the mask becomes more complex. In this section, you animate the mask so that the **Ghost.avi** media clip never interferes with the **No_Ghost.avi** media clip.

Create a Start Point for the Mask

1. If you are carrying on directly from the last section, the Properties view for the White Matte clip should be open, and the Sixteen-Point Garbage Matte should be selected showing the 16 handles in the Monitor panel. If this is not the case, return to the last section and follow the instructions in **Step 3**.

2. If it is not already displayed, click the **Show Keyframes** button to display the keyframe area.

3. If some of the handles in the Monitor panel are outside the panel's borders, right-click in the middle of the Monitor panel and select **Magnification > 100%** (or a lower value if the handles are still outside the Monitor panel).

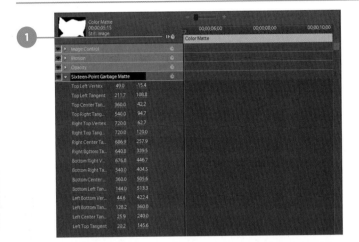

4. Move the **CTI** to about 00;00;06;05 (where the man is starting to get up off the sofa), then click the **Toggle Animation** button on for the **Sixteen-Point Garbage Matte**. Premiere Elements now creates a keyframe for each handle at your mask's starting point.

   NOTE At this point, we have not altered the opacity for the ghost and we have not added the Gaussian blur to the mask to feather its edges. This allows you a better view of the Ghost.avi clip while you are animating the mask. If you have added opacity changes to the Ghost.avi clip, turn them off by deselecting the eyeball next to the Opacity effect.

5. Drag each of the 16 points to surround the ghost. Don't move in too tight, but also, don't block any background that appears in the **No_Ghost.avi** clip. When you finish, your Sixteen-Point Garbage Matte should look something like the screenshot on this page.

   NOTE Remember, this is just the starting point for the mask; don't fuss over it too much at this stage.

6. Press the right arrow key a few times to advance the movie a few frames.

7. At around 00;00;06;18, the man getting up from the sofa has started to become headless. Clearly this ruins the effect you want, so move the handles in that area so that the man's head and shoulders become visible again (altering the handles in just that region to flow around the parts of the man that intrude into the mask). As you do so, Premiere Elements creates keyframes automatically for each handle.

8. When you are happy with this initial change, don't move the cursor any further and don't create any more keyframes. You do this in the next section. When you are ready to move on, press **Ctrl-S** to save your work so far.

The starting position for the mask

15

Create an End Point and
Animate the Mask

1. If it is not already open, click the **Properties** button to open the Properties view for the White Matte clip and select the **Sixteen-Point Garbage Matte** to highlight the handles in the viewer.

2. Drag the **CTI** up the Timeline until you reach a point where the man is almost fully standing and the ghost is blocked from view by the man (around 00;00;07;02).

3. Close the mask down to almost a straight line that runs down the right-hand side of the man.

   NOTE *In the example screenshot, some of the ghost is visible through the mask, but once you adjust the opacity later in this chapter, this is no longer a problem.*

4. Move the **CTI** back 10 frames by pressing the **left arrow** key 10 times. As you can see, the mask doesn't match the man; move only those handles necessary to correct this.

5 Move the **CTI** forward 5 frames by pressing the **right arrow** key 5 times. Note that some handles are animating nicely, but one or two, specifically around the man's head and neck area, need further fine-tuning. Make the necessary adjustments to these handles, but only move the ones that need tuning.

TIP *It is often better to animate a mask by creating a start and end point and then moving backward through the clip rather than forward. By doing this, you can avoid creating too many keyframes, which can slow down and even crash your computer.*

6 Rock backward and forward along the entire clip, adding keyframes as you see fit, until you are happy with the final animation. This is an intense piece of keyframing, but the more time you put in, the better it looks.

7 Make sure you press **Ctrl-S** on a regular basis to save your work at each step.

NOTE *Although it is possible to create all the keyframes you need by clicking forward a few keyframes at a time, you might end up with too many keyframes in this effect, thus causing the application to slow down and render times to increase. An easier method is to find the end point, where the effect is no longer needed, and place your final keyframes there. When you create a start and an end keyframe point, you can see where you need additional keyframes by simply moving the CTI backward and forward and adjusting the handles.*

5

15

Ghosts Using a Split-Screen Crop Effect

If you don't want to go to the extreme of using an animated mask, you can also create a Ghost effect by using the Crop effect. This does mean that your ghost and your scared human must each occupy one side of the screen and that neither should cross the midline. However, if you want to create a quick ghost effect, this is a very valid method for doing so.

Refining the Mask and the Ghost

Once you have the mask animated, it is time to add a few refinements to hide the edges of the mask and to make your ghost look a little more ghostly. In this next section you add a little blurring to the mask, a little ghosting to the ghost, and turn down the ghost's opacity.

Add a Blur to the Mask

1. If it is not already open, click the **Edit** tab to view the Edit workspace and click the **Effects** button to view the Effects panel.

2. Move the **CTI** to the start of the White Matte clip.

3. Type **blur** into the text field of the Effects panel.

4. Drag the Gaussian Blur effect to the White Matte clip.

5. Click the **Properties** button to open the Properties view and dial down the **Gaussian Blur** controls by clicking the small triangle.

6. Alter the amount of **Blurriness** to 25 (or to suit). You don't need any keyframes here!

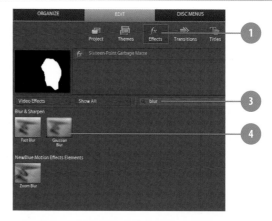

Add Ghosting to the Ghost

1. If it is not already open, click the **Edit** tab to view the Edit workspace and click the **Effects** button to view the Effects panel.

2. Move the **CTI** to the start of the **Ghost.avi** clip.

3. Type **ghost** into the text field of the Effects panel.

4. Drag the **Ghosting** effect to the **Ghost.avi** clip on the Ghost track.

   NOTE The Ghosting effect is one of the few Premiere Elements effects that has no controls. You take it as it is or not at all.

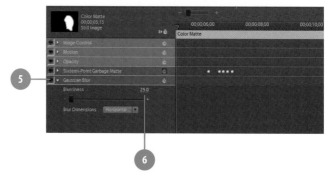

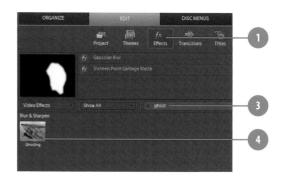

Adjust the Opacity of the Ghost

1 Click the **Ghost.avi** clip to select it, and then click the **Properties** button to open the Properties view.

2 Dial down the **Opacity** controls by clicking the small triangle.

3 Move the **CTI** to the start of the **Ghost.avi** clip and set **Opacity** to 0.0% for this first keyframe.

4 Turn **Toggle Animation** on for opacity.

5 Move the **CTI** 10 frames forward by pressing the **right arrow** key 10 times.

6 Set **Opacity** to 75% and Premiere Elements creates a keyframe at this point.

7 Move the **CTI** to 00;00;07;01 using the arrow keys or by entering the number **07;01** directly in the CTI readout.

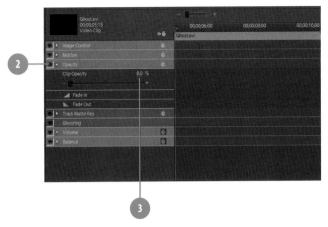

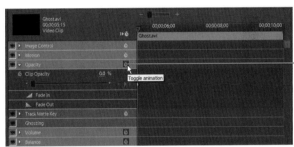

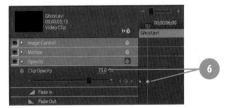

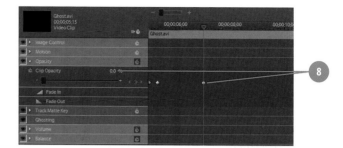

8 Set the **Opacity** to 0.0%.

NOTE *In this section you have not only reduced the overall opacity of the ghost, but you have also faded the ghost in from 0 percent and faded him back out to 0 percent creating his ghostly entrance and exit.*

Did You Know?

You can use the yellow rubberband to control opacity. Use the yellow rubberband that runs the length of every video clip to set opacity. Be sure that the rubberband is actually controlling opacity (see the sidebar on the next page). Then click the rubberband. When you hold the mouse button down the cursor changes to include small up and down arrows. Drag the rubberband down to decrease opacity, up to increase it. As you move the rubberband, Premiere Elements displays a small yellow box to show you the opacity amount.

You can choose what the rubberband controls. By default, the rubberband controls opacity, but you can set it to control other effects. To do so, click the settings menu control in the name bar at the top of the clip. It only appears at the head, or front, of the clip, so if you don't see it, scrub to the beginning. From the menu, select Opacity > Clip Opacity, as shown in the screenshot.

Understanding Opacity: How Opacity Works

Premiere Elements supports the friendly Ghost effect through the use of a function called *opacity*, which you may more readily understand as *transparency*. That is, it's the quality (or lack of) of "see-throughness," if you will, of a video clip.

When you use it by itself (that is, over an empty track or "nothingness"), you can decrease the opacity on a clip to make the clip appear darker. When you use it over another clip, the second clip acts as a background clip (as shown in the sequence of pictures here.)

When two clips are, for the most part, identical with only one element changing (specifically, it's becoming transparent, or losing opacity), it appears as if only that element with an altering level of opacity is changing, when, in fact, *everything* in that clip is actually changing.

An Apple Appears to Appear

Shown here are illustrations from two clips superimposed over each other. One is of a table without an apple; the other is of the same table, with an apple on top.

The opacity of the apple clip is set to gradually increase over time, from 0 percent to 100 percent. This makes it seem as if the apple is appearing out of thin air. (You can also accomplish this particular effect by cross dissolving from one clip to the other.)

This works because *all other elements*—the table, the placemats, the plants—are exactly the same in each shot. The only difference is the apple. This is simply an illusion, a kind of magic trick created with a camcorder and video editing software.

Requirements for Success

Even in the clips below, which were filmed literally within seconds of each other, you can begin to see the shadows shifting as the sun moves slowly in the sky. The sun is your enemy: this is rule number one whenever you plan to use the Opacity control in this way. As light and shadows change, the effect becomes less and less convincing. So here's requirement one: film as quickly as you can whenever you are creating scenes like these.

The second requirement for success is the tripod. Without one, you will fail. It's that simple. If there's even the slightest variation in angle or position from one clip to the other, the whole thing is ruined. It simply won't be believable. If you don't have a tripod or a monopod, find a way to rest the camcorder on a table, chair, shelf, or other rock-solid surface.

The apple magically appears as the opacity increases over time from 0 percent to 100 percent.

Flying Solo: Polishing the Project

What's a spooky clip without spooky music? Fly Solo now to add some spooky music, either from SmartSound or using **DarkCity30.mp3**, a twisted track provided courtesy of the folks at Twisted Tracks. We've included hints and tips, but by now, you should be very comfortable with adding SmartSound or other musical clips to the Timeline. As an optional extra, try adding a spooky ghost groan using the narration technique shown in Chapter 3.

Add a Touch of Spooky Music

1. View the **Edit** workspace (*Hint: Edit button*).

2. Create a SmartSound track and add it to the track *or* drag the **DarkCity30.mp3** and trim it to be no longer than the clips in the tracks above (*Hint: The sound file should be at the beginning of the Soundtrack track*).

3. Toggle off Keyframes for Volume and then adjust the volume level for either the SmartSound or the **DarkCity30.mp3** clip (Hint: open the Properties view; toggle off Keyframes; dial open Volume; set the volume level to a recommended 9.0 dB for the MP3 clip).

4. Click the **Fade Out** button for Volume in the Properties view so that the music fades out gracefully at the end of the movie.

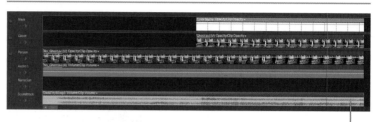

The included MP3 on the Timeline. Alternatively, you could create your own SmartSound track.

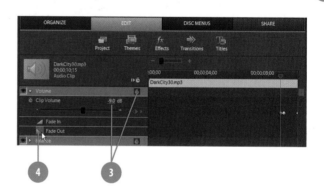

Add Fades

1 View the **Edit** workspace (*Hint: Edit button*).

2 Add a fade out for each clip on the Timeline (*Hint: right-click each clip in turn and select Fade > Fade Out Audio and Video*).

3 Press **Ctrl-S** to save your work.

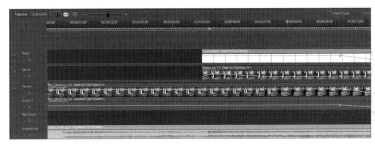

How your Timeline should look once you've added all the fades

15

Find a Huge Collection of Original Music at Twisted Tracks

Twisted Tracks creates royalty-free original music in a variety of different styles and genres, including "Blockbuster," "Horror," "High Energy," "Retro," "Noise," "Lounge," "Humorous," and "Triphop." You can download their music individually or as sets, or you can purchase complete DVD collections. You can also listen to any of their tunes online. Prices start at just a couple of dollars for the short loops. The folks at Twisted Tracks regularly offer a program on their site where by simply registering, you can download $50 worth of their music for free. Their music is fun, original, and priced well. You'll find more information at **www.twistedtracks.com**.

Making Adjustments, Rendering, and Exporting

Now that you've placed all the pieces of your production puzzle, you're ready to go. Of course, throughout this project you should always save as you go (**Ctrl-S**). Now, press **Enter** on your keyboard to render the project (it plays automatically once it's done rendering). Watch the playback. If you see anything you don't like, go in and tweak things, like the mask, and press the **spacebar** to play the clip again, or press **Enter** to render it again. When everything looks good, you're ready to export your project to a viewable movie file.

Finish the Project

1 Once you have played back your project and made the necessary adjustments, press **Enter** on your keyboard to render your project.

2 Once you have made all of your final adjustments, press **Ctrl-S** on the keyboard to save your project.

3 Finally, export your work as an AVI file. To export the clip, select **File > Export > Movie**, browse to a local hard drive and to the **HSMovies_Final Renders** folder you created in Chapter 1, and save the file as **Chapter 15_ The_Ghost.avi**.

NOTE *This final render will be used again in Chapter 21, as will many of your other final renders from the exercises in this book.*

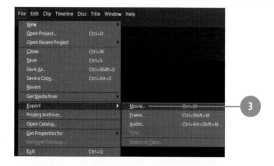

The finished movie, playing in Windows Media Player

Hollywood Movie Effects: Working with Clones!

MEDIA:
Clone_1.avi
Clone_2.avi
Clone_3.avi
234855_Waveringelectricsurge.wav

16

COMPLEXITY:	Simple	Moderate	Complex
SKILL LEVEL:	Easy	Intermediate	Advanced

Introduction

From almost the very start of television, having twins on the screen—who talk alike, walk alike, and sometimes even think alike (what a crazy pair!)—has been irresistible. With Premiere Elements 7, splitting the screen into two parts (or, if you are very, *very* careful, even more than two) is easy to do. The actor and his or her twin (which, of course, is the same actor again in a second location) can appear to hold a conversation and walk in and out of the scene in a convincing way.

One of the nice things about the Multiple You effect is, although it can be done using a blue or green screen, such equipment is not necessary. If you want to create the illusion of a clone (or a twin), the classic split screen works just fine. If you're careful, you can even create triplets (as demonstrated in this chapter). Anything beyond that, however, such as an army of clones, and you may find that you need a green screen so that you can strip away (key out) the background and layer the various clones over one another in the scene using the multiple tracks available in Premiere Elements. Either that, or you need to use animated garbage mattes and have the patience of a saint!

In this chapter, however, you concentrate on the much easier technique of splitting the screen using the Crop effect and creating the illusion of look-alikes engaged in the casual act of de-atomizing one of their own clones with the power of the Lightning effect. It was just one of those days!

Flying Solo: Preparing the Project

The first steps in creating this effect are the same as those for virtually all the projects in this book: begin a project, name the tracks, and import your media clips. For this project, you need three video clips, which you can find on the DVD that comes with this book. In Chapter 1, you learned the necessary techniques to do all these tasks, so Fly Solo now and see how much you can remember. Hints and tips are listed to help you out, but if you get really lost, just peek back at the Chapter 1 section "Preparing the Project" for more detailed instructions.

Start a Project, Customize the Timeline, and Import the Media

1 Start **Premiere Elements** and create a **New Project** called **Chapter 16_Clone_Attack** (*Hint: New Project at the splash screen or File > New > Project if Premiere Elements is already open; save in the Peachpit folder created in Chapter 1*).

NOTE *The sample files supplied on the DVD are for use on an NTSC Timeline. If your default Project settings are not NTSC, change them now by clicking the* **Change Settings** *button and selecting* **NTSC > DV > Standard 48kHz**.

2 If the Timeline is set to **Sceneline**, switch it to the **Timeline** (*Hint: Timeline button!*).

NOTE *You need to switch to the* **Timeline** *because for this project you are working with multiple clips on multiple video tracks.*

3 Deselect the Audio tracks 2 and 3 (*Hint: right-click Track Header; deselect Show Audio Tracks*).

4 Rename tracks 1 and 2 to the following (*Hint: right-click the track name; select Rename*):

◆ Video 1: **Clone_1**

◆ Video 2: **Clone_2**

◆ Video 3: **Clone_3**

Filming Tips

By now you are probably used to reading about locking down tripods and carefully avoiding moving shadows (or shadows in general) or moving objects such as plants and pets and other annoyances in the background that suddenly sparkle to life when you start filming. In this chapter you won't be disappointed because all of this is part of the first golden rule you need to remember if you decide to re-create this scene for yourself.

The second golden rule for creating a scene like this is that you need to keep the camera running. If you touch that Record button, even if only for the barest sliver of a second to turn it off, you will probably move the camera a fraction of an inch in one direction or another. That spells disaster for you later. So much disaster, in fact, that you will have to go back and shoot it all over again!

The third golden rule is to be quick. Unless you are filming in a studio setting, you are dependent on light levels from the sun. These change constantly as you put the film together, and changing light levels cause walls to look a different shade and skin to shift color! You can fix some of this in Premiere Elements, but if you can avoid breaking it in the first place, you'll be doing yourself a massive favor.

The sequence that you work on here has no dialogue at all. Conversation in such situations is very difficult and you should avoid it until you have mastered the basics of cloning. The secret, then, is to script out the conversation ahead of time so that the actors know where to look and what to say. Then, when you've pieced the scene together in Premiere Elements, it looks normal and natural as the clones point, talk, and look at each other in the course of conversation.

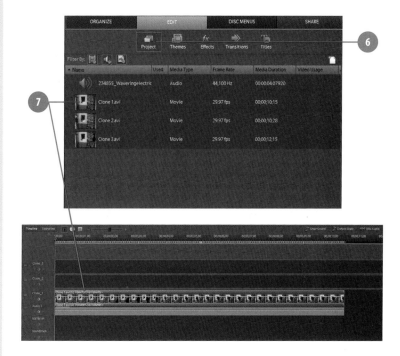

5 Import the **Clone_1.avi**, **Clone_2.avi**, **Clone_3.avi**, and **234855_Waveringelectricsurge.wav** media clips from the DVD (*Hint: Get media; DVD (Camcorder or PC DVD Drive) button; Advanced button; select DVD drive; UnCheck All; check required AVI clips*).

TIP *You can find complete instructions for importing media into Premiere Elements 7 in the Chapter 1 section, "Adding Media to Your Project."*

6 Once you've finished the import process, switch to the **Edit** workspace and open the **Media** panel (*Hint: Edit tab; Project button*).

7 Drag the **Clone_1.avi** media clip to the Clone 1 track on the Timeline.

TIP *Make sure the start of the media clip is at the head of the track.*

8 Use the **zoom** controls so the **Clone_1.avi** media clip occupies about two thirds of the Timeline. Move on to the next section when your Timeline looks similar to the one shown on this page.

Did You Know?

You can purchase sound effects for just a few dollars. Web sites such as **www. audiosparx.com** sell a massive range of audio special effects such as the Wavering Electrical Surge you use in this chapter. Though such sound effects cost only a few dollars, they can add massively to the quality of your projects.

16

Marking the Clones Entrance Points

You now need to add the two clones to your Timeline, placing them in such a way that they act together, moving their hands in a synchronized action. To get this right, you need to experiment a little; you can make this easier by using Timeline and clip markers. Timeline markers are something you have seen in various sections of this book, but in this chapter, you will learn how to add markers to a clip in the Media panel (**Clone_2.avi** and **Clone_3.avi**). This is an excellent technique to learn when it comes to streamlining the accuracy with which clips are added to the Timeline.

Create a Reaction Marker

1. Move the **CTI** until you see **Clone_1.avi** just beginning to react as though he is being electrocuted (*Hint: 00;00;05;10*).

2. Create a marker at this point by pressing the **Asterisk** key on the keyboard's number pad.

3. If you need to refine this marker point, move the **CTI** a few frames up or down the Timeline and drag the marker toward it.

Add Clip Markers to Clone_2.avi and Clone_3.avi

1. If it is not already open, switch to the Edit workspace by clicking the **Edit** tab, then open the Media panel by clicking the **Project** button.

2. Double-click **Clone_2.avi** to bring up the Preview window for that clip.

3. Move the **CTI** in the Preview window to approximately where the clone has raised his hands to attack (*Hint: 00;00;03;02*).

4. Create a marker at this point by pressing the **Asterisk** key on the keyboard's number pad.

5. Close the Preview window by clicking the **X** in the top-right corner.

6. Repeat Steps 2–5 with **Clone_3.avi**, but this time create the marker at 00;00;04;25.

Press the Asterisk key on the keyboard's number pad to add a marker at the CTI point.

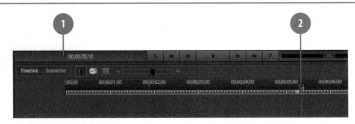

Add Clone_2.avi and Clone_3.avi to the Timeline at the Marker Points

1. Drag **Clone_2.avi** to the Clone 2 track on the Timeline, maneuvering the clip up or down the Timeline until the Clip marker and the Timeline marker line up.

   NOTE *You won't actually see the Clip marker while you're dragging the clip, but when they line up, a thin black line topped with an arrow head appears.*

2. If you see the Videomerge message, click **No**.

3. The **Clone_2.avi** clip should now be on the Timeline with its Clip marker lined up with the Timeline marker above.

4. Repeat Steps 1 and 2 to add **Clone_3.avi** to the Clone 3 track, maneuvering the clip up or down the Timeline until the Clip marker and the Timeline marker line up.

5. Move on to the next section when your Timeline resembles the screenshot shown.

Did you know?

Your clones can pass through the cropping areas of other clones as long as they don't "exist" in the frame at that time. In this example, Clone 1 walks through an area in which Clone 3 appears, but because you add an Opacity effect later in the chapter, you do not experience any problems associated with breaking a golden rule of cloning.

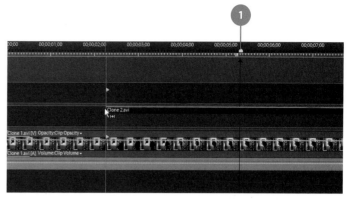

When the marker on the clip and the marker on the Timeline line up, a thin black line topped with an arrow head appears.

The two markers lined up on the Timeline

16

Applying the Crop Effect to All Clips

You now have all your clips lined up on the Timeline so they react as though they were all filmed at the same time and so it seems as if you really are looking at clones. Except, of course, for the top clip, Clone_3.avi, which obscures the other two clips for most of the project. To overcome this problem and bring this sequence to life, you will apply the **Crop** effect to all the clips on the Timeline, and then adjust each Crop effect so that you can see all three clones in the Monitor panel at the same time.

Apply the Crop Effect

1. If it is not already open, switch to the Edit workspace by clicking the **Edit** tab, then open the **Effects** panel by clicking the **Effects** button.

2. Type **crop** in the text box to reveal the Crop effect.

3. Drag the **Crop** effect from the Transform Video Effects and drop it onto the **Clone_2.avi** clip on the Clone 2 track.

4. Repeat the last step to add the **Crop** effect to the **Clone_3.avi** clip on the Clone 3 track and the **Clone_1.avi** on the Clone 1 track.

5. Press **Ctrl-S** to save your work so far.

   NOTE *Strictly speaking, **Clone_1.avi** creates the backdrop, and as such, it doesn't need a Crop effect. However, in the next section, you use the **Crop** effect as a crude garbage matte to remove unwanted objects from the top and bottom of the screen.*

Adjusting the Crop Effect for Each Clip

Now that you have applied the Crop effect to all the clips on the Timeline, you need to adjust the **Clone_3.avi** clip because the Clone 3 track is the topmost clip on the Timeline. Once you have edited the crop on **Clone_3.avi**, adjust the crop on **Clone_2.avi** and **Clone_1.avi**.

Make the Adjustments for Each Crop

1. Move the **CTI** over the **Clone_3.avi** clip and then click the clip to make it active.

2. With the clip selected, click the **Properties** button to open the Properties view and then dial open the **Crop** controls by clicking the triangle.

    NOTE *If the CTI is not over the **Clone_3.avi** clip, you will not see any changes you make to the Crop effect in the Monitor panel.*

3. Adjust the **Crop** effect by using the sliders; the following settings are the ones we recommend:

    ◆ Left: **73.8%**

    ◆ Top: **10.0%**

    ◆ Right: **0.0%**

    ◆ Bottom: **10.0%**

    TIP *We suggest a value of 10 for the top and bottom crop to rid the viewing area of some distracting objects at the top and bottom of the picture. Crop is often used in this way; you can also use it to create a pseudo-widescreen effect.*

4. Move the **CTI** over the **Clone_2.avi** clip and then click the clip to make it active.

5. The Properties view should still be open. If it isn't, click the **Properties** button to open the Properties view and then dial open the **Crop** controls by clicking the triangle.

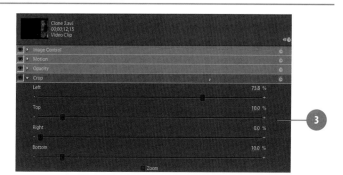

6 Adjust the **Crop** effect to suit by using the sliders; the following settings are the ones we recommend:

◆ Left: **0.0%**

◆ Top: **10.0%**

◆ Right: **76.2%**

◆ Bottom: **10.0%**

7 Now click **Clone_1.avi** on the Clone 1 track and repeat Step 5 to view the Crop controls and enter the following suggested crop settings:

◆ Left: **0.0%**

◆ Top: **10.0%**

◆ Right: **0.0%**

◆ Bottom: **10.0%**

NOTE *You only need a value of 10 for the top and bottom crop parameters to tie in with the values added to Clone 2 and 3. Left and right do not need any cropping because this clip forms the backdrop for the movie.*

Did you know?

You don't need to click the triangle next to the Crop effect. Instead you can click the Crop effect name bar and then adjust the crop directly in the Monitor panel. However, the control handles can sometimes be difficult to spot, depending on the background video. Look closely, and if in doubt, use the sliders!

After you apply and tweak the Crop filters, you can see all three clones!

Adding a Little Image Control

With all three clones now visible on the Timeline, it's easy to see that the left clone (**Clone_2. avi**) has a different brightness level than the other two clones. This is a problem that results from changing light levels because light is being blocked by Clone 2! Fortunately this is easy to correct using the Image Control effect, which comes attached to every clip by default.

Make Adjustments to Light Levels

1. Move the **CTI** over the **Clone_2.avi** and then click the clip to make it active.

2. The Properties view should still be open; if not, click the **Properties** button to open the Properties view and then dial open the **Image Control** controls by clicking the triangle.

3. Adjust the effect to the following suggested settings:

   ◆ Brightness: **4.7**

   ◆ Contrast: **113.7**

   ◆ Saturation: **112.9**

The readjusted image now has a closer match to the light levels of the neighboring clip.

16

Fine-Tuning the Entrance of the Clones

As is the way when you create material of this kind, it's difficult—some might say somewhat implausible—to expect that all your clone clips will be the same length. At the moment, there is a problem with Clone 1 being obscured by the presence of Clone 3. And Clone 2 is there before Clone 1 can react to him. That's not right either. In this next section, you simply trim the excess Clone 3 material out of the way, and then add a **fade in** to both the **Clone_2.avi** and the **Clone_3.avi** clips, giving them a much punchier entrance.

Adjust the Clone_3.avi Clip and Add a Fade In

1. Move the **CTI** to a point where **Clone_1.avi** is no longer being obscured by **Clone_3.avi** (*Hint: 00;00;03;12*).

2. Hold down **Ctrl**, then grab the head of the **Clone_3.avi** clip and drag it toward the CTI.

   NOTE *If you attempt to drag the head of the Clone_3.avi clip, it does not move up the Timeline; instead the end of the clip moves down the Timeline, shorting the clip but leaving the head in exactly the same place.*

3. Right-click the **Clone_3.avi** clip and select **Fade > Fade In Audio and Video**.

4. Repeat Step 3 for the **Clone_2.avi** clip adding a **Fade In** for this clip.

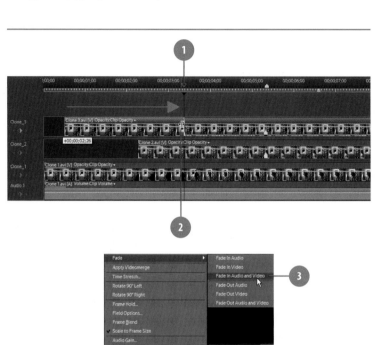

Adding Some Lightning Power

Evil clones are one thing, but at the moment, they don't look so evil. What they need is the power of lightning to make them a little bit frightening! In this next step you add lightning to the movie, adjusting the start and end points and trimming the values to make them a little less frantic. However, before you can add the lightning, you need to create a placeholder for it to live on; this is because the Lightning effect is difficult to reduce to zero, meaning that if you add it to the **Clone_3.avi** clip, the Lightning effect appears just as soon as the opacity fade is finished. Fortunately a very quick workaround actually offers many surprising benefits.

Add the Placeholder for the Lightning

1. Move the **CTI** to where both clones begin their attack (*Hint: 00;00;05;09*).

2. Click the **Add Default Text** button to open the Titler.

3. If **Add Text** is not highlighted (by default, it should be) highlight all the text by dragging the mouse across it, and then press **Delete** on the keyboard to remove it.

4. Click anywhere on the Timeline to exit the Titler, and place the new, blank title on a track above Clone 3.

   NOTE *Premiere Elements creates a new track when you exit Titler if the track immediately beneath it is occupied.*

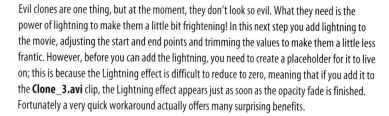

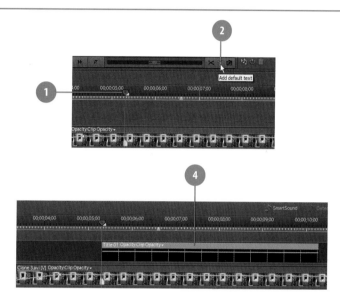

16

Add the First Bolt of Lightning to the Placeholder

1. If it is not already open, switch to the Edit workspace by clicking the **Edit** tab, then open the **Effects** panel by clicking the **Effects** button.

2. Type **light** in the text box to reveal the Lightning effect.

3. Drag the **Lightning** effect from the Effects panel and drop it onto the **Title 01** clip on the Video 4 track.

4. With the clip still selected, click the **Properties** button to open the Properties view and then dial open the **Lightning** controls by clicking the triangle.

5. Adjust the **Lightning** effect to suit your needs by using the sliders; the following settings are the ones we recommend:

    ◆ Segments: **8**

    ◆ Amplitude: **15**

    ◆ Detail Level: **5**

    ◆ Detail Amplitude: **0.5**

    ◆ Branching: **0.00**

    NOTE *Leave the other settings as they are, although if you want, you can scroll down to the bottom and alter the outside or inside color of your lightning.*

6. Click the **Lightning** name bar to highlight the start and end points in the Monitor panel.

    NOTE *The start point by default always appears on the left and the end point is always on the right, regardless of which way your actor is pointing. This can be confusing at first, but remember that the lightning branches out from the start point, not the other way round!*

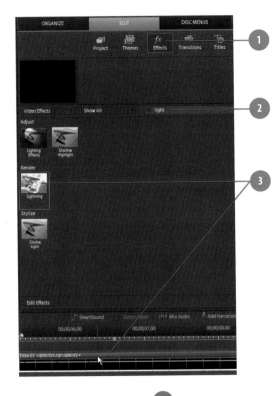

The End point position after being moved in Step 7

The Start point position after being moved in Step 7

7 Move the **start point** into the right hand of Clone 3 and then move the **end point** to the head area of Clone 1.

> **TIP** *Clone 1 moves his head a little, so place the **end point** slightly inside the head area.*

8 Finish this section by trimming the tail of the **Title 01** clip to about where Clone 3 starts to lower his hands (*Hint: 00;00;09;15*).

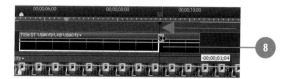

Add a Second Bolt of Lightning to the Placeholder

1 Select the **Title 01** clip on the Video 4 track by clicking it once.

2 Click the **Properties** button to open the Properties view and then dial closed the **Lightning** controls by clicking the triangle.

3 Right-click the **Lightning** name bar and choose **Copy** from the contextual menu.

4 Right-click in an empty area of the Properties view and choose **Paste** from the contextual menu.

5 Click the second **Lightning** name bar to highlight the **start** and **end points** of the second lightning bolt in the Monitor panel.

6 Move the **start point** into the left hand of Clone 3 and then move the **end point** (for a little variety) to the chest area of Clone 1.

> **NOTE** *To see the start and end points in the Monitor panel, you must move the **CTI** over the Title 01 clip.*

16

7 Finish this section by dialing open the **Opacity** controls for the Title 01 clip and by adding a **fade in** and a **fade out** by clicking the appropriate buttons.

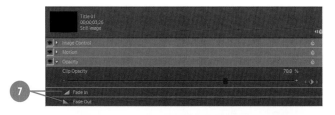

The copy of the original lightning bolt with the start and end point adjusted

Creating a Duplicate Lightning Placeholder for Clone 2

Clone 2 must be feeling a bit left out, so in this section you copy and paste the **Placeholder** clip—Title 01, complete with the Lightning effect—and then create a new track for it to live on. Finish this section by fine-tuning the start and end points of the new lightning placeholder clip.

Copy and Paste the Placeholder Clip

1. Right-click the **Title 01** clip on the Video 4 track and from the contextual menu choose **Copy**.

2. Move the **CTI** to the end of the Title 01 clip and press **Ctrl-V** on the keyboard.

3. Hold down **Ctrl**, and drag the newly created title up above Video 4, allowing Premiere Elements to create a new track for you (Video 5).

   NOTE *Dragging this clip to the new position without holding down the Ctrl key can cause all other clips on the Timeline to jump out of position.*

4. Right-click the **Title 01** clip on the Video 5 track (the upper title) and select **Rename** from the contextual menu.

5. When the Rename box appears, change the name to **Title 02** and click **OK**.

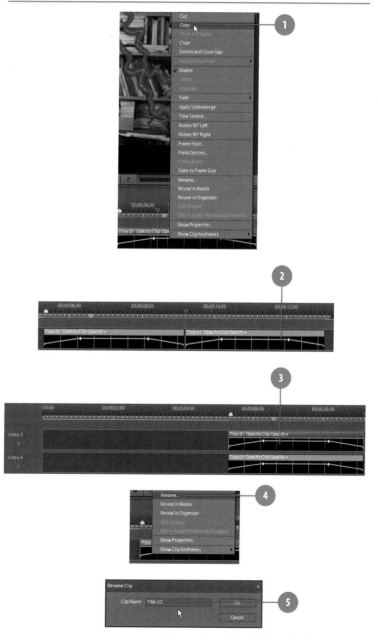

16

Adjust the Start and End Points for the Lightning Effect

1. Click the **Title 02** clip to select it.

2. Click the **Properties** button to open the Properties view and then dial closed the **Lightning** controls if they are open by clicking the triangle.

3. Click the first **Lightning** name bar to highlight the start and end points of the first lightning bolt in the Monitor panel.

    NOTE *Make sure the CTI is over the Title 02 clip otherwise you will not see the start and end points in the Monitor panel.*

4. Move the **start point** into the left hand of Clone 2 and then move the **end point** to the left head area of Clone 1.

5. Click the second **Lightning** name bar to highlight the start and end points of the second lightning bolt in the Monitor panel.

6. Move the **start point** into the right hand of Clone 2 and leave the **end point** roughly where it is.

The copied placeholder (left) with the start and end points altered

Polishing the Visual Effect

You now have a very convincing scene, with Clones 2 and 3 appearing, de-atomizing Clone 1, and then disappearing from whence they came! Spooky stuff. But the project needs some finishing touches. For starters, Clone 1 doesn't actually de-atomize, he just stands there. To make this more realistic, you need to adjust the length of the **Clone_1.avi** clip and then add an **Opacity** fade out. However, doing this causes a problem. Once Clone 1 vanishes, so does the background, leaving a black hole in its place. To fix this, create a freeze frame from the very start of the Timeline, and then insert it *under* the Clone 1 track. Finish by adding fades to the Clone 2 and 3 clips.

Trim Clone_1.avi and Add an Opacity Fade Out

1 Drag the tail end of the clip down the Timeline until it lines up with the tail end of the two Placeholder title clips above.

2 Right-click the **Clone_1.avi** clip, and from the contextual menu, choose **Fade > Fade Out Audio and Video**.

3 Press **Ctrl-S** to save your work.

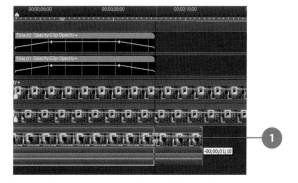

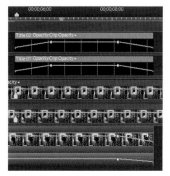

The trimmed clip complete with fade out

Create a Freeze Frame
of an Empty Room

1 Move the **CTI** to the very start of the Timeline.

2 Click the **Clone_1.avi** clip to select it.

3 Click the **Freeze Frame** button below the Monitor panel.

4 Choose the **Export** button and then select a save location for the BMP file and close the **Freeze Frame** box by clicking the small X in the upper-right corner.

5 If it is not already displayed, click the **Edit** tab to switch to the Edit workspace and then click the **Project** button to view the Media panel.

NOTE *The BMP still image file that you just created has been automatically imported into your Media panel.*

6 Right-click the track header and select **Add Tracks**.

7 In the Video Tracks area, change the **Placement** setting to **Before First Track** and then click **OK** to create a track *under* the Clone 1 track.

8 Drag the **freeze frame** from the Media panel to the new track (Video 1) with the head of the freeze frame about level with the first opacity keyframe on the **Clone_1.avi** clip.

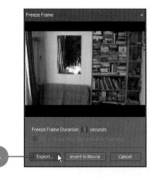

The newly created freeze frame

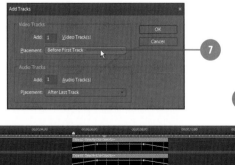

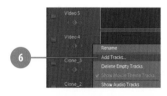

Trim Clone_2.avi and Add an Opacity Fade Out

1. Drag the tail end of the **Clone_2.avi** clip down the Timeline until it lines up with the tail end of the **Clone_3.avi** clip above.

2. Right-click the **Clone_2.avi** clip, and from the contextual menu, choose **Fade > Fade Out Audio and Video**.

3. Right-click the **Clone_3.avi** clip, and from the contextual menu, choose **Fade > Fade Out Audio and Video**.

4. Press **Ctrl-S** to save your work.

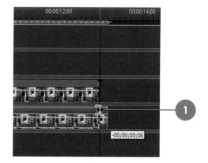

Both clips with the Fade Out added

16

Flying Solo: Adding Sound and Music

Once the visuals are complete, you need to add some sound effects and perhaps some spooky music. These techniques are ones you learned in previous chapters of this book, so Fly Solo now and complete this project before rendering it out in the final section of this chapter.

Add Some Sound Effects

1 Switch to the **Media** panel (*Hint: Edit tab; Project button*).

2 Move the **CTI** to the start of the Title 01 and Title 02 clips (*Hint: 00;00;05;10*).

3 Add the **234855_Waveringelectricsurge. wav** clip to the Narration track at the CTI point.

NOTE *In this case, one sound effect should be sufficient for all the lightning strikes seen on screen.*

4 Test and reposition the sound effect as necessary.

NOTE *In this case, the Sound effect is long enough for the on-screen visuals and it also fades out by itself, requiring no additional work from you.*

Add Some Music

1 Move the **CTI** to the very start of the Timeline.

2 Open the **SmartSound** interface (*Hint: Click the SmartSound button*).

3 Open the **SmartSound Maestro** box (*Hint: "Click here to select Music"*).

4 Select your choice of music (we suggest Futuristic; Subterfuge).

5 Alter the **Duration** and select the variation (*Hint: 00;13;15; Below*).

6 Click **OK** and save the file to your hard drive. Premiere Elements then adds the tune to the Soundtrack track.

NOTE *SmartSound automatically adds a musical flourish of the length you define to the end of tracks it creates, so often you do not need to add a fade out.*

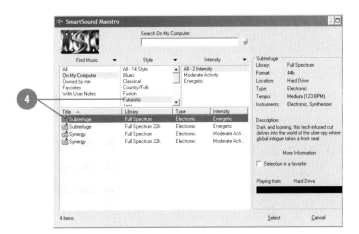

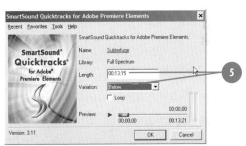

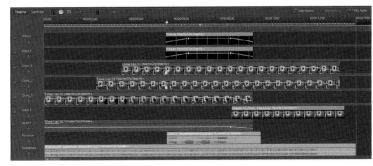

The finished Timeline. Impressive!

16

Acquiring and Using Sounds

Adding sounds to a project after you have completed filming in the phase known as *post production* (or simply *post*) is an important and often neglected part of assembling your final movie. Sound editing is a unique skill. Finding, creating, and adding sound effects is a unique skill *within* that skill known as *Foley work*, done by *Foley artists*.

In this chapter, you use sound effects to enhance the visual aspects of a visual effect you create, but the more traditional use of sounds is to enhance a film. For example, if you film a conversation between two people walking along a beach, you might deliberately mic the scene to clearly capture just their conversation and as little as possible of the background sounds. Later, you would want to add in, in a controlled way, the sounds of waves and seagulls, and so on.

Skillful editors are known for the way they weave sound into a scene, especially sounds in the distance such as church bells or a siren that you might not even be consciously aware of.

Finding Sounds

You can gather the sounds you need for your production in a number of ways. The simplest is to "film" the sounds with your camcorder at the scene. Just spend a few minutes before and after you have finished taking the video footage you need to capture additional footage for its sound value. Premiere Elements 7 lets you bring in (capture) footage as audio only.

As mentioned previously, if you are at the beach, capture some extra footage of the sound of the waves, children playing, dogs barking, and so on. You can use these audio clips to add in the background of your production later in your studio during post.

In addition to collecting these sounds, you can also create some of the sounds you need—such as a slamming door, glasses tinkling, car horns, and so on—by using your camcorder again and filming the sounds as they occur.

Sound Collections

Another source for sounds, besides creating them yourself, is prepackaged sound effect CDs. You'll find these at most CD stores as well as at online stores such as Tower Records, Amazon, and the like. These are typically inexpensive (around $10) and contain a wide variety of royalty-free clips.

You can find very good sound effects collections at your local library, as well. These tend to be theme-based, such as Halloween (horror) sounds, cartoon sounds, and the like. The sound effects in such collections might be copyrighted, so if you use them in any of your productions that are not just for personal use (other than for your own home movies, in other words), be sure to acknowledge the source.

Using Internet Sounds

Perhaps the best source for sound effects is the Internet. A quick search for "sound effects" brings up pages of sources. Among the more popular are AudioSparx (www.audiosparx.com), where we acquired the sound effects for this chapter.

On this site, you can search by category or keyword as well as listen to a sample of each sound. If you like what you hear, download the file to your hard drive. Some of these sites offer sound effects collections on CD or DVD, often with search software built in. If you like a company's product, consider buying a full set of their audio wares this way; then you will have it on hand without having to search the Internet.

Copyrights and Permissions

Again, as with any files you use in your productions that you didn't create yourself, verify that the sounds you use are, in fact, in the public domain (which means they are not protected by copyright and essentially belong to all of us) or be sure to get permission to use them from the owner/creator.

Rendering, Exporting, and Creating

Your final step in any project is to render and save. However, in this chapter you are going to render, save, and then combine two projects together (this one and the one from Chapter 4—Clone Attack titles). In this section, you render this project, create a brand new project, and add the AVI you created from Chapter 4 and the one from this chapter to the Timeline, adding an impressive previously- prepared titles sequence to this already impressive project.

Export the Project

1 Once you have played back your project and made the necessary adjustments, press **Enter** on your keyboard to render your project.

2 Once you have made all of these adjustments, press **Ctrl-S** to make a final save of your project.

3 Export your work as an AVI file. To export the clip, select **File > Export > Movie**, then browse to a local hard drive and the folder you created in Chapter 1 (**HSMovies_Final Renders**) and save the file as **Chapter 16_ Clone_Attack.avi**.

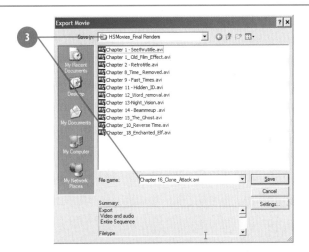

Join Two Projects Together

1 From the menu, choose **File > New > Project** and create a project called **Clone_Attack_With_Titles**.

2 Select the **Organize** tab and then click the **Get Media** button. From this panel, select **PC Files and Folders** as the device from which you are importing.

3 When the Add Media window appears, browse to the **HSMovies_Final Renders** folder and with the **Ctrl** key held down, click **Chapter 4 - Star Wars Title.avi** and **Chapter 16_ Clone_Attack.avi**.

4 Drag the **Chapter 4 - Star Wars Title.avi** clip to the Video 1 track on the Timeline, with the head of the clip at the start of the Timeline.

5 Drag the **Chapter 16_Clone_Attack.avi** clip to the Video 1 track on the Timeline, with the head of the clip at the tail of the previous clip on the Timeline.

6 Play back the project and enjoy. Add closing credits if you wish, then save the final version and export it as an AVI.

Did You Know?

Creating movies in this style (one project for the titles, another one for the action, and so on) avoids projects that have a single Timeline hours long! In fact most Timelines become unstable when they are very long and loaded down with effects, either audio or visual. A much better way to create a project is to divide it into scenes; each scene is a separate project. When you have completed all the scenes you need, assemble the rendered AVI files on a new Timeline as the complete movie. Render times are more bearable, the application is less prone to crashes, and making one tiny little change to a project is less likely to have a disastrously global effect to the Timeline! To summarize, work in units and stay tear-free before bedtime!

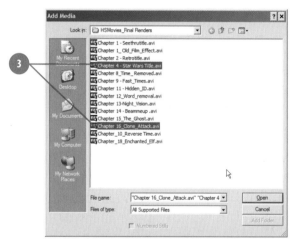

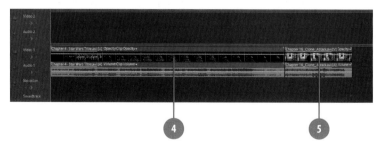

Hollywood Movie Effects:
Lighting Up Light Sabers

MEDIA:

Chapter_10_Reverse Time.avi
13905_Lasersaberbeingturnedon.wav
13902_Lasersaber.wav
Beam.bmp

17

COMPLEXITY:	Simple	Moderate	**Complex**
SKILL LEVEL:	Easy	**Intermediate**	Advanced

Introduction

In Chapter 3 you created a *Star Wars*-like opening title, in Chapter 10 you altered the flow of time to give your actor Jedi-like telekinesic powers to move objects, and then in Chapter 16 you created a mini-movie of dimension-hopping clones wielding lightning destruction, another well-known power of The Force. Therefore, this book can't let you go without giving you one last Jedi weapon: the Light Saber!

The Light Saber, first wielded to deadly effect by Alec Guinness in a Tatooine bar, is now the signature of the Jedi, and no self-respecting movie fan of *Star Wars* will get far without one, or preferably two, flashing swords of laser-zinging destruction.

In this chapter, you learn how to create the illusion of a Light Saber using an ordinary BMP image file and the Corner Pin effect. Now read on, young Jedi; your journey is almost complete, but if you lose your way, remember to use the hints…. Use the hints, Luke…. Use the hints….

What You'll Learn

Flying Solo: Preparing the Project

Flying Solo: Adding the Beam.bmp Clip, then the Corner Pin Effect

Keyframing the Light Saber

Adding Some Polish to the Beam

Fading the Saber In and Out

Adding Sound FX to the Saber

Making Adjustments, Rendering, and Exporting

Flying Solo:
Preparing the Project

Despite the revered nature of creating this holiest of holy *Star Wars* effects, the first steps are the same basic steps you use for virtually all of the projects in this book. However, because this book demonstrates two variations of creating the Light Saber effect, you have two Project preparations to go through; the first, which you perform now, is simply to load the AVI you created in Chapter 10 and the second where you make some track and Timeline adjustments. Fly Solo now and complete the following tasks. Hints and tips are listed to help you out, but if you get really lost, take a peek back at the Chapter 1 section "Preparing the Project" for more detailed instructions.

Start a Project, Customize the Timeline, and Import Some Media

1. Start **Premiere Elements** and create a new project called **Chapter_17_Light_Saber_1**.

2. Deselect the audio tracks 2 and 3 (*Hint: right-click Track Header; deselect Show Audio Tracks*).

3. Rename tracks 1 and 2 to the following (*Hint: right-click the track name; select Rename*):

   ◆ Video 1: **Movie**

   ◆ Video 2: **Saber**

4. From the DVD that came with the book, import the following media clips: **13905_ Lasersaberbeingturnedon.wav**, **13902_Lasersaber.wav**, and **Beam.bmp** (*Hint: Get Media; DVD [Camcorder or PC DVD Drive] button; Advanced button; select DVD drive; select Show Audio or press Ctrl-U; UnCheck All; Check files that you need!*).

5. From your hard drive, import the AVI you created in Chapter 10: **Chapter_10_Reverse Time.avi** (*Hint: Get Media; PC Files and Folders; HSMovies_Final Renders folder*).

   TIP *If you have not completed the exercises in Chapter 10, you can also find a version of the* **Chapter_10_Reverse Time.avi** *on the DVD.*

6. Add the **Chapter_10_Reverse Time.avi** clip to the Movie track on the Timeline.

7. Use **Ctrl-S** to save your work so far.

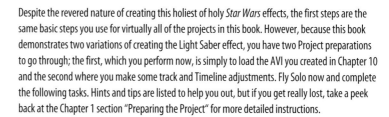

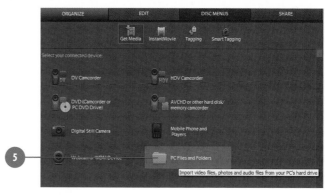

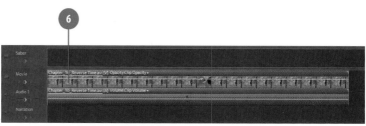

Flying Solo: Adding the Beam.bmp Clip, then the Corner Pin Effect

In this section you add the **Beam.bmp** clip to the Timeline and then place the Corner Pin effect on the clip. This is something you should be more than capable of, so Fly Solo now to complete this part of the chapter.

Add the Beam.bmp Clip to the Timeline

1. Move the **CTI** to where the Jedi closes his hands around the sword handle (*Hint: 00;00;10;08*).

   TIP *You may find it easier to place a marker at each "key" CTI location, such as 00;00;10;08, by pressing the Asterisk key on the keyboard numberpad when the CTI is in the correct place.*

2. If it is not already open, switch to the **Media** panel (*Hint: Edit tab; Project button*).

3. Drag the **Beam.bmp** clip to the Saber track at the CTI point. If you see the Videomerge box, click **No** because you do not use that effect in this chapter.

Add the Corner Pin Effect to the Beam.bmp Clip

1. Open the **Effects** panel and locate the Corner Pin effect (*Hint: Edit tab; Effects button; type corner*).

2. Drag the **Corner Pin** effect onto the **Beam.bmp** clip.

3. Extend the **Beam.bmp** clip to the length of the AVI underneath.

4. Press **Ctrl-S** to save your work so far.

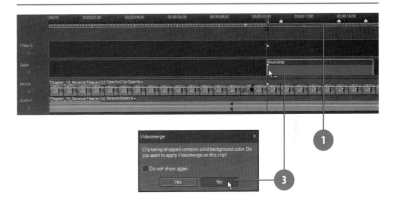

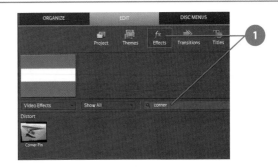

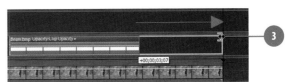

17

Keyframing the Light Saber

You now keyframe the Corner Pin effect to re-create the illusion of the **Beam.bmp** launching from the handle as the Light Saber activates. You then keyframe the **Beam.bmp** to the movement the actor makes with the handle of the saber.

Create a Saber Activating

1 Send the **CTI** to the start of the **Beam.bmp** clip by pressing **Page Up** or **Page Down** on the keyboard.

2 Click the **Beam.bmp** clip once to select it.

3 If it is not already open, click the **Properties** button to open the Properties view and click the triangle to open the Corner Pin controls.

4 Toggle the keyframes area open using the **Show Keyframes** button.

5 Click the **Corner Pin** name bar to show the four points of the Corner Pin effect in the Monitor panel.

6 Move the top right and bottom right points to the top of the Light Saber handle.

> **TIP** *You may want to zoom in on the Monitor panel by right-clicking inside the Monitor panel and selecting **Magnification > 400%** from the contextual menu; then use the scroll bars to read the area you need to see.*

7 Move the top-left and bottom-left **Corner Pin** points so that they are directly above the handle, creating a beam of light extending upward from the handle to just above the actor's head.

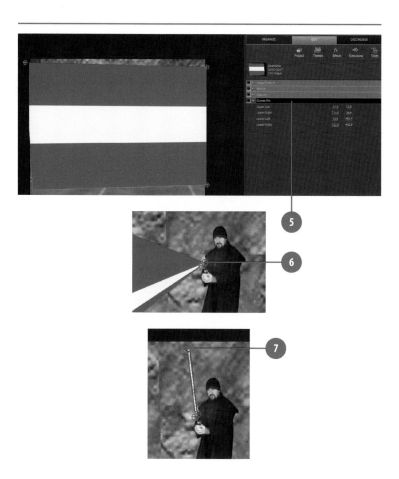

8 Move the **CTI** forward to 00;00;08;07.

9 Toggle animation on for the Corner Pin effect to create keyframes at this point.

10 Finally, use **Page Up** to send the CTI to the head of the **Beam.bmp** clip, and then move the top two Corner Pin points downward to sit on top of the bottom two points.

NOTE *Premiere Elements creates new keyframes at the opening point, and when you play back this clip, the light beam launches out of the handle.*

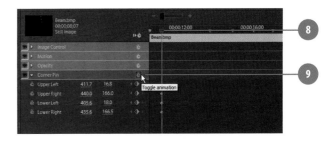

17

Follow the Movement of the Saber to the Left

1 Select the **Beam.bmp** clip and highlight the Corner Pin effect name bar, with the four Corner Pin points showing in the Monitor panel.

2 Move the **CTI** forward five frames.

3 Alter the bottom two points of the Corner Pin effect so that they line up again with the sword handle.

4 Alter the top two points of the Corner Pin effect so that they are directly over the handle, but at an angle, as shown in the screenshot.

TIP *Try to make sure the length of the beam doesn't deviate from the starting position. Also, try to drag the points in straight lines because this can affect the way keyframes play back. If your keyframes become too entangled, then it may be best to delete some and start again.*

5 Repeat Steps 2 to 4, moving the CTI five frames forward each time and creating new positions for the Corner Pin effect until you have reached the end of the **Chapter_10_ Reverse Time.avi** clip.

TIP *To create a flare or fan smear movement for the laser, make sure the top clips are slightly further apart while the sword handle is moving, and only bring them together when the sword handle is no longer moving.*

Adjust the top two Corner Pin points to show a flare as the laser moves from point to point.

Closing Down the Sword

1 The last movement of the sword handle should be around 00;00;17;05. At this point, close down the laser sword.

2 Move the **CTI** 10 or 15 frames beyond this point.

3 Pull down the two upper **Corner Pin** points until they cover the two lower Corner Pin points.

Did you know?

The more keyframing you do, the better the effect looks. However, you don't need to add a keyframe to each of the four Corner Pin points for each frame of the movie. Premiere Elements can calculate where the keyframe was and where it needs to be and work out, in most cases, where the rest of the keyframes need to be. Sometimes you need to do a little bit of tweaking, but if you have a massive Timeline with a massive Light Saber fight going on, you need to be aware that keyframes eat up memory and rendering time, and sooner or later you will run out of one and get an error with the other.

17

Adding Some Polish to the Beam

As it stands, this is a pretty cool-looking effect, but there is room for improvement. In this section, you add the Gaussian blur to diffuse the edges of the beam and then add the Alpha Glow effect to give your saber a truly dangerous Jedi look.

Add Effects to the Beam.bmp Clip

1 Make sure **Beam.bmp** clip is selected and that the CTI is somewhere that displays the full beam.

2 Open the **Effects** panel by clicking the **Effects** button, then type **blur** into the text field to reveal all the blur effects available to you.

3 Drag the **Gaussian Blur** onto the **Beam.bmp** clip.

4 If it is not already open, click the **Properties** button to open the Properties view and click the triangle to open the opacity controls.

5 Reduce the amount of blur to 5%.

6 Repeat Step 2, but this time enter **glow** in the text field.

7 Drag the Alpha Glow effect to the **Beam.bmp** clip.

8 Alter the **Glow** to around 13 and the **Brightness** to 111. Leave the Start Color as is, but change the end color to a shade similar to the outer color of your saber beam (in this case, light blue) and place a check in the Use End Color box.

NOTE *The Alpha Glow effect won't show up until you move the CTI up and down the clip.*

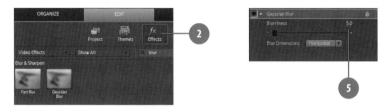

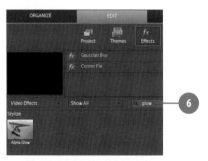

The laser beam with fan movement showing and Gaussian Blur and Alpha Glow effects added

Fading the Saber
In and Out

Once again, to finish off this effect, you need to add opacity fade in at the start of the effect to tidy it up. Once you've done that, you can push on to the end of this chapter where you add Sound FX and music to the movie.

Add Fades to the Beam.bmp Clip

1. Make sure the **Beam.bmp** clip is selected and that the CTI is at the very start of this clip.

2. Zoom right in on the **Timeline** to see the first few frames of the Title 01 clip.

3. If it is not already open, click the **Properties** button to open the Properties view and click the triangle to open the opacity controls.

4. Turn **Toggle Animation** on for Opacity.

5. Reduce the **Opacity** to 0%.

6. Move the **CTI** five frames into the clip by pressing the **right arrow** on the keyboard five times and increasing **Clip Opacity** to 100%.

7. Move the **CTI** to the very last frame of the clip and reduce **Clip Opacity** to 0.0%.

8. Move the **CTI** five frames backward and increase **Clip Opacity** to 100%.

> **NOTE** *Premiere Elements creates a new keyframe for you at this point.*

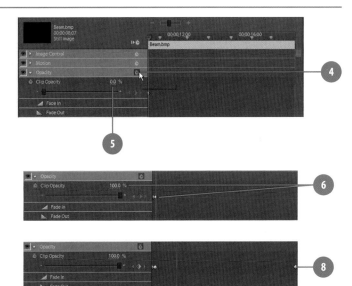

17

Adding Sound FX to the Saber

What's a Light Saber without one of the most famous sound effects in science fiction history? Very little. In this section you add a number of sound effects to the laser: one to launch it, another for the background hum, and a number of others to give the audio indication that the laser is moving through the air.

Add Light Saber Sound Effects

1 Select the **Beam.bmp** clip and move the CTI to the very start of this clip.

2 Drag the **13905_Lasersaberbeingturnedon.wav** to the Narration track, and make sure the head of the sound effect is level with the head of the **Beam.bmp** clip.

3 Drag the **13902_Lasersaber.wav** so it falls directly after the previous sound file, but hold down the **Ctrl** key while dragging to avoid all your other clips jumping out of order.

4 This sound file isn't long enough to cover all movement of the Light Saber, so right-click the **13902_Lasersaber.wav** clip and select **Time Stretch** from the contextual menu.

5 Change the **Speed** to 50.00% (to double the length of the sound file) and place a check in the **Maintain Audio Pitch** box to prevent the tone of the sound file from changing when the speed is altered.

6 Click this altered **13902_Lasersaber.wav** clip and press **Ctrl-C** on the keyboard, then move the **CTI** to the end of the clip and press **Ctrl-V** on the keyboard to create a copy of the clip.

7 Move the **CTI** to the end of this new sound clip, and press **Ctrl-V** again to create a third version of this sound file on the Timeline, then repeat this to create a fourth and final version of this sound file.

8 Play back the Timeline and make any adjustments you think you need to make.

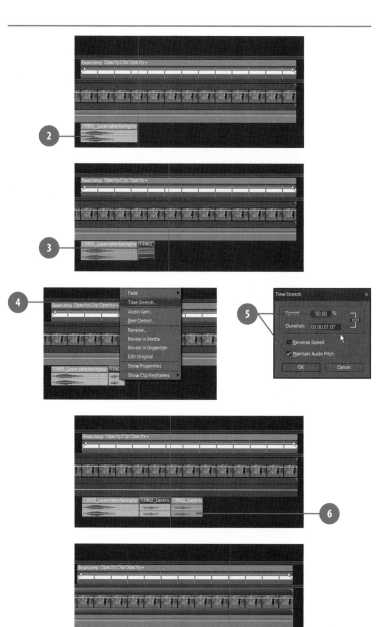

Create a Closing Saber Sound Effect

1. Return to the media panel and double-click **13905_Lasersaberbeingturnedon.wav** to open it in the Preview window.

2. Reduce the overall length of the clip to about 00;00;01;00 by dragging the Set Out marker to the left.

3. Close the Preview window, then drag (with the **Ctrl** key held down) the **13905_Lasersaberbeingturnedon.wav** from the Media view to the Narration track so the clip appears directly after the last sound file in the row.

4. Right-click the clip and select **Time Stretch** from the contextual menu.

5. When the Time Stretch box appears, leave all the settings as they are, but place a check in the **Reverse Speed** box.

NOTE *Use the opening sound in reverse to create a closing sound for the saber. This is a classic video editing trick that allows you to create two sound effects for the price of one.*

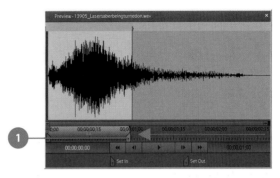

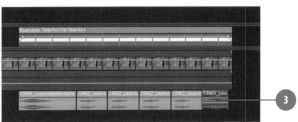

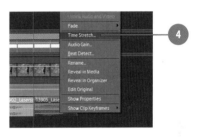

Did you know?

We downloaded all the Light Saber effects you use in this exercise from www. AudioSparx.com. AudioSparx has an almost inexhaustible supply of sound effects just like these, all of which are available for a few dollars.

17

Making Adjustments, Rendering, and Exporting

Well, you've done it! That was a lot of keyframing, but the end result should be something you are pleased with. If not, then return to the project and do some fine-tuning. Listen closely to those sound effects. Work, work, work. Detail sells this effect, so the more effort you put in, the better the effect looks. Once you are happy, render and export your project.

Finish the Project

1 Once you have played back your project and made the necessary adjustments, press **Enter** on your keyboard to render your project.

2 Once you have made all of these adjustments, press **Ctrl-S** to make a final save of your project.

3 Finally, export your work as an AVI file. To export the clip, select **File > Export > Movie,** then browse to a local hard drive and save in the **HSMovies_Final Renders** folder you created in chapter 1. Save the file as **Chapter_17_Light_Saber.avi**.

TIP *This final render may be used again in Chapter 21, as will many of your other final renders from the exercises in this book.*

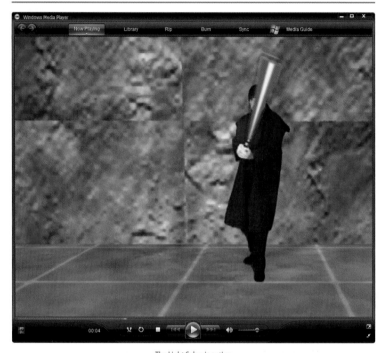

The Light Saber in action

Hollywood Movie Green Screen Techniques: The Enchanted Elf Effect

MEDIA:
elf.avi
elfgarden.bmp
elfish_song.wav

18

COMPLEXITY:	Simple	Moderate	Complex
SKILL LEVEL:	Easy	Intermediate	Advanced

Introduction

It's a magical, mysterious world out there: Harry Potter is flying on a turbo broomstick; Gandalf and Frodo are going to extremes for a supernatural ring; and the children of the wardrobe are sacrificing everything for Narnia. All around us there seem to be more dwarfs, giants, fairies, and elves than we can shake a staff at. In this chapter, you jump on board the gilded bandwagon as it rolls magically past by creating your own little magic. Here, you fashion out of thin air, or so it seems, an enchanting little elf who is ready to charm or annoy (depending on how you feel about elves).

Although you can use stage makeup, props, CGI animation, and special effects software to create this effect, who has that kind of time and money? More importantly, it's not necessary. Premiere Elements 7 gives you all the tools you need to create this effect. The Enchanted Elf effect looks at various green screen techniques that can be handled by Premiere Elements, and once you have these under your belt you can use them for lots of different projects in many different ways.

This chapter introduces you to the shrinking power of Premiere Elements. Using this technique, you can shrink anything—your dog, your house, your friends—and feature them as elves or fairies, or in miniature *Honey, I Shrunk the Kids* situations. Second, this chapter introduces you to Premiere Elements' color-changing abilities. You change a child with normal coloring into a green elf. Again, using this technique, you can change anyone or anything—again, perhaps your dog or cat—to any color you want: orange, red, blue, purple.

This chapter also uses a technique we introduced earlier in this book: the split screen. Here, you use the split screen to create a multidimensional background for the elf to interact with. You only create a single split in this project, but in your own projects you can create multiple splits to allow your character to move in front of and behind objects in the background. This is a sophisticated technique that, with a little planning, is relatively easy to pull off.

What You'll Learn

Flying Solo: Preparing the Project

Using Videomerge on a Green Screen Clip

Appling Color and Contrast Effects to the Elf Clip

Adjusting the Videomerge Effect

Colorizing the Elf

Adding the Foreground Clip

Creating a Multidimensional Environment with the Garbage Matte Effect

Shrinking and Adjusting the Elf's Starting Location

Making the Elf Vanish

Flying Solo: Adding and Mixing Some Playful Elfish Music

Making Adjustments, Rendering, and Exporting

Flying Solo:
Preparing the Project

Setting up a project should be easy enough for you now, so Fly Solo to put down the foundations for this cool-looking project. For this movie, you need two media clips, **elf.avi** and a still backdrop, **elfgarden.bmp**. In this section, you set up the Timeline, rename the tracks, and add the **eflgarden.bmp** background to the Timeline.

Prepare the Project

1 Start **Premiere Elements** and create a new project called **Chapter_18_Enchanted_Elf**.

2 The Timeline should be set to Timeline view (*Hint: Timeline button to the left of the interface*).

> **NOTE** *You need to switch to **Timeline** because you will be working with multiple clips on multiple video tracks.*

3 Deselect the audio tracks for Video 2 and 3 (*Hint: deselect Show Audio Tracks*).

4 Rename (*Hint: right-click the header*) and change each track to the following:

- ◆ Video 1: **Background**
- ◆ Video 2: **Elf**
- ◆ Video 3: **Foreground**

5 Import the **elfgarden.bmp**, **elf.avi**, and **elfish_song.wav** media clips from the DVD (*Hint: Media Downloader; Show Audio; Uncheck All*).

> **TIP** *You can find complete instructions for grabbing media into Premiere Elements 7 in the Chapter 1 section "Adding Media to Your Project." Don't forget you need to uncheck all before you make your selection!*

> **NOTE** *The default settings of the Media Downloader are set not to show Audio media clips. To see any Audio media clips, you need to click the **Show Audio** button or press **Ctrl-U** on the keyboard while the Media Downloader is open. Watch out, Media Downloader rechecks all the files when you do this and you need to uncheck them all again!*

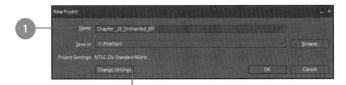

Make sure you set the project settings to NTSC-DV-Standard 48kHz when you're using files from the book's DVD.

Filming Tips

Creating the backdrop for this particular project can be as simple as taking a well-lit photograph. Creating the green screen footage, however, can be anything but simple. The main worry here is correct lighting. Ideally, it should be evenly spread over the green screen with the actor casting as few shadows as possible. Look out for wrinkles in the green screen; these can cast shadows and illuminated spots caused by something behind the green screen (perhaps a window) shining through the material.

Once you have this all sorted out, which may take a looooong time, make sure you mount the camera on a tripod to ensure the correct framing of the shot all the way through the shoot.

Run through the session a couple of times with the actor and don't forget the golden rule: always film your rehearsals just in case one of them turns out to be the best take! Videotape is cheap these days, and keeping the camera running is a much easier way to ensure that you get the footage you need.

6 Switch to the **Edit** workspace (*Hint: Edit tab*).

7 Drag the **elfgarden.bmp** clip to the Background track.

> **IMPORTANT** *Be sure to line up the head (start) of both media clips with the front of the Background track.*

8 Zoom the Timeline using the zoom slider to expand your view of the Media clip on the Timeline.

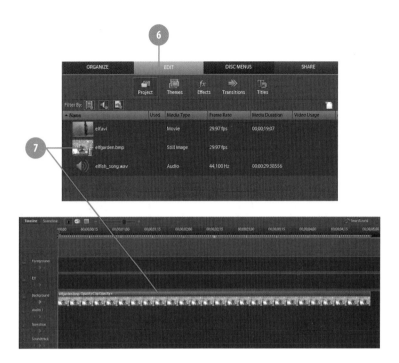

Using Videomerge on a Green Screen Clip

One of the cool new features of Premiere Elements 7 is Videomerge, which automatically detects if a media clip has a solid background color. It then attempts to "key-out" that solid color (in this case green) revealing the background on the lower track. Essentially, this is a one-stop shop for simple green screen keys. In this section, you add the **elf.avi** clip to the Timeline and apply the Videomerge effect.

Add the Elf Clip and Apply the Videomerge Effect

1. If it is not already open, click the **Edit** tab to switch to the Edit workspace and click the **Project** button to display the Media panel.

2. Drag the **elf.avi** clip to the head of the Elf track so the clip is at the very beginning of the track, as shown in the illustration.

3. Once you drop the **elf.avi** clip onto the Timeline, you see this message: "Clip being dropped contains solid background color. Do you want to apply Videomerge on this clip?" Click **Yes** to apply this effect. The green background should now be removed using just the Videomerge's default settings.

   NOTE *Removing the green background from green screen (or indeed blue screen) material is called creating a "clean key." In this case the key is not totally "clean," but you will tune it up later in this chapter.*

4. Finally, drag out the **elfgarden.bmp** clip until it is the same length as the **elf.avi** clip.

5. Press **Ctrl-S** to save your work so far.

The instant result of using Videomerge. In this case, not a bad key.

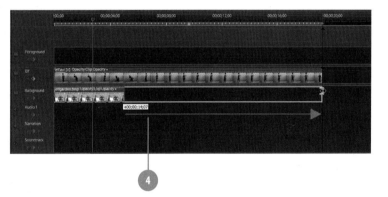

18

Applying Color and Contrast Effects to the Elf Clip

A best practice when working with green screen clips is to apply the **Auto Color** and **Auto Contrast** effects. This helps even out the colors and contrasts in the clip, allowing the Videomerge effect to successfully remove all of the green background. Premiere Elements' Auto Color and Auto Contrast effects make the colors in the clip richer and more vibrant, thus enhancing the green background as well.

Apply the Auto Color and Auto Contrast Effects

1 If it is not already open, click the **Edit** tab to switch to the Edit workspace and click the **Effects** button to switch to the Effects panel.

2 In the text box on the **Effects** portion of the Media panel, type **auto**.

3 Select the **Auto Color** effect and drag it onto the **elf.avi** clip on the Elf track.

4 Leave the **Auto Color** settings at the defaults.

5 Select the **Auto Contrast** effect and drag it onto the **elf.avi** clip on the Elf track.

6 Leave the **Auto Contrast** settings at the defaults.

TIP *You can find more advice on troubleshooting the removal of a green screen background in Chapter 10.*

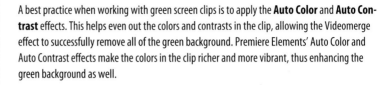

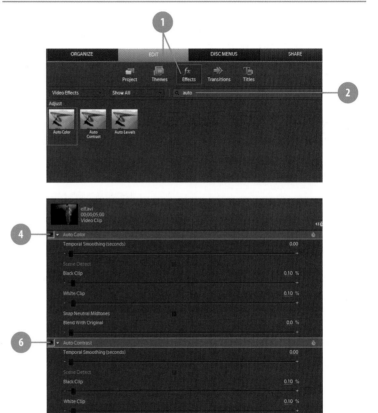

Did You Know?

It's a study in contrasts. When you are using a green or blue screen effect in your future projects, apply the **Auto Color** and **Auto Contrast** effects, play with the effects' controls, and see what you come up with. Click the effect's toggle (the **eyeball**, shown at the left) to see what the clip looks like with the effect turned on and off. Although brightening a clip and increasing the color saturation and contrast can improve how a clip responds to keying out the background, "results may vary," as they say on the infomercials. So, try the effect and if you like it, keep it. If you don't or aren't sure, click the **eyeball** off and leave it turned off. Remember, video editing is both a science and an art, and it sometimes takes experimentation to get just the look you want.

Before...

...and after adding the Auto Color and Auto Contrast effects

18

Adjusting the Videomerge Effect

Now that you've adjusted the clip for color and contrast, you can try tweaking the Videomerge effect a little more to try and get an even cleaner key. Here are settings that are optimal, but play around with them until you are happy. It's your project after all.

Fine-Tuning Videomerge

1. Click the **Properties** button to open the Properties view, and then dial down the **Videomerge** effect controls by clicking the triangle.

2. Adjust the effect as follows:

   ◆ Presets: **Detailed**

   ◆ Tolerance: **0.57**

   ◆ Invert Selection: **Unchecked**

Colorizing the Elf

You now need to change the elf so that she is elfin leaf green. Otherwise, she does not appear to be real. Ironically, after all the trouble you took to remove every last pixel of green from the **elf.avi** clip, here you go making the whole thing green after all! After you've applied the **Tint** effect, use the two color swatches and eyedroppers in the **Properties** view, mapping the green tint to the Map White channel.

Apply the Tint Effect

1 If it is not already open, click the **Edit** tab to switch to the Edit workspace and click the **Effects** button to switch to the Effects panel.

2 In the text box type **tint**.

3 Select the **Tint** effect and drag it onto the **elf.avi** clip on the Elf Movie track.

4 Click the **Properties** button to open the Properties view, and then dial down the **Tint** effect controls by clicking the triangle.

5 Click the **Map White To** color swatch (leave the black as is, that is, the black should stay mapped to black).

6 The **Color Picker** dialog displays. In the very bottom box, enter the following value: **55FF00**.

7 Set the **Amount To Tint** to 50.0%.

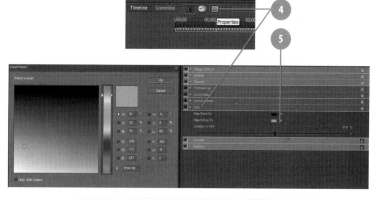

18

Adding the Foreground Clip

You are going to reuse the Background clip as a foreground clip to trick the viewer's eye into thinking the elf is really in the world by making it seem as though she is moving among the objects. You do this by adding the Background clip to the Foreground track and then cropping it to create the illusion you want.

Use the Background Clip Again, but Now as a Foreground Clip

① If it is not already open, click the **Edit** tab to switch to the Edit workspace and click the **Project** button to switch to the Media panel.

② Once again, select the **elfgarden.bmp** clip in the Media panel and drag it onto the Timeline, this time onto the Foreground track. Be sure that you drop it so the head (front) of the clip is at the very beginning of the track.

③ Adjust the length of the **elfgarden.bmp** clip on the Foreground track so that it matches the duration of the **elf.avi** clip.

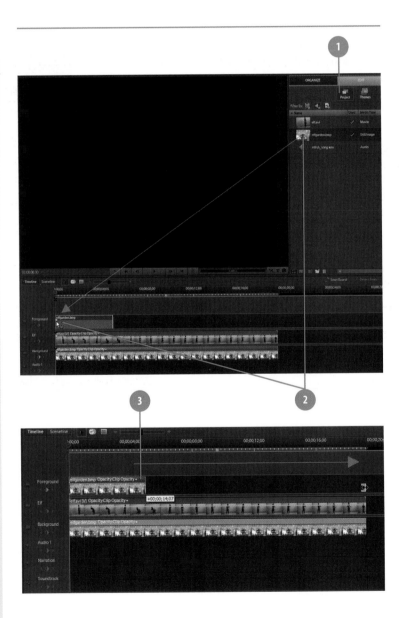

Creating a Multidimensional Environment with the Garbage Matte Effect

Premiere Elements can work with multiple video tracks (up to 99 tracks, should you need them), allowing you to create layer upon layer of backgrounds or images. Here, you use another copy of the background image and remove everything but the watering can to make the watering can appear to be in the foreground. If you want, you can add another track above (**Video 4**) and crop it so the bonsai plant can be, effectively, another object in the scene.

Use the Garbage Matte Effect to Create an Illusion of a Foreground

1. If it is not already open, click the **Edit** tab to switch to the Edit workspace and click the **Effects** button to switch to the Effects panel.

2. In the text box on the Effects panel, type **garbage**.

3. Select the **Eight-Point Garbage Matte** effect and drag it onto the **elfgarden.bmp** clip on the Foreground track on the Timeline.

4. Click the **Properties** button to open the Properties view, and then click the **Eight-Point Garbage Matte** effect so that it highlights the name text. Eight handles appear around the **elfgarden.bmp** clip in the Monitor panel.

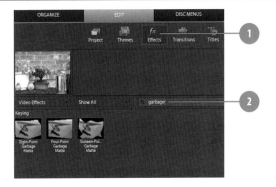

18

5 If you cannot see all the handles, right-click inside the Monitor panel and select **Magnification > 100%** (or lower).

6 Select the handles one by one and move them to surround the watering can as shown in the illustration.

NOTE *The more points your garbage matte uses, the more accurate a mask is created and the better the illusion. However, more points take much longer to set up.*

5

Did You Know?

You can create as many layers as you want. Here's how creative you can get with this: Film your elf standing on a chair, peeking about. Then have her jump off, run around a bit, and exit. In post, you can hide the chair behind the plant. As a result, the elf appears to jump down from the plant. When the elf exits, she appears to run between the bonsai plant and the watering can.

6

The foreground watering can masked using the Eight-Point Garbage Mattte

Shrinking and Adjusting the Elf's Starting Location

In this task, you shrink the elf down to elf size. This simple procedure in Premiere Elements 7 uses the scale setting in the Motion effect (an effect that all clips have by default). You reposition the elf in the Monitor panel so that the small green creature appears to peek out from behind the watering can. You will not believe how effective you can be with this illusion, even when you create it on your home computer!

Shrink the Elf Down to Elf Proportions

1. Click the **elf.avi** clip on the Elf track to select it.

2. Click the **Properties** button to open the Properties view, and then open the **Motion** effect settings by clicking the triangle.

3. Drag the scale slider to the left and stop at about 40%.

   TIP *In the next task, you hide the elf behind the watering can, so eyeball the relative size of the elf as you shrink her. You want the elf to be slightly smaller than the base of the watering can.*

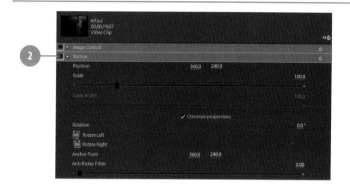

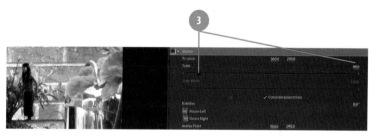

Move the Elf to Add Believability to Her Hiding Place

1. Move the **CTI** to the start of the Timeline.

2. Make sure the **elf.avi** clip is still selected, and in the Properties view for the clip, make sure Motion is still selected.

   TIP *A box appears around the **elf.avi** clip in the Monitor panel, enabling you to drag it across the screen.*

3. With your mouse, click anywhere inside the box on the Monitor panel and drag the **elf.avi** clip until the elf appears hidden behind the watering can. An ideal starting location shows these settings in the Position parameters: **514–385**.

The **elf.avi** dragged down and to the left, just behind the Eight-Point Garbage Matte around the watering can. The elf now has the illusion of peeking around the corner.

Did You Know?

It's a piece of cake to add more layers.
Because you can have up to 99 video tracks in a Premiere Elements project, you can use the techniques you learn in this chapter to create additional layers. For example, you can add a flowerpot in front so that the elf can run from her hiding place behind the watering can to a new hiding place behind the pot. You can also create objects in the elf's environment that the elf can either pick up or push aside using the same technique, or you can film the object first against a green screen. Have the actor (in this case, the Elf) act out by lifting the object or pushing it. Then, in post, place the object in the right position and use keyframes to make it appear as if the Elf affects the object. As with most of the concepts introduced in this book, how far you take this one is limited only by your imagination.

Making the Elf Vanish

In the clip, **elf.avi**, the actor playing the elf is surprised by the sound of approaching humans and so she decides to vanish. Because she has elfin powers, all she needs to do is snap her fingers and she's gone. The clip, **elf.avi**, ends when the elf snaps her fingers. To make it appear as if she's suddenly disappeared, all you need to do is keep the background on screen for a few seconds longer, and then fade it to black.

Adjust the Ending Points

1. With your mouse, grab the tail end of the **elfgarden.bmp** clip in the Background track and drag it out a few seconds more so that it's longer than the **elf.avi** clip in the Elf Movie track.

   NOTE *The **elfgarden.bmp** clip on the Background track should now be about 21 seconds and 6 frames long (00;00;21;06).*

2. Right-click the **elfgarden.bmp** clip on the Background track and select **Fade > Fade Out Video** from the contextual menu.

3. Move the **CTI** to 00;00;18;03.

4. Click once on the **elf.avi** clip to select it.

5. Click the **Split Clip** button or press **Ctrl-K** to split the clip at this point.

6. Delete the right-hand section of the **elf.avi** clip. This creates the illusion of the elf vanishing immediately after she snaps her fingers.

   TIP *Listen carefully for the finger snap and position the CTI at that point before you trim the **elf.avi** clip.*

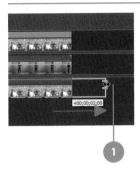

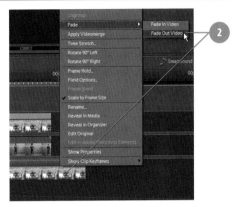

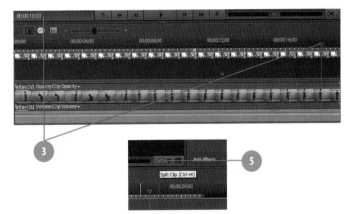

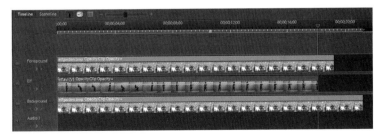

This is how your Timeline should look at the end of this exercise.

18

Flying Solo:
Adding and Mixing Some
Playful Elfish Music

This goes without saying, but you can't create a video clip that features an elf without having a bit of elfish music playing in the background. In video editing, music that plays softly in the background plays "under" (as in "under" the visual aspects of the movie). On the DVD we supply with this book, there is a bit of elf music, **elfish_song.wav** (generated by SmartSound Quicktracks: Synergy; Emergent). Fly Solo now and add this music to your movie, then reduce the volume a little before you finish it off with a fade out.

Add the Music to the Project and Adjust the Audio on the Elf Clip

1 Switch to the **Edit** workspace (*Hint: Edit tab*).

2 Add the **elfish_song.wav** clip to the Soundtrack track so that the front of the clip is at the front of the track.

3 Trim the **elfish_song.wav** clip to be the same size as the **elfgarden.bmp** clip on the Foreground track.

4 Open the **Properties** view and dial open the volume controls.

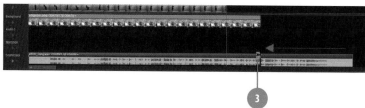

5 Set the **Clip Volume** to -12.0 dB.

IMPORTANT *By default, the Volume property already has its Animation Toggle turned on, so you get keyframes when you change volume here. Your options for reducing the audio level of the entire clip are to either turn off the Animation Toggle first or use the Audio Mixer while the video is not playing.*

6 Add a **Fade Out**.

TIP *Rather than use the MP3 on the DVD, why not create your own SmartSound track (Synergy; Emergent) for the exact length of the Timeline. This has the advantage of having its own natural fade at the end of the movie.*

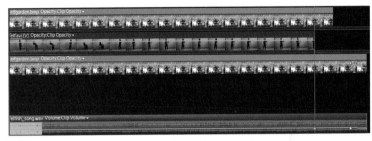

The finished Timeline complete with all fades

Making Adjustments, Rendering, and Exporting

You're now ready to render all of your effects, save your project one more time, and create your output file. Before you do, you might want to play the clip (press the **spacebar** on your keyboard or click the **Play** button on the Monitor panel) to see how it looks. If you need to, make any final tweaks. For example, you might need to slightly adjust the point at which the elf vanishes. Then, you are ready to save, render, and make your movie.

Finish the Project

1. Once you have played back your project and made the necessary adjustments, press **Enter** on your keyboard to render your project.

2. Once you have made all of your final adjustments, press **Ctrl-S** on the keyboard to save your project.

3. Finally, export your work as an AVI file. To export the clip, select **File > Export > Movie**, then browse to a local hard drive and to the **HSMovies_Final Renders** folder you created in Chapter 1, and save the file as **Chapter_18_Enchanted_Elf.avi**.

   TIP *If Export is grayed out, check that the Timeline is selected.*

   NOTE *This final render will be used again in Chapter 21, as will many of your other final renders from the exercises in this book.*

The finished project running in Windows Media Player. Notice the elf's size, color, and the illusion that she's hiding behind the watering can.

Hollywood Movie Green Screen Techniques: The Nightly News Effect

MEDIA:

144_Background1.mov
144_Lowerthird2.mov
anchor.avi
hawaii.avi
Hawaii_reporter.avi

19

COMPLEXITY:	Simple	Moderate	Complex
SKILL LEVEL:	Easy	Intermediate	Advanced

What You'll Learn

Flying Solo: Preparing the Project

Flying Solo: Creating the TV News Background Text

Adding the Anchorman

Resizing and Moving the Anchorman

Adding the Lower-Third Graphic

Adding Lower-Third Text for the Anchorman

Flying Solo: Creating the Hawaii Reporter Scene

Adding a Cross Dissolve to End the News Feature Report

Flying Solo: Adding a Little Music

Flying Solo: Mixing the Music Levels

Making Adjustments, Rendering, and Exporting

Introduction

The Nightly News effect takes advantage of the incredible resources available today to give anyone's "basement tapes" the look and feel of a professional studio production. It seems as if the entire world is uploading their videos to One True Media, Mydeo, YouTube, and even the Current cable network, and we are all evolving into better videographers and video editors simply by being exposed to others' videos. We are getting better, too, because we are all, to some degree, creating more small video clips than ever before. And why not? The world is watching! Now back to our main story…

By using the Green Screen Key in Premiere Elements 7, you can remove, or *key out*, the green background behind the actor to reveal any location that you choose. Although the location in the background can be a still photograph, especially in cases where the actor is standing in front of a building or monument, using video clips adds to the realism. One factor to consider is the lighting. If the light on your actor appears to be coming from the east, and the light in the background clip is coming from the west, it looks strange, especially if shadows are noticeable. In this chapter, you learn how to use Premiere Elements to brighten your reporter and help match the actor to the Background clip.

Overlays, lower thirds, and what are variously referred to as "backdrops," "motion loops," or "motion backgrounds" are available from a variety of sources across the Web. Not only do these look professional, they are professional. The exact same broadcast-quality backgrounds, overlays, and lower thirds that you can use in your productions are being used by *Entertainment Tonight*- and ESPN-type shows nationwide.

The Nightly News effect is a great effect for having fun with kids who want to create a news broadcast—from developing the stories, to creating a basic set (chair, table, paper, and pen), to "broadcasting" the finished news program on your television. Students can also use the techniques learned here for school television broadcasts or they can incorporate them into school projects.

Flying Solo: Preparing the Project

By now, the first step in this project must be frighteningly familiar. You need to begin a project, name the tracks, and import your media clips; in this case, you need the **anchor.avi** and **Hawaii_reporter.avi** clips, as well as the background and foreground graphics clips, **144_Background1.mov** and **144_Lowerthird2.mov**. In Chapter 1, you learned the necessary techniques to perform all these tasks, so Fly Solo now and see how much you can remember. Hints and tips are listed to help you out, but if you get really lost, take a peek back at the Chapter 1 section "Preparing the Project" for more.

Start a Project, Customize the Timeline, and Import the Media

1 Start **Premiere Elements** and create a **New Project** called **Chapter 19_Nightly News** (*Hint: use the New Project button at the splash screen or File >New >Project if Premiere Elements is already open; save in the Peachpit folder you created in Chapter 1*).

NOTE *The sample files supplied on the DVD are for use on an NTSC Timeline. If your default Project Settings are not NTSC, change them now by clicking the **Change Settings** button and selecting **NTSC > DV > Standard 48kHz**.*

2 If the Timeline is set to Sceneline, switch to the **Timeline** (*Hint: Timeline button!*).

NOTE *You need to switch to **Timeline** because for this project, you are working with multiple clips on multiple video tracks.*

3 Add one video track to the Timeline (*Hint: right-click Track Header; select Add Tracks*).

4 Deselect the audio tracks 2 and 3 (*Hint: right-click Track Header; deselect Show Audio Tracks*).

5 Rename tracks 1 and 2 to the following (*Hint: right-click the track name; select Rename*):

◆ Video 1: **Background**

◆ Video 2: **News_Title**

◆ Video 3: **Video**

◆ Video 4: **Lower_Thirds**

1

6 Import the **144_Background1.mov**, **144_Lowerthird2.mov**, **anchor.avi**, **hawaii.avi**, and **Hawaii_reporter.avi** media clips from the DVD (*Hint: Get Media; DVD [Camcorder or PC DVD Drive] button; Advanced button; select DVD drive; UnCheck All; Check files that you need!*).

TIP *You can find complete instructions for grabbing media into Premiere Elements 7 in the Chapter 1 section "Adding Media to Your Project."*

7 Once the clips appear in the panel, switch to the **Edit** workspace (*Hint: Edit tab; Project button*).

8 Drag the **144_Background1.mov** clip to the Background track on the Timeline. Repeat to add a second copy of the **144_Background1. mov** clip directly after the first.

TIP *Make sure the start of the media clip is at the head of the track.*

NOTE *You are adding the clip twice to the Timeline because the duration of the file isn't sufficient for the intended project, but two copies of the clip are exactly right.*

9 Use the **Zoom In** or **Out** controls so the **144_Background1.mov** clip occupies around two-thirds of the Timeline.

INFORMATION *144_Background1.mov is one of the many great graphic loop clips available from Digital Juice (**www.digitaljuice.com**).*

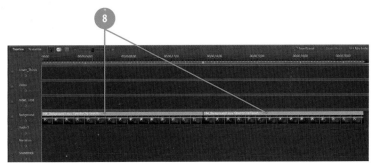

Flying Solo: Creating the TV News Background Text

The graphic loop clip from Digital Juice, **144_Background1.mov**, is a fantastic background that only needs some text to create a truly authentic News Background screen. In this section, Fly Solo to finish off the convincing background for your newscaster project by adding a title clip, altering the font and size, and dragging it into position. It's something you have done many times in this book, but hints and tips are available in case you get lost. Once your background is in place, move on to add an anchorman to the scene in the next task.

Create the News Background Text

1. Open the Titler (*Hint: Add Default Text button*).

2. Type **The Nightly News with Joe** in the text box. Press **Enter** on your keyboard after the words **Nightly** and **News**.

   TIP *If the **Add Text** text box becomes unhighlighted before you start typing, click inside it and drag across the default text with your mouse to highlight it.*

3. Change the font to **Times New Roman** (*Hint: Titler Properties view*).

4. Set the text to be right justified (*Hint: Right Align Text button*).

5. Use the **Selection tool** (*Hint: the "arrow" button*) to move the text to the upper-right corner of the panel, as shown in the illustration. Be sure to stay within the safe text zone, which is represented by the inside white box.

6. Highlight **Nightly News** and change the font size to **115**.

7. Highlight **The** and change the font size to **55**.

8. Highlight **with Joe** and change the font size to **55**, as well.

9. Exit the Titler (*Hint: Done button*).

10. Extend the **Title 01** clip to the length of the two clips below (*Hint: grab the tail; drag it to the right*).

Adding the Anchorman

Now that you have your background in place—complete with the spinning globe, other backdrop elements in motion, and your title text—it's time to bring in the star of your show, Joe the Anchorman. Joe was filmed against a green screen, so when you add him to the Timeline, you see the Videomerge message. Use this to strip away the green background, revealing the spinning globe and titles underneath. You also need to apply the **Non Red Key** to get rid of the persistent green glow around the actor; you may have become familiar with this process from completing other such projects in this book.

19

Add the Anchor Clip to the Timeline

1. Click the **Edit** tab to switch to the Edit workspace and click the **Project** button to view the Media panel.

2. Move the **CTI** to the 8-second mark on the Timeline (*00;00;08;00*).

3. Drag the **anchor.avi** clip from the Media panel to the Video track at the CTI point (*Hint: the 8-second mark*).

    TIP *If you find that any of the other clips move around the Timeline during this step, hold down the **Ctrl** key when you drag the **anchor.avi** clip to your Timeline.*

4. When you drop the clip onto the track, Premiere Elements detects that this clip uses a green screen and as a result, the Videomerge message appears. Click the **Yes** button to apply this effect.

5. With the **anchor.avi** clip selected on the Timeline, click the **Properties** button to open the Properties view and then dial open the **Videomerge** controls by clicking the triangle.

6. Adjust the **Tolerance** to 0.42.

    TIP *Don't worry for the moment about the large green "bump" that appears in the middle of the Monitor panel. You deal with this in a later step.*

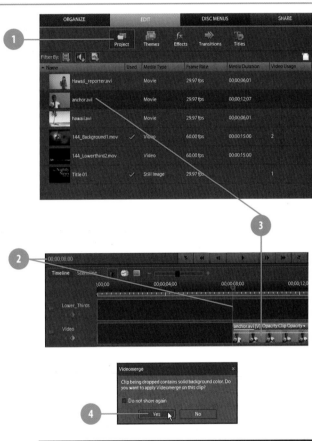

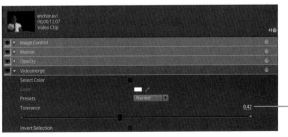

Apply the Non Red Key

1. Click the **Edit** tab to switch to the Edit workspace and click the **Effects** button to view the Effects panel.

2. Type **red** in the text box to display the Non Red Key.

3. Drag the **Non Red Key** onto the **anchor.avi** clip on the Video track.

4. With the **anchor.avi** clip selected on the Timeline, click the **Properties** button to open the Properties view. Click the triangle next to the Non Red Key to view the effect's controls.

5. Make the following changes to the settings for the Non Red Key:

   ◆ Threshold: **35%**

   ◆ Cutoff: **35%**

   ◆ Defringing: **Green**

   ◆ Smoothing: **High**

The Anchorman with all traces of green removed

Did You Know?

You can defringe green or blue. Sometimes, as a result of lighting or other factors, you may end up with more of a bluish tinge to a clip. Whenever that happens, choose **Blue** from the Defringing menu.

Did You Know?

You can view a white silhouette. If you want to see how well a Green Screen Key is keying out the green, select the **Mask Only** check box. When you do, the **Monitor** panel changes to show a white cookie cutter shape of the actor. If the settings are correct, you should see no artifacts (holes) within the white silhouette. If you do, tweak the **Threshold** and **Cutoff** settings until all you see is a pure white silhouette.

Adjust the Brightness

1 With the **anchor.avi** clip still selected, click the triangle next to Image Control in the Properties view to reveal the effect's controls.

TIP *If the effect controls for Image Control are already showing, you can skip this step.*

2 Make the following changes for the Image Control settings:

◆ Brightness: **5.0**

◆ Contrast: **105.0**

Did You Know?

There can be too much of a good thing. As you work with the Image Control effect controls, including Brightness, Contrast, Hue, and Saturation, use a light touch. Although the keying effects allow you to make big adjustments up or down to get the effect you want (removing the green, for example), controls such as Brightness can have an immediate positive or negative effect on a clip even when you just adjust one or two steps up or down. Be especially careful adjusting the Hue or Saturation settings on any clip that has had a keying effect applied, such as the Green Screen Key effect. Again, even a minor adjustment here can alter the green that the Green Screen Key effect was keying on.

Resizing and Moving the Anchorman

As it stands, the anchorman is a little too large; his head clips the title. In this section, you adjust his scale and reposition him slightly on screen. By doing so, you create a better on-screen composition and allow more of the cool background to be seen.

Move and Shrink the Anchorman

① If the **anchor.avi** clip is no longer the selected clip, reselect it now.

② Click the **Properties** button to open the Properties view and then click the triangle next to the Motion effect to view its controls.

③ Make the following changes for the **Motion** settings:

- ◆ Position: **237.4   260.1**

- ◆ Scale: **66.8**

Did You Know?

You can make your initial adjustments right in the Monitor panel. After you click the **Motion** effect in the Properties view for the **anchor.avi** clip, a white box appears around the clip in the Monitor panel. You can optionally drag a corner of the box to resize the clip, and then click in the center of the box to move the clip to its new position. Use the **Position** and **Scale** controls to fine-tune those settings after you've made your manual adjustments on the Monitor panel.

Adding the Lower-Third Graphic

Most news and sports programs now use the lower-third graphic as a backdrop for displaying the reporter's name or location, the name of the person being interviewed, or any other pertinent information for the story. Your lower-third clip is called **144_Lowerthird2.mov** and you can simply drag it to the Timeline and make an adjustment or two. Adding this graphic also allows you to cover up the green bump displayed by the **anchor.avi** clip.

Add the Lower Third

1 Click the **Edit** tab to switch to the Edit workspace and click the **Project** button to view the Media panel.

2 Drag the **144_Lowerthird2.mov** clip from the Media panel onto the Lower_Thirds track. Position the clip so that the head (start) of the clip is aligned with the head of the **anchor.avi** clip.

3 If the Videomerge box appears, click **No**.

4 Trim the length of the **144_Lowerthird2. mov** clip by dragging the tail of the clip so that it is the same length as the **anchor.avi** clip below.

TIP *Depending on your screen resolution, you may need to use the vertical scroll bar at the end of the Timeline to fully view clips placed on the upper Timeline tracks.*

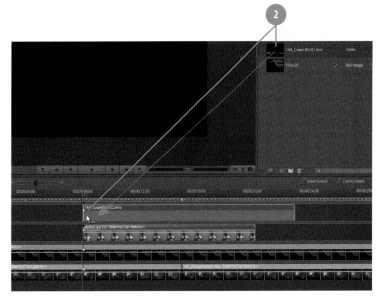

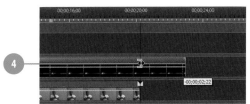

Adjust the Lower Third

1 Click the **Edit** tab to switch to the Edit workspace and click the **Effects** button to view the Effects panel.

2 Type **horiz** in the text box on the Effects panel to bring up the Horizontal Flip effect.

3 Select the **Horizontal Flip** effect from the Video Effects Transform category and drag it onto the **144_Lowerthird2.avi** clip on the Lower_Thirds track.

TIP *The Horizontal Flip effect flips the 144_ Lowerthird2.avi clip so that the globe is on the right side of the screen. This is a better look for your set, because you already have the big gold globe spinning away on the left, behind the anchorman. By the way, note that the Horizontal Flip effect has no effect controls to adjust in the Properties view. However, in the following steps, you use the Properties view to change the 144_Lowerthird2.avi clip's position to hide that unsightly bump on the reporter clip, and you can also stretch the lower third to cover the whole screen.*

4 Click the **Properties** button to open the Properties view for the **144_Lowerthird2. avi** clip, and twirl down the triangle next to Motion to reveal the effect's controls.

5 Make these changes for the **Motion** setting:

- Position: **358.3   318.9**

- Uncheck: **Constrain Proportions**

- Scale Width: **105.5** (scale height unchanged at 100)

IMPORTANT: *These settings only work if Scale to Frame Size is ticked ON for this clip in the program preferences. This setting is ON by default, although people who work regularly with photos in Photoshop may have it turned off.*

The lower-third graphic, flipped horizontally, scaled up slightly, and repositioned

Understanding Overlays, Background, and Lower Thirds

Animation Clips

What are *animation clips* in terms of broadcast-ready clips used in video productions? These are simply precreated computer art variously referred to as overlays or backdrops or motion backgrounds—Digital Juice calls them "jump backs"—that are used to enhance a production and give an ordinary-looking clip some "pizzazz" or "punch."

Now that we are all in the business of producing small, fun, and informative clips, it doesn't hurt to add an overlay or lower third when needed to give our productions a little "somethin' somethin'" and add a real professional touch to our videos. In fact, these clips are very effective when you add them to a simple video of a soccer game, bike race, or other action-oriented "extreme" sports moment in which you or your family are involved.

Digital Juice

There are many companies on the Web that create unique and high quality still and animated clips for the television industry, independent producers, wedding videographers, and home video producers. These are clips we all need but don't have the time or expertise to create ourselves.

One of the best is Digital Juice (**www. digitaljuice.com**). They also provide music software, sound effects, royalty-free video, and other packages both professional and amateur video producers find useful. Digital Juice has provided the animation clips used in this chapter. If you like these, they have many more available that you can download immediately or have shipped to you on DVD.

Digital Juice Sample Clips

215_Jumpback from Jump Backs 5: Sports:
An example of a sports-themed back drop or motion background

150_Overlay3 from Editor's Toolkit 7: Wedding Tools II:
An example of a wedding- or romance-themed overlay

226_Lowerthird2.mov from Editor's Toolkit 9: Christmas Tools:
An example of a holiday-themed lower third

Muvipix.com

A cool alternative to Digital Juice and one especially relevant to Premiere Elements users is Muvipix, a great source for Motion backgrounds and DVD templates, a number of which are offered for free and even more of which are available for an affordable annual fee. Muvipix is run by Premiere Elements enthusiasts and is worth checking out if only for the thriving and helpful community, as well as the wealth of tips and tricks specifically aimed at the Adobe program. If you are serious about using Premiere Elements to the max, you need to check out this web site today.

Adding Lower-Third Text for the Anchorman

You now need to add some text to the lower-third graphic at the bottom of the screen to introduce the name of the anchorman. As noted earlier, you usually use lower-third text to identify the person on the screen, and often their location. But you can also use it to convey highlights from other news stories, sports scores, and so on. This type of text typically crawls across the bottom of the screen, from right to left (so that you can read it from left to right). You can also use the Titler's scroll facility, but the text presets offered in the Premiere Elements 7 Titler are much more fun, and have a bigger wow factor.

Type the Text and Choose a Style

1. Press **Page Up** to move the CTI to the start of the **anchor.avi** clip, and then click the **Add Default Text** button to open the Titler.

2. Replace the default text, **Add Text**, with **Joe, Your Anchorman**.

3. Select **Times New Roman** and **Bold Italic** from the fonts menu in the Properties view.

4. Resize the text to **32** points.

5. Click the **Selection tool** and drag to reposition the text so that it is positioned over the lower-third graphic.

6. Add a little movement and style to the text by selecting from one of the many presets and clicking the **Apply** button (*Hint: we suggest FocusIn*).

7. Click anywhere on a blank area of the Timeline to exit the Titler.

> NOTE *Although you have run out of "upper" tracks on the Timeline, Premiere Elements automatically creates one for the title you just created so long as you positioned the CTI at the start of this section.*

8. Grab the tail of the **Title 02** clip and drag it across the **Video 5** track until it matches the length of the **anchor.avi** clip.

> NOTE *In this case, the **Title 02** clip is the same length as the **anchor.avi** clip so that the text displays for as long as the anchorman is on the screen. If you want the text to appear later or end sooner, just adjust the start and end points accordingly.*

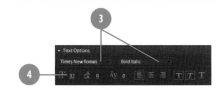

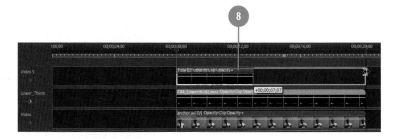

Flying Solo: Creating the Hawaii Reporter Scene

With the Anchorman scene complete, it's time to add the on-location reporter, who is of course anywhere but the place she is pretending to be—in this case, Hawaii. To pull off this visual illusion, Fly Solo and use all the skills you learned in the previous section for adding the backdrop scenery (a beach in this case), adding a green screen reporter and blending her with the backdrop, adding the lower-third graphic, and lastly, creating some lower-third text. It sounds complex, but it is nothing more than you have already done, and hints and tips are in the text to help you on your way.

Add the hawaii.avi and Hawaii_reporter.avi Clips

1. Switch to the **Media** panel (*Hint: Edit tab; Project button*).

2. Add the **hawaii.avi** clip to the Background track, directly to the right of the **144_Background1.mov** clip (*Hint: drag*).

3. Allow the clips on the Background track and the News_Title track to be split and sent further up the Timeline.

4. Add the **Hawaii_reporter.avi** clip to the Video track. Again, you want it directly to the right of (and touching) the **anchor.avi** clip.

5. If the Videomerge prompt appears, click **No**.

   NOTE *In this case, where the green screen has many folds and creases, the Videomerge effect is not the correct keying effect to use if you want to remove the green screen. Instead, use the Green Screen Key effect, which gives clearer results.*

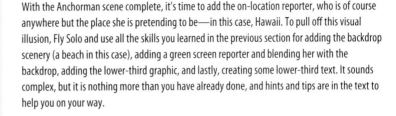

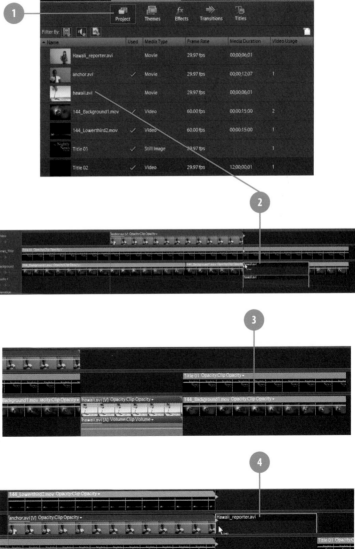

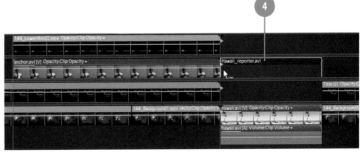

6. Switch to the **Effects** panel and locate the **Green Screen Key** effect (*Hint: Effects button; type Green in the text field*).

7. Remove the green screen background from the **reporter.avi** clip (*Hint: drag the Green Screen Key on the reporter.avi clip; Properties view; Threshold 44.7%: Cuttoff 26%*).

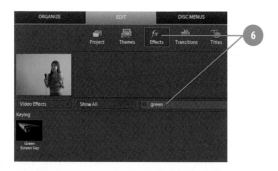

Did You Know?

You are using A and B clips. When you have two clips side-by-side like this on the Timeline, the arrangement creates one of the basic editing situations in film and video. The **anchor.avi** clip is referred to as the *A clip*. It is the current, but outgoing, clip. The **Hawaii_reporter.avi** clip is called the *B clip*. It is the incoming, and soon to be current clip. Finally, the cut between these two clips, then, is the classic *A/B cut*.

Adjust the Brightness to Give the Actor an Outdoor Look

1. Select the **Hawaii_reporter.avi** clip to make it the active clip.

2. Set the **Brightness** to 5.0 (*Hint: Properties view; Image Control*).

3. Press **Ctrl-S** to save your work so far.

The clip with the green screen removed and the actor brightened to give the appearance of being outdoors

Add the Lower-Third Graphic

1. Switch to the **Media** panel (*Hint: Edit tab; Project button*).

2. Add the **144_Lowerthird2.mov** clip above the **Hawaii_reporter.avi** clip.

   TIMESAVER *You can choose to simply copy the **144_Lowerthird2.avi** clip already on the Timeline and paste the copy again in line on the Timeline. It's a bit of a coin toss here as to which method is quicker. Use whichever method you prefer.*

3. If the Videomerge prompt appears, select **No**.

4. Resize the **144_Lowerthird2.mov** clip to be the same length (duration) as the **Hawaii_reporter.avi** clip.

5. Switch to the **Effects** panel and locate the **Horizontal Flip** effect (*Hint: Effects button; type Hori in the text field*).

6. Add the **Horizontal Flip** effect to the **144_Lowerthird2.mov** clip.

7. Change the **Scale Width** to 105.0 (*Hint: Properties button; Motion controls; uncheck Constrain proportions; enter new value*).

8. Change the **Position** to 360.0   283.0.

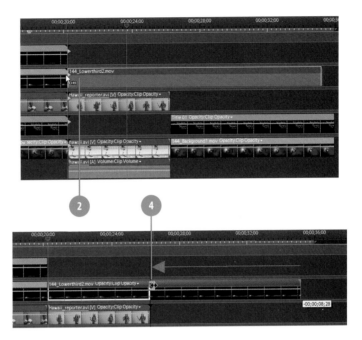

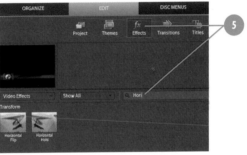

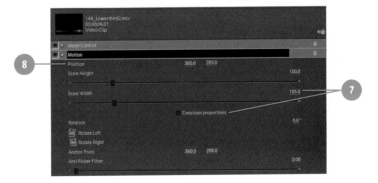

Add the Lower-Third Text

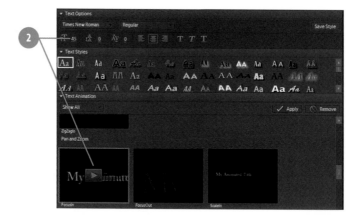

1 Move the **CTI** to the start of the **reporter.avi** clip (*Hint: Page Up or Page Down*).

2 Add the following text over the **144_ Lowerthird2.mov** clip: **on Location in Hawaii** (*Hint: Add Default Text button; select Font [Times New Roman]; alter Font Size [45]; apply Text Animation [FocusIn]*).

3 Reposition the text of the lower-third graphic (*Hint: Selection tool*).

4 Exit the Titler and adjust the length of the title to be the same length as the **Hawaii_ reporter.avi** clip.

5 Press **Ctrl-S** to save your work so far.

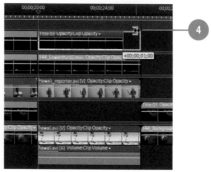

Adding a Cross Dissolve to End the News Feature Report

The nightly news looks great and has all the elements you would expect from it; all you need to do is add a transition from the Hawaii reporter back to the Nightly News logo. In this next section, add a dissolve transition to the **hawaii.avi** and **Hawaii_reporter.avi** clips, and then finish by adding a fade out to the end of the **Title 01** clip and the **144_Background.mov** clip.

Add a Dissolve

1 If the Edit workspace is not displayed when you press the **Edit** tab, then click the **Transitions** button to display the **Transitions** view.

2 Enter **cross** into the text field to display the Cross Dissolve.

3 Drag the **Cross Dissolve** transition onto the tails of the following clips:

- ◆ **Hawaii_reporter.avi**

- ◆ **hawaii.avi**

- ◆ **144_Lowerthird2.mov**

- ◆ **Title 02**

4 Drag the **Cross Dissolve** transition onto the head of the **Title 01** clip to the right of the **Hawaii_reporter.avi** clip.

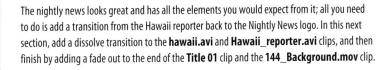

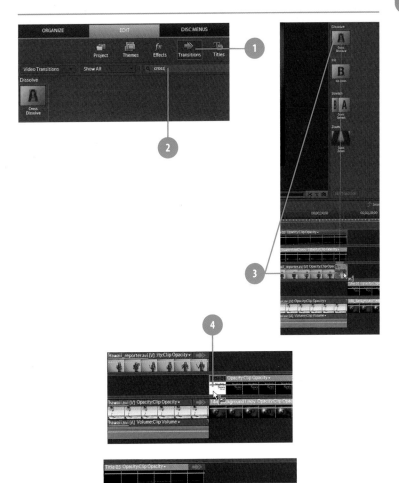

A cross dissolve added to five different clips on the Timeline

Add a Fade Out

1. Right-click the **Title 01** clip at the far right of the Timeline.

2. From the contextual menu, select **Fade > Fade Out Video**.

3. Repeat Steps 1 and 2 for the **144_Lowerthird2. mov** clip.

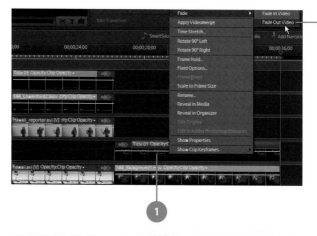

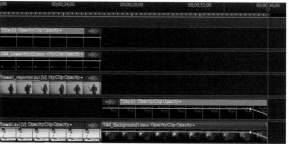

Both clips with a Fade Out added

Flying Solo:
Adding a Little Music

The project is almost finished. Almost! However, one of the most important ingredients is missing. Music! Fly Solo now and use SmartSound to add a *stinger* (a short dramatic piece of music) to your new titles, a little tropical music for your Hawaii reporter, and lastly, a stinger tune to exit the project. If you do get lost, check out the hints and tips. If you get very lost, refer to Chapter 3 for full details on how to use SmartSound with Premiere Elements 7.

Add an Intro Stinger

1 Move the **CTI** to the very start of the Timeline and use the Timeline scroll bar to show the Soundtrack track at the bottom of the Timeline.

2 Open the **SmartSound Maestro** dialog (*Hint: SmartSound button; click here for music*).

3 Select:

◆ **On My Computer**

◆ **Orchestral**

◆ **Olympic**

4 Click **Select** to exit back to the SmartSound Quicktracks dialog and enter **00;08;24** for the Length and select **Launch** as the variation.

5 Click **OK** to save this to your computer and add it to the Timeline.

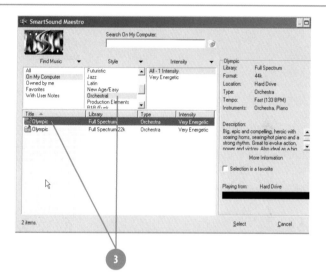

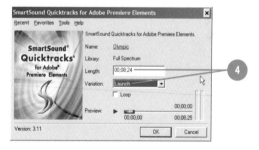

Add Some Island Music

1. Move the **CTI** to the very start of the Hawaii.avi clip (00;00;20;08).

2. Open the **SmartSound Maestro** dialog (*Hint: SmartSound button; click here for music*).

3. Select:
   - ◆ **On My Computer**
   - ◆ **World**
   - ◆ **Island Party**

4. Click **Select** to exit back to the SmartSound Quicktracks dialog and enter **00;05;29** for the Length and select **Jammin** as the variation.

5. Click **OK** to save this to your computer and add it to the Timeline.

Add an Exit Stinger

1. Move the **CTI** to the end of the **Hawaii_reporter.avi** clip (00;00;26;08).

2. Open the **SmartSound Maestro** dialog (*Hint: SmartSound button; click here for music*).

3. Select:
   - ◆ **On My Computer**
   - ◆ **Orchestral**
   - ◆ **Olympic**

4. Click **Select** to exit back to the SmartSound Quicktracks dialog and enter **00;09;21** for the Length and select **Launch** as the variation.

   TIP *To find the duration of a clip on the Timeline, hover the mouse over the clip and it appears as a pop-up.*

5. Click **OK** to save this to your computer and add it to the Timeline.

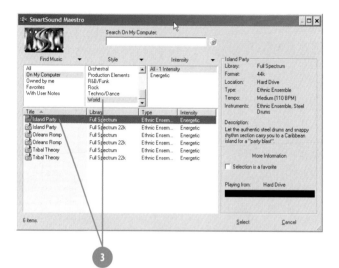

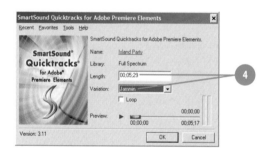

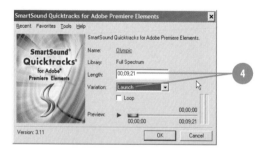

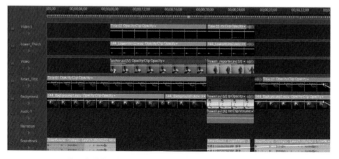

The whole Timeline complete with three SmartSound audio clips

Flying Solo:
Mixing the Music Levels

Play back the Timeline now and you can see the startling difference a few minutes of using SmartSound can make. However, although the intro and exit music are about the right volume level, the Island Party music is swamping our Hawaii reporter. In this section, you adjust the volume of that clip.

Adjust the Music's Volume
to Match the Clips

1 Click once on the **SmartSound - Island Party - Jammin [00;05;17]** clip to select it.

2 Open the **Properties** view by clicking the **Properties** button.

3 Dial open the **Volume** control by clicking the triangle.

4 Toggle animation **OFF** by clicking on the Toggle animation button, then set the **Volume** to -10 dB (negative).

Making Adjustments, Rendering, and Exporting

You're done! It goes without saying that you've been pressing **Ctrl-S** on your keyboard (or selecting **File > Save** from the Premiere Elements menu) all along, but do it one last time here. Also, it doesn't hurt to render as you go, either (press **Enter** on your keyboard, or select **Timeline > Render > Work Area** from the menu). Once you have finished making any last minute changes, export the project as a finished file format.

Finish the Project

1 Once you have played back your project and made the necessary adjustments, press **Enter** on your keyboard to render your project.

2 Once you have made all of your final adjustments, press **Ctrl-S** on the keyboard to save your project.

3 Finally, export your work as an AVI file. To export the clip, select **File > Export > Movie,** then browse to a local hard drive and to the **HSMovies_Final Renders** folder you created in Chapter 1, and save the file as **Chapter 19_NightlyNews.avi**.

TIP *If Export is grayed out, check that the Timeline is selected.*

NOTE *This final render may be used again in Chapter 21, as will many of your other final renders from the exercises in this book.*

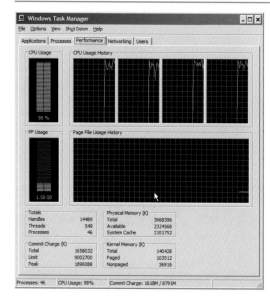

If you have more than one core in your computer's CPU, Premiere Elements 7 takes advantage of that when it is rendering a complex Timeline.

The finished project broadcasting in Windows Media Player

Hollywood Movie Green Screen: The Super Hero Effect

MEDIA:

ACB101.mov
superboy.avi
superwind.wav

20

COMPLEXITY:	Simple	Moderate	Complex
SKILL LEVEL:	Easy	Intermediate	Advanced

Introduction

Superman returns! One of the most popular special effects of all time is creating the illusion of a superhero flying through the clouds or over the sea or across a city skyline. With Premiere Elements 7, and any acceptable green screen or blue screen, this dream can be yours to achieve: human, or superhuman, flight!

In this chapter, you learn how to re-create this most famous of special effects, and in doing so, you find out how to deal with less-than-perfect green screen shots, and how royalty-free video clips can add real punch to your projects without sinking your bank account.

What You'll Learn

Flying Solo: Preparing the Project

Flying Solo: Adding the Cloud Background

Flying Solo: Adding Superboy

Cleaning Up the Green Screen Key

Adjusting the Direction and Speed of the Clouds

Setting Our Hero's Flight in Motion

Adding a Little Rotation to Our Hero's Flight Motion

Flying Solo: Adding Super Music and Super Sound Effects

Making Adjustments, Rendering, and Exporting

Flying Solo: Preparing the Project

Setting up a project should be easy enough for you now, so Fly Solo again to put down the foundations for this cool-looking project. Start the project, rename the tracks, and then import the media clips you need to complete this. As always, hints and tips are in the text should you get lost.

Set Up the Project

1. Start **Premiere Elements** and create a new project called **Chapter_20_Superhero**.

2. The Timeline should be set to Timeline view (*Hint: Timeline button to the left of the interface*).

   NOTE *You need to switch to the **Timeline** because you will be working with multiple clips on multiple video tracks.*

3. Deselect the audio tracks for Video 2 and 3 (*Hint: deselect Show Audio Tracks*).

4. Rename (*Hint: right-click the header*) and change each track to the following:

   ◆ Video 1: **Background**

   ◆ Video 2: **Greenscreen**

5. Import the **ACB101.mov**, **superboy.avi**, and **superwind.wav** media clips from the DVD (*Hint: Media Downloader; Show Audio; UnCheck All*).

   NOTE *To see any Audio media in the Media Downloader clips, you need to click the **Show Audio** button or press **Ctrl-U** on the keyboard while the Media Downloader is open. Watch out, Media Downloader rechecks all the files when you do this and you need to uncheck them all again!*

6. When your Timeline and Media panel look similar to the screenshots shown here, press **Ctrl-S** to save your work so far, then proceed to the next section.

Filming Tips

Virtually every child would love to see themselves flying across the sky on the television screen, and virtually every child alive knows how to act this one out: stretch out across a dining room chair, place arms in flight mode, look around at the "earth" below. It's almost as if we are born with the ability to "fly," at least in the special effects superhero definition of the word.

When you're ready to shoot your own superhero scene, be sure to set up a green or blue screen background as flat (wrinkle-free) and as evenly lit as possible. Make any additional equipment (such as a table or a chair) green screen–friendly; that is, paint it green-screen green. Plastic patio furniture or kids' furniture can often work well as is, if the color is right. The Chroma Key can key out any color, so you can match the background color (a sheet or paint) to the furniture, if that's an option.

When you create your own clip, consider dressing your hero in a super costume (or at least a cape) instead of leaving him or her in street clothes, as we've done in this project. You could optionally add a fan to cause the cape to ripple in the wind—just be careful not to cause ripples in the green screen.

Hey! If it were easy, everyone would be doing it...

Flying Solo: Adding the Cloud Background

For your superhero to fly free and powerful through the sky, as only a true hero with superpowers can, you first need to add the supplied Artbeats clip, **ACB101.mov**, to the Timeline. This is a swooping flight through a blue sky filled with puffy white clouds. It's perfect for a relaxing flying break for a busy superhero. Fly Solo now, just like Superman, but a bit more earthly, and add the clouds to the Timeline. Hints and tips are here to guide you.

Add the Clouds

1. Switch to the **Edit** workspace to view the **Media** panel (*Hint: Edit tab; Project button*).

2. Drag the **ACB101.mov** clip to the Background track.

   IMPORTANT *Be sure to line up the head of the **ACB101.mov** clip with the start of the Background track.*

3. Zoom the Timeline in or out so the clip occupies about two-thirds of the screen (*Hint: the Zoom slider*).

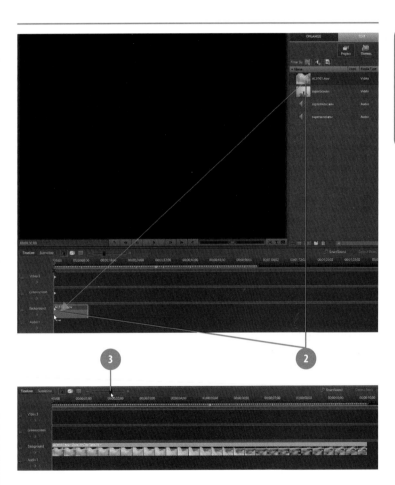

Flying Solo:
Adding Superboy

Now that the clouds are in place, it's time for Superboy to fly into action. Join him by Flying Solo and adding the **superboy.avi** clip to the Timeline, then turn down the invitation to add Videomerge. Hints and tips are there to guide you.

Drag with No Videomerge

1 Switch to the **Edit** workspace (*Hint: The Edit tab!*).

2 Add the **superboy.avi** clip to the Greenscreen track.

> **TIP** *Place the **superboy.avi** clip at the start of the Timeline.*

3 When prompted, click **No** to Videomerge.

Royalty-free footage refers to any video (or music or sound effects) footage that you purchase to use in your own projects. By the way, the *free* in royalty-free doesn't mean that you don't have to pay for it. It means that you don't have to pay *again* each time you use it; you only pay for the initial purchase. After that, you can pretty much use the footage over and over for whatever you want; this is called *unlimited use*.

However, typically some restrictions for such use apply. For example, if you use the footage in a for-profit project, you may need to credit the clip's producers or you may need to limit how much royalty-free content you include. In addition, it's usually the case that you don't have the right to resell or to repackage the clip.

About Artbeats

Artbeats is one of the most respected sources in the industry for royalty-free content. Their source material is actually 35mm film, which they digitize into high-quality footage and distribute in two formats: NTSC (the format used in the United States and Canada) and PAL (the format used in most of Europe, as well as in Japan).

To help you create some of the projects in this book, as well as to give you a taste of the kind of clips they have available, Artbeats has supplied the **ACB101.mov** clip included on the DVD with this book. You'll find hundreds more clips for purchase in many more categories at **www.artbeats.com**.

Cleaning Up the Green Screen Key

Videomerge isn't an appropriate tool to use to remove the green screen background in this case, mainly because you have several shades of green to deal with known as *hotspots.* You need to complete the *key,* or the removal of color, using the Chroma Key. In this section, you use most of the green screen skills you have learned in this book by applying a garbage matte to throw away some of the hotspots, then you add the Auto Color and Auto Contrast effects to even out the various tones of green that are left. Finally, you add the Chroma Key twice and then the Non Red Key once to thoroughly clean away the green.

Apply a Garbage Matte

1. If it is not already open, click the **Edit** tab to switch to the Edit workspace and click the **Effects** button to view the Effects panel.

2. Type **garbage** in the text box to bring up the various garbage matte effects.

3. Select the **Four-Point Garbage Matte** effect and drag it onto the **superboy.avi** clip on the Greenscreen track.

4. Click the **Properties** button to open the Properties view for the **superboy.avi** clip, and then click the **Four-Point Garbage Matte** text label to highlight the four points in the Monitor panel.

5. Move the four points to surround the actor; make sure his feet and hands don't pass through the edges of the garbage matte.

Apply Auto Color and Auto Contrast

1. If it is not already open, click the **Edit** tab to switch to the Edit workspace and click the **Effects** button to view the Effects panel.

2. Type **auto** in the text box to bring up the Auto Color and Auto Contrast effects.

3. Select the **Auto Color** effect and drag it onto the **superboy.avi** clip on the Greenscreen track.

4. Select the **Auto Contrast** effect and drag it onto the **superboy.avi** clip on the Greenscreen track.

5. Leave both effects at their default settings.

The Superboy clip with the Four-Point Garbage Matte effect

20

Apply and Tune the Chroma Key

1 If it is not already open, click the **Edit** tab to switch to the Edit workspace and click the **Effects** button to view the Effects panel.

2 Type **Chroma** in the text box to bring up the Chroma Key.

3 Select the **Chroma Key** and drag it onto the **superboy.avi** clip on the Greenscreen track.

4 Click the **Properties** button to open the Properties view for the **superboy.avi** clip, and then open the controls for the Chroma Key by clicking the triangle.

5 Select the **eyedropper tool** and click the green screen background just above the head of the actor in the Monitor panel.

6 Adjust **Similarity** to a value of 30% and **Blend** to a value of 10% (Default).

7 Set **Smoothing** to High.

Did You Know?

The Chroma Key can key any color. *Chroma* actually means color. Therefore, unlike with the Blue Screen Key or the Green Screen Key, you can actually use the **Chroma Key** to key out any color in the color spectrum that you want to remove from the background. You can use the eyedropper tool to select the color directly from the background. Alternatively, you can click the color swatch to bring up the **Color Picker** dialog. From here, you can pick the color from the color spectrum or enter the numeric value for the color if you know it. You can enter the numeric color as RGB (red, green, blue), HSB (hue, saturation, brightness), HSL (hue, saturation, luminance), YUV (luminance, blue, red), or even as a hexadecimal number.

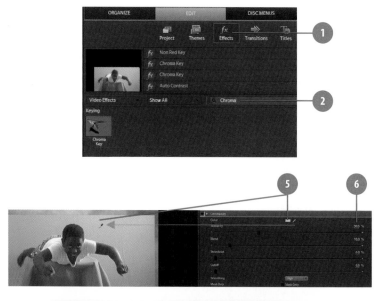

After the first application of the Chroma Key effect, some green still remains.

Apply and Tune the Chroma Key Again

1 Following the instructions in the previous exercise, add the Chroma Key again.

2 For the second time, sample an area of the green screen that is still visible and adjust **Similarity** to a value of 9.4% with a **Blend** value of 3.3%.

> **TIP** Before you begin altering the sliders, toggle **Mask Only** on by placing a check in the Mask Only box.

3 Set **Smoothing** to High.

> **TIP** If you find you can't remove all the green, try resampling a different area with the eyedropper.

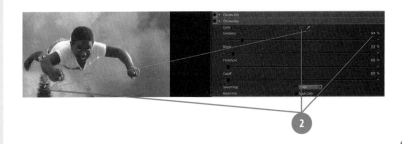

Apply and Tune the Non Red Key

1 If it is not already open, click the **Edit** tab to switch to the Edit workspace and click the **Effects** button to view the Effects panel.

2 Type **Non** in the text box to bring up the **Non Red Key**.

3 Select the **Non Red Key** and drag it onto the **superboy.avi** clip on the **Greenscreen** track.

4 Click the **Properties** button to open the Properties view for the **superboy.avi** clip, and then open the controls for the **Non Red Key** by clicking the triangle.

5 Change **Defringing** to **Green**, leave all other settings at the defaults.

The final clean key of the **superboy.avi** clip

20

Adjusting the Direction and Speed of the Clouds

If you play back this little movie, you will notice the clouds are unfortunately moving in the wrong direction, killing the effect. With Premiere Elements 7, you can provide an easy fix; simply reverse the clip. While you are messing with time, you should also slow the clip down just a bit so that it lasts as long as (actually, just a bit longer than) the **superboy.avi** clip. Otherwise, he flies against the sky background for awhile, and then suddenly, against a mysterious black background.

Use Time Stretch to Make the Changes

1 Right-click the **ACB101.mov** clip in the Background track.

2 From the contextual menu select **Time Stretch**.

3 In the **Time Stretch** dialog, set the **Speed** to 50%.

4 Mark the **Reverse Speed** check box.

5 Click **OK**.

TIP *Since the **ACB101.mov** clip does not contain any audio, you don't need to worry about the **Maintain Audio Pitch** setting.*

6 Move the **CTI** to 00;00;12;00 and click the **Split Clip** button below the Monitor or press **Ctrl-K** on the keyboard to split the clip at this point.

7 Select the clip on the right of the split, then press **Delete** on your keyboard to remove it from the Timeline.

Did You Know?

You decrease speed to increase duration. It may seem a bit counter-intuitive at first, but when you want to make a clip last longer, you enter a smaller number for the Speed setting. For example, if you increase the speed of a clip to 200 percent; the clip's speed increases but the clip's duration is cut in half. Decreasing the speed to 50 percent increases the clip's duration and the clip lasts on screen for twice as long.

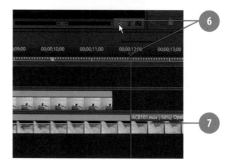

Setting Our Hero's Flight in Motion

In this task, you really make Superboy fly about the clouds; this sells the effect a great deal more than just having him stay in a static position in the center of the screen. You do this by resizing and moving him to set up a full motion flight path using the **Motion** effect in Premiere Elements.

Set Superboy's Starting Location and Size

1 Select the **superboy.avi** clip on the green screen track.

2 If it is not already open, click the **Properties** button to open the Properties view and open the **Motion** controls by clicking the triangle.

> **TIMESAVER** *Be sure the CTI is in the home position at the start of the Timeline. If it isn't, drag it there with your mouse or simply press **Home** on your keyboard.*

3 Click the **Show Keyframes** button on the Properties view to reveal the workspace for adding keyframes.

> **TIP** *The **Show Keyframes** button, once clicked, becomes the **Hide Keyframes** button and its function changes to match.*

> **TIMESAVER** *Adjust the horizontal size of the Properties view as needed so that you can work most effectively with keyframes. To do so, drag the left side of the panel to the left. You want to see as much of the Properties view Timeline as possible.*

4 Set the position and scale to the following:

◆ Position: **-80** (negative); **40**

◆ Scale: **0.0**

5 Click the **Toggle Animation** button to turn on the animation functionality of Premiere Elements.

> **TIP** *Premiere Elements automatically places the necessary keyframes at this point for all of the Motion-related settings.*

Set a Midpoint Marker for Adjusting Superboy's Location and Size

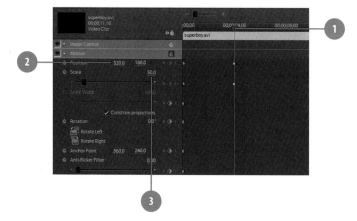

1 Drag the **CTI** over to the 4-second mark (00;00;04;00).

2 Set the **Position** property for the clip as follows:

◆ Position: **320; 180**

3 Set the **Scale** property for the clip as follows:

◆ Scale: **50**

TIMESAVER *After you adjust the position of the* **superboy.avi** *clip, Premiere Elements automatically drops a keyframe for the Position property. After you adjust the scale, Premiere Elements then drops keyframes for both Scale and Scale Width.*

Did You Know?

You can change the magnification of the Monitor panel. When you deal with scenes where objects move on and off the screen, you may find it easier to zoom the monitor out by right-clicking the Monitor panel and selecting the desired magnification.

Did You Know?

Place a keyframe whenever and wherever you want to make a change. As you work on your projects, whenever you need to make an animation (time)-related change—such as when you need to change the size of an object, its orientation (rotation), or its location. Remember, the more keyframes you use, the more control you have over the object (clip) that you are morphing. Remember, too, that Premiere Elements fills in the blanks, so to speak (known as *tweening*) between each of the keyframes and their settings, in sequence.

Set the Final Locations and Sizes for the Super Hero

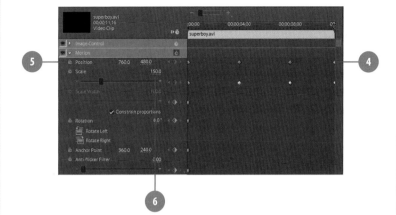

1 Drag the **CTI** over to the 8-second mark (00;00;08;00).

2 Drag the **superboy.avi** clip over to the left of the Monitor panel, as shown in the illustration. The clip should now be roughly at this position:

- ◆ Position: **250; 315**

3 Adjust the scale as follows:

- ◆ Scale: **100.0**

TIMESAVER *Premiere Elements automatically places keyframes for you for the* **Position**, **Scale**, *and* **Scale Width** *properties.*

4 Drag the **CTI** to the end of the **superboy.avi** clip (00;00;11;16).

5 Drag the **superboy.avi** clip over to "off camera" down in the bottom-right of the Monitor panel. The clip should now be roughly at this position:

- ◆ Position: **760; 480**

6 Adjust the scale as follows:

- ◆ Scale: **150.0**

TIMESAVER *Again, after you adjust the position of the* **superboy.avi** *clip, Premiere Elements automatically places a keyframe for the Position property. This is also true when you adjust the scale. Premiere Elements places keyframes for both the Scale and Scale Width properties.*

20

Adding a Little Rotation to Our Hero's Flight Motion ▶

Move the **CTI** to 00;00;06;16 and look at Superboy's left hand (on the right of the screen). It appears to be cut off. This is because, during filming, his hand dipped below the level of the camera. You can solve this two ways: first, increase the **superboy.avi** clip scale at this point so the missing hand is masked by the edge of the frame (however, be aware that this interferes with the motion path you just set up), or second, use the Rotation settings in the Motion effect. Using rotation has the advantage of adding some extra zing to the effect, so in this next step, you add rotation to three places in the flight path, the last being to mask the missing hand problem.

Add Rotation to Superboy

1. If it is not already open, select the **superboy.avi** clip and click the **Properties** button to open the Properties view. Dial down the Motion settings by clicking the triangle.

2. Move the **CTI** to 00;00;03;06 (just before he makes his swoop to the left) and enter a rotation setting of **15.0**.

3. Move the CTI twice to the following points on the Timeline and alter the Rotation values given below:

   ◆ CTI: **00;00;04;21**

   ◆ Rotation: **-7.7** (negative)

   ◆ CTI: **00;00;06;03**

   ◆ Rotation: **9.0**

   NOTE *You don't need to correct the rotation after the third keyframe because the actor's movement suggests a tilt back to the right.*

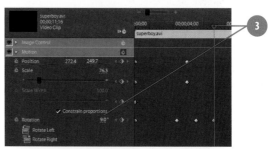

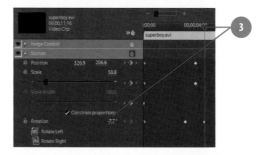

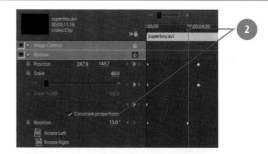

Superboy, flying fast and proud with added rotation!

Flying Solo: Adding Super Music and Super Sound Effects

You can't have a superhero streaking through the sky without some kind of wind sound effect or a stirring soundtrack to remind your audience of how super he is. We've included a wind sound effect on the DVD, and you can generate the super music you need with SmartSound. You should already be comfortable with the techniques and skills required to add a sound file to the Timeline and to create a SmartSound track, so Fly Solo now and finish off this project in style.

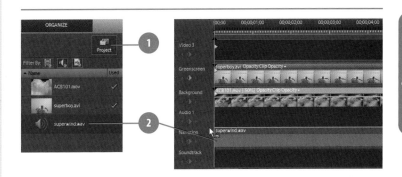

Add Sound FX

1 Switch to the **Edit** workspace to view the **Media** panel (*Hint: Edit tab; Project button*).

2 Drag the **superwind.wav** clip onto the Narration track.

> **IMPORTANT** *Be sure you line up the head of the **superwind.wav** clip with the start of the Narration track.*

3 Untoggle the keyframe animation for the volume level of the **superwind.wav** clip and increase the dB level (*Hint: Properties view; Animation toggle; Volume [+10dB]*).

Add Some Music

1 Move the **CTI** to the very start of the Timeline.

2 Open the **SmartSound** interface (*Hint: Click the SmartSound button*).

3 Open the **SmartSound Maestro** dialog (*Hint: Click here to select music*).

4 Select your choice of music (*Hint: we suggest Futuristic; Subterfuge*).

5 Alter the duration and select the variation (*Hint: 00;12;15; Jetstream*).

6 Click **OK** and save the file to your hard drive. Premiere Elements then adds the tune to the Soundtrack track.

> **NOTE** *SmartSound automatically adds a musical flourish to the end of tracks it creates, to the length you specify, so often you do not need to add a fade out.*

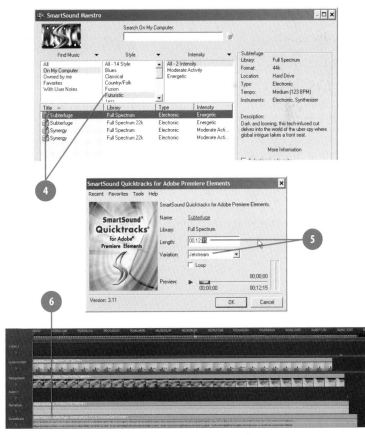

The finished Timeline complete with sound FX and musical accompaniment

Making Adjustments, Rendering, and Exporting

You've done a super job! All the pieces are in place. You've learned how to create the illusion of a superhero in flight using the Chroma Key, motion effects, and keyframes—not to mention sound effects and music. Save your work one more time and then render and export your project so that you can show people what you've created.

Finish the Project

1 Once you have played back your project and made the necessary adjustments, press **Enter** on your keyboard to render your project.

2 Once you have made all of your final adjustments, press **Ctrl-S** on the keyboard to save your project.

3 Finally, export your work as an AVI file. To export the clip, select **File > Export > Movie,** then browse to a local hard drive and to the **HSMovies_Final Renders** folder you created in Chapter 1, and save the file as **Chapter_20_Superhero.avi.**

NOTE *This final render may be used again in Chapter 21, as will many of your other final renders from the exercises in this book.*

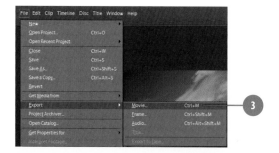

The finished project "flying" along in Windows Media Player

Hollywood Movie Trailer: Creating a Movie Trailer Using InstantMovie

MEDIA:

Various AVIs from your own projects
Or:
Chapter 1_ Old_Film_Effect.avi
Chapter 13-Night_Vision.avi
Chapter 15_The_Ghost.avi

21

COMPLEXITY:	Simple	Moderate	Complex
SKILL LEVEL:	Easy	Intermediate	Advanced

Introduction

One of the cool new features in Premiere Elements 7 is the InstantMovie function, which can take your movies—those AVI files you created at the end of each chapter—and bundle them all together with some cool graphics and music to create a really neat-looking movie trailer.

In this chapter, you use this new feature with the rendered AVI files you created in each of the chapters. You don't need to use them all, just the ones you want to or the ones we recommended in the instructions. It's up to you.

Once you have completed this chapter, you will have created a truly exciting and original trailer based on all your hard work.

What You'll Learn

Flying Solo: Preparing the Project

Organizing and Choosing Your Clips

Selecting a Theme for Your InstantMovie

Customizing the Final Output of InstantMovie

Let It Rip: Creating, Rendering, and Exporting

Flying Solo: Preparing the Project

You only need to prepare a little bit to set up a project for InstantMovie. You are only going to use one track, so there is no real advantage to renaming it, or indeed creating extra tracks. Actually, all you need to do is create a new project and then import the AVI files that you want to include in your InstantMovie trailer. In this case, we encourage you to use your own rendered versions from the various chapters that you have worked on, but if for some reason you don't want to do this, you can use the three AVIs (renders taken from exercises in this book) you will find on the DVD. Fly Solo now to set up the basic project and import the files you want to work with.

Start a Project and Import Some Media

1 Start **Premiere Elements** and create a new project at the splash screen called **Chapter_21_InstantMovie_Trailer**. Save this in the Peachpit folder you created in Chapter 1.

> **NOTE** *InstantMovie only uses one track, so leave the original track names as they are; they will do just fine for this chapter.*

2 Do one of the following:

◆ Import the AVIs you saved to the **Peachpit\HSMovies_Final Renders** folder (*Hint: Get Media; PC Files and Folders; HSMovies_Final Renders folder*).

◆ Import the following AVIs from the DVD: **Chapter 1_ Old_Film_Effect.avi**, **Chapter 13-Night_Vision.avi**, and **Chapter 15_The_Ghost.avi** (*Hint: Get Media button; DVD [Camcorder or PC DVD ROM]; Advanced button; Uncheck all; check required files*).

> **INFORMATION** *We recommend that you use a minimum of three AVIs during this initial learning period, but you should try more once you have the hang of the InstantMovie workflow.*

3 Use **Ctrl-S** to save your work so far.

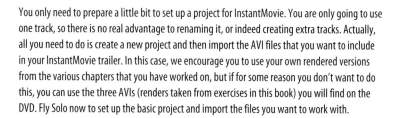

Importing AVIs you created and saved on your hard drive

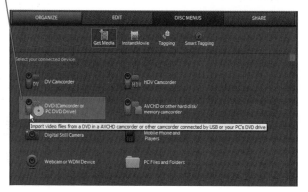

Importing AVIs stored on the DVD that came with this book

Organizing and Choosing Your Clips

InstantMovie loads clips into its instant movie-making engine in the order they are displayed in the Assembly workspace. You can sort this in two ways: Oldest or Newest. You also have the option of "opening" a clip and deleting scenes you don't want included in the instant movie, which gives you some level of control over what is included and what is not. In this section, you switch the play order, then choose which clips to include.

Switch to Oldest

1   If it is not already open, click the **Organize** tab to switch to the Assembly workspace.

2   Ensure that the Video Filter is set to **Show**.

3   Click the **Media Arrangement according to date** button to the right of the workspace, and select **Oldest First**.

Choose Which Clips to Include

1   If it is not already open, click the **Organize** tab to switch to the Assembly workspace.

> **NOTE** *To see this exercise correctly, you need to have at least three video clips in the Assembly workspace.*

2   Click the **InstantMovie** button.

3   Hold down **Ctrl** on the keyboard and click once on each clip you want to include in your instant movie.

> **TIP** *Instead of **Ctrl-click**, you can use **Ctrl-A** to select all the clips in the Assembly workspace.*

4   Click the **Next** button in the lower-right of the Assembly workspace.

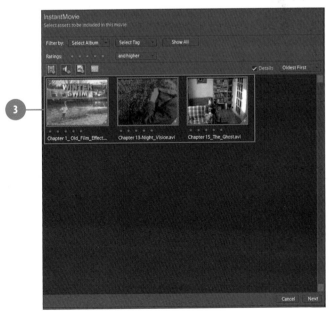

Selecting a Theme for Your InstantMovie

Themes are a little more than you might think. They are not just clever menu openings with some snazzy transitions, although a good deal of that is in there; they also constitute the look and feel of your instant movie. Choose well; if you have lots of action, avoid the Wedding Doves template; if it is a birthday, think about using the Birthday Party template! If you are not sure which to choose, then remember, you can preview an InstantMovie theme, and in this next section you do this and then choose a theme before moving on.

Previewing and Selecting an InstantMovie Theme

1. You should be looking at the **Theme** panel; if not, back up and complete the previous section.

2. Scroll down the **Theme** panel until you find a theme you like.

3. Hover the mouse cursor over the theme and a small Play button appears. Press the **Play** button to preview the theme.

4. Once you find your perfect theme, click it once to select it, then click the **Next** button.

Customizing the Final Output of InstantMovie

The final screen you encounter before you create your instant movie is the Customize panel. Here you determine what text to use in the opening and closing titles, which music to use, the duration of that music, the sequence order, and the content. In this next section, you customize all these options.

Customize Credits

1 In the **Opening Title** area, type in any text you want the audience to see before the instant movie begins.

> **NOTE** *You can make your opening titles more than one line, but you will see more consistent results if you keep them to a single line where possible.*

2 Enter any closing text in the **Closing Title** area. This closing text will almost always be scrolling white text on a black background.

> **INFORMATION** *If you leave the opening or closing title text as the default, Premiere Elements uses what it has, so it is best to delete all the default text if you have no ideas.*

Customize Music

1 Click the triangle next to Music to display the options.

2 By default, Theme Music is ticked; this automatically generates a SmartSound music clip and adds it to the Timeline. Here are the other options:

- ◆ **My Music**: You select a music file stored on your hard drive.

- ◆ **No Music**: Silent running!

3 For the benefit of this part of the tutorial, leave the default, **Theme Music**, selected.

> **TIP** *At the bottom of the Music area is a slider that allows you to balance between the music InstantMovie adds and the music in your clips.*

Customize Duration

1 Click the triangle next to Duration to display the options.

2 For this example, choose **Use All Clips** to create a tune that is the same duration as your clips.

NOTE *By default, duration is set to* ***Match Music****. If your movie is too long, then Instant-Movie shortens it to match the duration of the music. If it is too short, InstantMovie duplicates some clips in order to match the duration of the music. InstantMovie warns you before it does either and gives you extra options should you want to correct this situation by adding more clips. The other options are:* ***Specify Duration****, which tells InstantMovie how long you want the tune to be, and* ***Use All Clips****, which tells InstantMovie to match the duration of the music to that of the clips you have selected.*

NOTE *In this example, you do not need to alter Sequence or Theme content, but for full details on these functions, please refer to the Adobe help file.*

Did You Know?

You can also add themes to any open Timeline. Less instant but still effective is your ability to add themes to any open project. When you add themes, the Credit and Music options remain the same as they would when you use InstantMovie from the Organize tab.

Let It Rip: Creating, Rendering, and Exporting

And that's it. Yes it really is that easy to create an instant movie with Premiere Elements 7. All you need to do now is set InstantMovie to work to create your InstantMovie trailer. If you don't like the finished result, just go back to the start, pick a new theme, and try again. The result takes seconds to generate, so you really don't have an excuse not to experiment.

Finish the Project

1 Once you are happy with all the settings in the last section, press the **Apply** button to begin the InstantMovie process.

> **IMPORTANT** *Once InstantMovie has analyzed your clips and generated the theme, it places it on the Timeline. It may also offer to render the Timeline if it is a particularly complex one. To avoid playback issues, accept this offer.*

2 Once you have played back your project and made the necessary adjustments, press **Enter** on your keyboard to render your project if necessary, then press **Ctrl-S** to make a final save of your project.

3 Finally, export the movie by selecting **File > Export > Movie** and saving it in the **HSMovies_Final Renders** folder under the filename **Chapter_21_InstantMovie_ Trailer.avi**.

Did You Know?

Once InstantMovie analyzes your clips you can look in the Assembly workspace and open a clip and see the various scenes it contains. To do this, just click the small arrow on the right of the clip frame. Once the scenes display, you can delete one or all of them, removing them from the next instant movie you create.

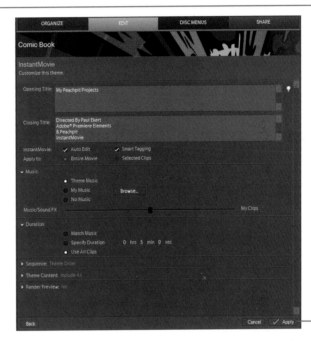

InstantMovie first analyzes the clips...

... then adds the Comic Book theme to various places in the movie.

If the movie is particularly complex, Premiere Elements 7 offers to render the Timeline before you play it back.

Congratulations! You have reached the end of the book. We hope that you have both enjoyed and benefited from the journey, and we wish you luck in your own future Hollywood Movie Projects. Oh, and don't forget to have fun!

The finished Timeline

An example of the Comic Book theme

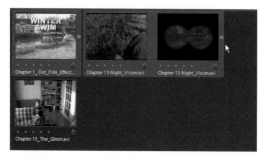

Once InstantMovie has analyzed your clips, the next time you look in the Assembly workspace, you can open a clip and see the various scenes that clip contains.

The opening credits InstantMovie created using the Comic Book theme and a project imported into the Organize workspace.

Index

synchronizing beat with unnumbered markers, 47

Web resources for, 68, 196

Muvipix.com, 301